FORTRESS

# INTRODUCTION TO
# THE GOSPELS

FORTRESS
# INTRODUCTION TO THE GOSPELS

Mark Allan Powell

Fortress Press ◆ Minneapolis

# For Michael Aaron Powell

FORTRESS INTRODUCTION TO THE GOSPELS

Picture of St. Matthew (from the Ebbo Gospels, Carolingian Manuscript, Epernay, France) featured on page 10 is courtesy of Scala/Art Resource, NY.

Greek New Testament on page 31 is from *Novum Testamentum Graece* (Deutsch Bibelgesellschaft Stuttgart: Germany, 1898 and 1979).

Cover design by David Meyer.

Interior design by Debbie Finch.

Library of Congress Cataloging-in-Publication Data

Powell, Mark Allan, 1953–
    Fortress introduction to the Gospels / Mark Allan Powell.
      p.  cm.
    Includes bibliographical references.
    ISBN 0-8006-3075-0 (alk. paper)
      1. Bible. N.T. Gospels—Introductions.   I. Title.
    BS2555.2.P67   1998
    226'.061—DC21
                                         97-22995
                                              CIP

Manufactured in the U.S.A.                                       AF 1-3075

09 08                                                      12

# CONTENTS

◆─────────────────────────────────────◆

# FIGURES

# Four Stories of Jesus

◆

Matthew, Mark, Luke, and John—these are the names given to the first four books included in the second part of the Christian Bible, which is known as the New Testament. They are commonly called "the four Gospels." All four relate the career of Jesus, the central figure of the Christian faith. The New Testament actually contains twenty-seven books, all of which reflect upon the significance of Jesus, but only these four describe his life and ministry.

The names given to these books were added at a later time. The books themselves are anonymous, but were written in Greek by Christians who lived in the Roman Empire during the last half of the first century. Jesus himself was born at the beginning of the first century—that, of course, is why it is called the first century in cultures influenced by Christianity. Thus, these four Gospels were written a generation or so after the time of Jesus himself, but nevertheless before Christianity had become the developed, institutionalized religion that it is today.

◆

## The World of the Gospels

Since the Gospels were written in a place and time other than our own, we sometimes need help understanding the stories they tell. They relate tales concerning centurions, Samaritans, Sadducees, and magi—people whom

Figure 1

---

Four Pictures of Jesus

*The Gospel of Mark* is interested in Jesus primarily as the one who died on the cross for sins. Jesus gave his life as a ransom for many (Mark 10:45).

*The Gospel of Matthew* is interested in Jesus primarily as the one who abides with his people always until the end of time. Jesus founded the church, in which sins are forgiven, prayers are answered, and the power of death is overcome (Matt. 16:18-19; 18:18-20).

*The Gospel of Luke* is interested in Jesus primarily as the one whose words and deeds liberate those who are oppressed in any way. Jesus came to seek and to save the lost and to bring release to all those he described as "captives" (Luke 4:18; 19:10).

*The Gospel of John* is interested in Jesus primarily as the one who reveals what God is truly like. Jesus was the Word of God made flesh, and he revealed through his own words and deeds all that can be known of God (John 1:14; 14:8).

---

we are not likely to encounter in our world today. We also hear about tax collectors and lawyers, who *are* still with us, but in the world of the Bible these professions evoked different associations than they do today. Tax collectors were viewed as traitors to their country, since they were collecting taxes on behalf of a conquering power. Lawyers did not sue people, but were experts at interpreting the Scriptures (the "law" of God). If we read the Gospel stories without realizing these things, we are likely to miss the point.

The world of the Gospels can be a strange environment to the uninitiated. People beat their breasts (Luke 18:13; 23:48), tear their clothing (Mark 14:63), and wash each other's feet (John 13:3-15). Jesus criticizes a group of people called the Pharisees for making "their phylacteries broad and their fringes long" (Matt. 23:5). He criticizes another Pharisee for neglecting to kiss him when he came to visit (Luke 7:45). Fortunately, a wealth of information is available to us regarding the world of the Gospels. For example, detailed descriptions of many places, people, and events are offered by the Jewish historian Josephus (37–c. 100 c.e.).[1] For students, numerous resources exist to provide the information needed. Bible dictionaries, for instance, are available in both single-volume and multi-volume editions to offer brief or in-depth explanations of manners, customs, and concepts that are no longer immediately understandable.[2] Similarly, Bible atlases offer maps, photographs, time lines, and other useful aids.

## Scholarship and the World of the Gospels

Our knowledge of the world of the Gospels has been aided over the years through a variety of academic fields of research.

*Archaeology.* Archaeologists have uncovered physical evidence from the place and time of the Gospels that supplies background information for interpreting the gospel stories.[3] Among the most important discoveries are numerous ancient documents from this period. The Dead Sea Scrolls reveal the thoughts and values of one first-century Jewish community.[4] Less famous, but possibly even more significant is the Nag Hammadi library of fourth-century gnostic Christians discovered in 1945, a find that yielded among other treasures our first complete copy of a volume called *The Gospel of Thomas* (see appendix, "The Other Gospels").[5] Such discoveries, in addition to physical excavations of biblical sites, have greatly increased our understanding of the biblical world.

*Sociology.* In recent years, Bible scholars have found another major ally in coming to understand the world of the Gospels: fields of study associated with the social sciences.[6] These entail a variety of approaches and disciplines, some of which are still being defined. *Social history* involves the interpretation of events in light of the social impact that historical transitions have on communities. For example, one result of the Jewish homeland becoming part of the Roman Empire was an exchange of populations. Business opportunities and other factors prompted non-Jewish people to move into Palestine in unprecedented numbers and Jewish people to move out of their homeland and to settle throughout the empire. Social historians would seek to define the effects that such migrations have on group identity and then to examine the Gospels to determine whether those issues are addressed in the stories they tell. The process is analogous to asking "the place of Franklin's *Poor Richard's Almanac* in preindustrial America or the relation of Steinbeck's *Grapes of Wrath* to the Great Depression."[7]

A related field, *sociology of knowledge,* tries to understand what people in a given culture take for granted about the world and how this relates to their patterns of social organization.[8] Examples might be beliefs about the extent to which life (or the future) is predetermined, or ideas concerning what constitutes wisdom (knowing right from wrong or understanding how things work). Especially significant is the investigation of what happens when competing sociologies collide, or when people convert from one way of knowing to another. John's Gospel, for instance, represents faith as coming to know what his community calls "the truth" (8:32). Sociologists would say this means more than just adding new religious propositions to a prior list of convictions. Rather, John's Gospel calls for its readers to abandon their preconceived notions about life and to entertain an entirely different vision of reality.

*Cultural anthropology.* Also derived from the social sciences, cultural anthropology employs models for understanding key phenomena that often occur within cultures. The goal is to understand what happens in a particular culture within a broader framework.[9] For example, almost all cultures designate certain days as special ("holidays"), but it is revealing to note whether the special days within a given culture mark events of primary significance to the individual (birthdays), the nation (Independence Day), or a prominent social subgroup (Christmas, Hanukkah). Similarly, cultural anthropologists study such matters as kinship relations, power structures, gender roles, economic systems, and strategies for education. The method of study always involves cross-cultural comparisons, asking, for instance, what purpose a phenomenon in one culture is expected to fulfill based on what we know from the study of other cultures. With regard to the Gospels, cultural anthropology has emphasized the significance of honor and shame within the Mediterranean world, explained the social dimensions of purity codes that label people "clean" or "unclean," and clarified the socioeconomic dynamics of peasant culture in which, without a middle class, most persons experience both the hardships and solidarity of poverty.

## Basic Dynamics of the Biblical World

Orienting ourselves to the world of the Gospels involves recognition of religious, political, and social dynamics.

*Religious.* The religious world of the Gospels is primarily that of the Jewish people, though we should not rashly assume that the beliefs or values of Jewish people in that era were identical with those of Jewish people today.[10] Perhaps the most outstanding characteristic of first-century Judaism was its diversity of belief and practice. Indeed, the very phrase "first-century Judaism" is anachronistic, implying a uniform religion that simply did not exist at that time. Recent discoveries such as the Dead Sea Scrolls have confirmed the presence of many different groups of Jewish people with conflicting religious ideas. The two Jewish groups that figure most prominently in the Gospels are the Sadducees and the Pharisees. The Sadducees are associated with the Temple in Jerusalem where sacrifices were offered to God under their auspices. The Pharisees are associated mainly with synagogues scattered throughout the area where they interpreted the Scriptures at regular sabbath services. These Scriptures included the books that Christians now call "the Old Testament," and familiarity with them is assumed throughout the Gospels. Another group of Semitic people, the Samaritans, claimed to be the true descendants of Abraham (the ancestor of the Jewish people) and the true followers of Moses (their lawgiver). They had their own temple (near the center of Palestine, at Gerizim) and their own copies of Scripture, but were viewed as heretics and foreigners by most Jewish people.

*Political.* The political world of the Gospels is that of an occupied land.[11] In 64 B.C.E.[12] the Roman general Pompey conquered Jerusalem. The areas where Jesus would later live and work (Galilee, Samaria, Judea) were all brought under the control of the Roman Empire. Typically, Roman rule involved the imposition of a king, governor, or other such figure appointed by Caesar, but also preserved certain institutions of native rule. According to the Gospels, a council of Jewish leaders (mostly Sadducees) called the Sanhedrin had authority in Jerusalem in some matters, but the Roman governor Pontius Pilate supposedly had the final say. The power struggles between these Jewish and Roman authorities (who's really in charge?) form a backdrop to the Gospels' stories of the trial and execution of Jesus and remain fuel for controversy even today in discussions of who was to blame for his crucifixion.[13]

*Social.* The social world of the Gospels must be understood as an intersection of cultures, a world in which Jewish traditions and values came to be influenced or challenged by those of other cultures.[14] For example, the Jewish people portrayed in most of the Gospels often understand sickness to be the result of possession by an evil spirit and healing to involve exorcism. These ideas do not derive from their Scriptures (there are no exorcisms in the Old Testament) but apparently were acquired from Persia or some other Eastern culture with which they had contact. Even more significant, however, is the degree of influence on these people from the Greek and Roman cultures, an influence that is usually called *Hellenism.* Hellenistic thought tended to focus upon the individual and to emphasize acquisition of knowledge and wisdom (including knowledge of the self). It also tended to be dualistic, that is, to make distinctions (good or evil, matter or spirit) that facilitated the organization of knowledge. These tendencies were not altogether absent from the Jewish tradition, but in general the latter had emphasized the community over the individual, stressed obedience over knowledge, and preferred paradox to precision. In short, the social world of the Gospels facilitated the development and integration of ideas from a variety of backgrounds. Two examples of such development within both Jewish and early Christian tradition are (1) *apocalyptic* thought, which saw the world as a battleground between God and Satan;[15] and (2) *Gnosticism,* which taught that people's spirits could be saved from the evil material world through the acquisition of secret knowledge.[16]

◆

# Genre

What is a Gospel anyway? Most modern readers are familiar with many different genres of literature—biography, poetry, science fiction, romance, and so forth—and they usually find it easy to identify the category to which a particular work belongs. But no one writes Gospels anymore. When we first approach these books we may find they are unlike anything else that we have ever read.

Scholars sometimes compare the Gospels to *historical fiction*. They depict real people and real events but the stories they recount are told with a flair more closely associated with novels than historical reporting. The authors of these books knew the art of storytelling, and their narratives develop in ways that are intended to be rhetorically effective. They employ such literary devices as irony, symbolism, and foreshadowing. They solicit our empathy so that, as the stories unfold, we may feel drawn into the drama.

The organization of the Gospels begs comparison to modern fictionalizations of history. None of the authors seems to be particularly concerned with recording the order in which events actually happened. This explains why, when the four Gospels are set side by side, their chronology of events is often inconsistent. For example, the account of Jesus overturning tables in the Jerusalem Temple is found near the beginning of John's Gospel (2:13-17), but in the Gospel of Mark this event occurs during the last week of Jesus' life (11:15-17). In both cases, the placement of the episode seems to be determined more by literary considerations than historical ones.

All four of the Gospels can be studied with methods similar to those employed by literary critics in their analysis of contemporary novels or short stories. New Testament scholars often talk about the plot of a particular Gospel, or they may discuss a Gospel writer's distinctive approach to characterization or conflict development. Still, the analogy between these works and modern historical fiction is primarily stylistic. Most Christians today would be offended by the notion that the Gospels are fiction, and rightly so. The authors of these books did not intend them to be read simply as literature, but clearly hoped their readers would accept the stories as accurate accounts. Comparisons to historical novels are helpful up to a point, but if taken too literally they become anachronistic, imposing modern categories on ancient documents.

How would the Gospels have been viewed by their original readers? The Greco-Roman world, like our own, knew many types of stories. There were comedies and tragedies. There were fables, myths, and legends. There were heroic epics, historical monographs, and (in the Jewish milieu) apocalyptic reports of heavenly visions. Against such a background, the Gospels are probably most similar to *ancient biographies.*[17]

They are not like modern biographies, for they make no pretense of offering an objective or balanced perspective on Jesus' life. They do not reveal their sources or offer any way for readers to check the reliability of what they report (no footnotes!). Their treatment is far from comprehensive: they offer little insight into Jesus' personality or motivation (How did he come to think the way he did?), provide almost no information about his early life (Did he have formal education? Was he ever married?), and do not even bother to describe his physical appearance (Was he short or tall? Fat or thin?). Such matters, however, were not expected to be addressed in biographies of this period. Biographies of philosophers, for example, tended to focus on selected anecdotes that preserved a person's teaching for the benefit of those who considered themselves to be his followers. Such biographies were almost worshipful in tone and, like our Gospels, they sometimes provided extended accounts of the hero's death, which was thought to reveal his character most fully.

Even so, this classification is not without its problems. The communities in which these Gospels were produced did not view Jesus primarily as a philosopher, nor did they think of themselves as schools. To "believe in Jesus" or to "follow" him no doubt meant to accept his teaching and to practice his way of life, but it meant something else as well. It might have meant to believe that he was "the Son of God" (Matt. 16:16) or "the Savior of the world" (John 4:42). It might have meant to identify him as the Jewish Messiah who had fulfilled God's ancient promises to Israel (Luke 24:25-27) or to regard him as a cosmic figure who would soon return from heaven to judge all people and to determine their destiny (Mark 13:26-27). It might even have meant to conclude that Jesus was God, that is, the physical embodiment of the one who created all things (John 1:1-3, 14). Though some ancient biographies did present the philosopher-hero as a divine figure, no parallel exists for the multitude of categories applied to Jesus in the Gospels.

The distinctiveness of the Gospels also becomes apparent when we consider the perspective they offer on Jesus' death. In every case, the story of Jesus' crucifixion provides an opportunity for the Gospel writer to present Jesus facing this ultimate crisis in a way that demonstrates his integrity and commitment. But there is more. The Gospels present Jesus' death as the climax of history. When he was crucified, something happened, something that altered forever the very nature of human existence in a way that ultimately would affect the life of every person. The Gospels struggle for language to describe what happened, referring to Jesus' death as a "ransom" (Mark 10:45) or as the institution of a "new covenant" (Luke 22:20). They liken him to a sacrificial animal who "takes away the sin of the world" (John

1:29). They dramatize the significance of this event through reference to a ritual meal in which bread may be described as Jesus' flesh given "for the life of the world" (John 6:51) or wine identified as his blood poured out "for the forgiveness of sins" (Matt. 26:28). The superlative nature of these claims may be trivialized by identification of the Gospels as biographies.

Still, most scholars admit that to persons in the ancient world, these books probably looked more like biographies than anything else. Some are content to leave the matter at that; others prefer to say that the Gospels draw upon the genre of ancient biography but transcend or expand this genre in important ways.

◆

# Sermons in Story Form

The word *gospel* itself means "good news," and in the first century it appears to have passed rather quickly through four stages of application:

First, the term was used to describe the content of Jesus' preaching. As one writer puts it, "Jesus came to Galilee, proclaiming the good news of God" (Mark 1:14). We will examine what is meant by this in more detail in the next chapter, but for now may simply note that Jesus talked about God, and what he said about God was thought to be gospel or "good news."

Second, the word was used to describe the content of early Christian preaching regarding the death and resurrection of Christ. When the apostle Paul says that he preached "the gospel of God" (Rom. 1:1-5), he does not mean that he repeated what Jesus had said about God but that he told people what had happened when Jesus died and rose from the dead (see also 1 Cor. 15:1-8). This also was thought to be good news.

Third, as a combination of the above, the term *gospel* came to refer to preaching that summarized the ministry of Jesus in a way that included both what Jesus had said was the good news about God and what Christians had said was the good news about Jesus. A summary of such a sermon is found in Acts 10:34-43. Or, again, when Mark 14:9 says that an incident involving a woman anointing Jesus will be recounted "wherever the gospel is preached," we may conclude that what is meant by "gospel" now includes reports of events from Jesus' life, not just summaries of his essential message or announcements of his death and resurrection.

Finally, the word came to be used for books that offer in written form what had previously been proclaimed orally. The first such book was probably the one that we call the Gospel of Mark, and it uses this term in its very first verse: "The beginning of the good news [gospel] of Jesus Christ, the Son of God."

What this brief survey illustrates is that our written Gospels are only a short step removed from preaching, and this may explain some of the difficulty in ascribing them to a genre of written literature. The Gospels are sometimes described as "sermons in story form."[18] They may have looked like biographies to ancient readers, and they may look like historical fiction to modern readers, but buried within these outer forms are sermons trying to be heard.

The technical term scholars use for the authors of these books is *evangelists* (from the Greek word for gospel, *euanggelion*). Today, that term may summon images of zealous religious figures who berate people to change their ways. If we can set aside the caricatures of such a role that derive from association with celebrity figures ("television evangelists"), we may realize that this image is actually not too far off the mark. The Gospel writers do want to effect definitive changes in the ways we think and live.

Recognition of the essentially religious character of these works raises questions for how they are best approached within an academic setting. On the one hand, such a setting demands that these books be studied like any other, with rigorous objectivity that does not exempt them from critical scrutiny. On the other hand, to ignore the religious dimension would represent a failure to engage them on their own terms. Reading the Gospels merely as literature or as ancient historical documents allows interpreters to adopt a detached perspective that avoids consideration of the very factors that caused these books to be written and preserved in the first place. An objective, dispassionate reception is the last thing the Gospel writers would have wanted their books to receive. We are free to accept or reject, belittle or embrace, but whatever our response, we ought to understand what these books intend to do: they intend to convert us.

# CHAPTER ONE

# From Jesus to Us

Jesus lived in the northern portion of Palestine (modern Israel) in the region known as Galilee. He was a Jewish peasant who lived a relatively simple life. He wrote no books and he traveled less than fifty miles from his hometown. Much controversy surrounds the significance and meaning of his life, yet even today the time when Jesus lived is called "the first century" because of him.

The incredible influence of Jesus on Western civilization owes much to the religion that arose after his death. The Christian faith has found diverse forms of expression, but all traditional Christians have this in common: they believe that this Jewish peasant Jesus is living still, glorified in heaven where he rules the cosmos and hears their prayers. He is the Son of God, and the things he said and did on earth are remembered as the words and acts of God.

About half of the people living in the United States identify themselves as Christians, and on Sundays many of them go to their respective houses of worship. At a climactic point in the service, the worship leader will open a Bible and read familiar words regarding something that Jesus said or did, words taken from one of the four New Testament Gospels. But what Christian congregations experience on Sunday mornings is different from what they would have witnessed if they had actually been present with Jesus in Galilee. For one thing, they hear the words of Jesus proclaimed in English rather than in Aramaic, the ancient Semitic dialect that Jesus actually spoke, or in Greek, the language in which all four of the Gospels were written.

Figure 2

---

From Jesus to Us.

Stages in the Transmission of the Gospel Tradition

1. *The Historical Jesus*
   Jesus says and does things that are considered to be remarkable.

2. *Early Tradition*
   Written sources: People write down what Jesus said or did and preserve these documents.
   Oral tradition: People remember what Jesus said or did and share these memories with others.

3. *Redaction of the Gospels*
   The Gospel writers compile their books, editing the early written sources and oral traditions.

4. *Preservation of Manuscripts*
   People make copies of the completed Gospels and disseminate them throughout the world.

5. *Translation*
   Scholars translate copies of the Gospels into other languages, including English.

6. *Reception*
   Finally, we hear or read about what Jesus said and did in our modern editions of the Gospels.

---

New Testament scholars are interested in the process of development that leads from the historical time of Jesus to the impact that his words and deeds as reported in the Gospels have on people today. Six stages of transmission may be discerned (see figure 2), and each of these becomes the subject of particular types of research. Most scholars recognize that the Gospel tradition undergoes development as it passes through these stages of transmission. In other words, changes occur, and these changes may be evaluated either positively or negatively by people with different theological interests or religious commitments.

◆

# The Historical Jesus

Even though the Gospels cannot be read as modern biographies, they are often used by historians as resources for gathering biographical information. The person Jesus did exist, and he did say and do things that were deemed remarkable by his contemporaries. The task of separating historical facts about Jesus from faith claims and religious interpretations concerning him has been tagged "the quest of the historical Jesus." In the modern era, this quest has known three phases, as the topic came to prominence first in the nineteenth century, again in the 1960s, and then resurged yet again at the end of the twentieth century.[1]

The controversial group known as the Jesus Seminar has played a prominent role in recent studies. Founded in 1985, this organization of scholars meets twice a year to consider the historicity of matters related to Jesus. After discussion, members vote on selected matters and the results are broadcast widely through a variety of media. In past years, the Jesus Seminar has decided that Jesus really did tell the parable of the Good Samaritan reported in Luke 10:30-35, but that he did not actually teach his disciples the Golden Rule as found in Matthew 7:12 and Luke 6:31. More troubling to many Christians is the group's contention that such events as the virgin birth of Jesus or his resurrection from the dead cannot be regarded as historical occurrences.[2]

A number of recent scholars have attempted to provide the modern world with what the Gospels do not offer: reliable historical biographies of Jesus (see figure 3). Although there are points of overlap, controversy arises over such questions as the level of continuity or discontinuity Jesus shared with his Jewish contemporaries and the extent to which he was oriented toward the present or the future. Among the works surveyed in figure 3, Crossan sees Jesus as an unconventional Jew and Meier labels him a marginal one. Sanders and Wright place him in the tradition of Israel's prophets, while Borg considers him exemplary of a mystical variety of Judaism. Both Borg and Crossan emphasize Jesus' this-worldly orientation as a politically conscious social reformer. Meier and especially Sanders focus on his vision of a future in which God will transform what lies beyond the capacity of humans to effect. Wright thinks Jesus believed that he himself was bringing about that transformation.

How do these scholars determine which information concerning Jesus is to be regarded as historically authentic?[3] They are not content simply to sift through the Gospels in the form that we now have them. Rather, they rely upon the work of source critics and form critics (discussed below) to deter-

Figure 3

---

Modern Biographies of Jesus

Numerous studies of Jesus were produced by historical scholars in the last decade of the twentieth century. Here is a sample of some of their conclusions:

*Marcus Borg* sees Jesus as a Jewish mystic, a charismatic "Spirit person" who was intent on revitalizing Israel. He claimed an intimacy with God, referring to the deity as "abba," a term of familiarity similar to modern day "Daddy." Throughout his life, he experienced visions and other encounters with divine reality that he believed empowered him to accomplish the mission for which God had selected him. This mission involved initiating a religious movement that would prioritize compassion over concern for purity. Thus Jesus opposed "the politics of holiness" that categorized people in his day as clean or unclean, Jew or Gentile, and his religious vision led him to be identified also as a subversive social reformer. See *Jesus: A New Vision* (San Francisco: Harper & Row, 1987).

*John Dominic Crossan* views Jesus as a radical peasant who rebelled against political and religious authorities by defying their conventions. A Jewish Cynic, he taught a new wisdom through parables and aphorisms that pointed out the inherent inadequacies of usual ways of thinking. In conscious resistance to the economic and social tyranny of Roman-occupied Palestine, he proclaimed a vision of life oriented around God's radical justice and adopted a lifestyle intended to emulate this concept. He and his followers lived in poverty by choice. Even after he had gained some renown, he performed exorcisms without charge, claiming to heal people for free. In violation of accepted taboos he sought to demonstrate a radical egalitarianism by openly engaging in table fellowship with misfits and outcasts. See *The Historical Jesus: The Life of a Mediterranean Jewish Peasant* (San Francisco: HarperSanFrancisco, 1991).

*John Meier* describes Jesus as "a marginal Jew," that is, as a Jewish teacher who by circumstance and choice lived on the margins of his own society, speaking and acting in ways that made him appear "obnoxious, dangerous, or suspicious to everyone." He began life as the eldest son of an average peasant family, but as a young adult abandoned his job as a woodworker and left his home to become a disciple of John the Baptist, who called people to repent in preparation for some sort of imminent divine intervention. Later, he began a public ministry of his own, preaching that God was coming to gather his scattered people and to rule them as their King. Jesus also became widely known as a miracle worker, and

*(continued)*

Figure 3 *continued*

---

this reputation allowed him to claim that, in some sense, God's reign was already present. In light of this activity, he presented himself as an authoritative teacher of God's will, giving his followers clear directives on how God their King wanted them to live. See *A Marginal Jew*, 2 vols. (New York: Doubleday, 1991–94).

*E. P. Sanders* presents Jesus as an eschatological prophet whose essential mission was to announce a great future event that was about to take place. God was going to intervene directly in history in a way that would involve the elimination of all evil and the dawning of a new age. His vision for this transformation was decidedly Jewish: the selection of twelve disciples was intended to represent the restoration of the twelve tribes of Israel, and the demonstration in the temple was a symbolic act presaging that God would raise up a new temple to replace the corrupt one. The most radical aspect of Jesus' vision was that he promised inclusion in God's kingdom to sinners without demanding their repentance. He emphasized forgiveness, presenting God as loving and gracious. See *The Historical Figure of Jesus* (London: Penguin, 1993).

*N. T. Wright* describes Jesus as one who believed his vocation was to enact what Scripture said God would do. Viewing himself as both prophet and Messiah, he understood his own destiny as symbolizing that of Israel. Thus, he performed mighty works as signs of long-awaited fulfillment of prophecy and sought to create a community of followers that would represent reconstituted Israel. He came to believe that his vocation included dying as the representative of Israel. His death, he thought, would be a way of symbolically undergoing the judgment he had announced for Israel, and would also serve as a prelude to vindication by God. This vindication would initiate a new covenant with Israel and inaugurate God's reign as king of the world. In such ways, Jesus attempted to do and be, for Israel and for the world, what Scripture said God alone could do and be. See *Jesus and the Victory of God* (Minneapolis: Fortress Press, 1996).

---

mine the origins of the materials that have been incorporated into each of these books. Material that is believed to derive from an early source is likely to be considered more credible than that which comes from a later period. In addition, facts concerning Jesus are best attested when they can be confirmed from more than one source. For example, no historian would doubt that Jesus did in fact tell parables, since numerous parables (albeit different ones) are attributed to him in many different sources.

Historical scholars inspect the Gospel materials for anachronistic references that reflect the later interests of Christians rather than what can be reasonably attributed to Jesus himself. For instance, Matthew's Gospel por trays Jesus as telling his disciples to bring problems "to the church" for resolution (18:17), but historians do not believe the church existed as an identifiable institution until many years after Jesus' death. By the same token, descriptions of Jesus in the Gospels may be accorded authenticity precisely because they are dissimilar to what would have served the interests of the developing Christian religion. Depictions of Jesus as a person who socializes with such social outcasts as tax collectors (Mark 2:15) strike many as a tradition the church would have been more likely to suppress than invent. Hence, this detail about Jesus' life is usually accepted and allowed to serve as one piece of solid biographical data.

This use of the Gospels as resources for historical research is a far cry from more popular treatments that regard these books as Holy Scripture. Some historical scholars would insist that Jesus is significant to historians as well as to theologians and deserves to be studied as a historical figure apart from the presuppositions of religious belief. Other historical scholars approach this topic as avowed Christians who are committed to ongoing dialogue with the secular world. They wish to consider such questions as what should be written about Jesus in an encyclopedia or what should be taught concerning him in public schools. Some Christian scholars are committed to research of this nature because they believe their faith can only be confessed with integrity when they allow its historical foundations to be examined.

Ultimately, however, all of these scholars will recognize that the interests of history and theology overlap only in part. Christian theology claims that Jesus was crucified under the Roman governor Pontius Pilate, and this claim can be tested through historical investigation. But Christian theology also claims that through Jesus' death God acted to save human beings from their sins. This latter proposition offers an interpretation of the historical event that cannot be tested. The criteria of historical research offer no means for determining whether such an interpretation is true or false.

◆

# Early Tradition: Written Sources and Oral Transmission

Because the New Testament Gospels were not compiled until several decades after the time of Jesus, scholars are often interested in how the traditions concerning Jesus were transmitted during those intervening years. In particular, source critics attempt to identify and reconstruct early written materials that may have existed prior to these four Gospels and served as sources for their composition. Similarly, form critics seek to identify units of material that may have been passed on through oral tradition before they were incorporated into these Gospels.

Source critics began by making a distinction between the Gospel of John and the other three books, which they call the Synoptic Gospels. This distinction is based on the recognition that Matthew, Mark, and Luke contain a large number of parallel passages, that is, passages that are very similar or even identical to each other. Accordingly, source critics assume that these three Gospels must somehow be related—they either used the same sources or else one or more of them must itself have served as a source for the other(s). The dilemma scholars face in figuring out the details of this relationship is called the Synoptic problem. Over the last hundred years numerous scenarios have been proposed and tested, but in the latter half of the twentieth century a near consensus was reached.

The most widely accepted solution to the Synoptic problem is the *Two-Source Hypothesis* (see figure 4). Most scholars believe that Mark's Gospel was the first one written and that it served as a source for both Matthew and Luke. This explains the large volume of triple parallels between the three works. But there is more. Most scholars believe that Matthew and Luke also used another source, an early written collection of Jesus' sayings which has come to be referred to as *Q* (an abbreviation of the German word for source, *Quelle*). This explains the large amount of material that is parallel in Matthew and Luke, but is not found in Mark. For convenience, the material in Matthew that is not derived from either Mark or Q is referred to as *M,* and material in Luke that is not derived from Mark or Q is referred to as *L*. (Because of the latter two designations, the Two-Source Hypothesis is sometimes called the Four-Source Hypothesis. This is misleading, since most scholars do not use the labels *M* and *L* to refer to actual sources but to material of unknown origin.[4])

The most significant (and controversial) aspect of this theory is the proposal that Christians once possessed a written collection of Jesus' sayings that has since been lost. Numerous attempts have been made to reconstruct the Q document based on what is preserved in Matthew and in Luke (see figure 5). These reconstructions are always incomplete and somewhat hypothetical, but they offer a glimpse of what may have been the first book about Jesus. Historical Jesus scholars often regard material that can be ascribed to Q as especially significant for their work, asserting that this lost document provided more reliable information about Jesus than any book in the New Testament. Others interested in the origins of Christianity also value reconstructions of Q as providing a look at what was deemed most important for one community of the earliest Christians.

Figure 4

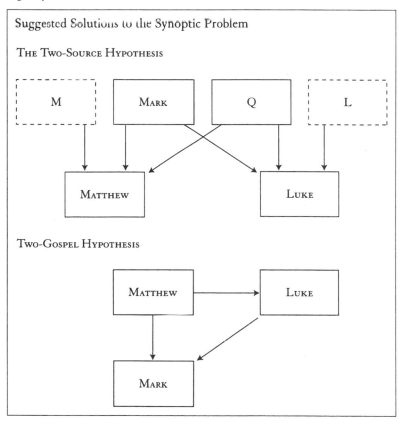

Suggested Solutions to the Synoptic Problem

THE TWO-SOURCE HYPOTHESIS

M    MARK    Q    L

MATTHEW    LUKE

TWO-GOSPEL HYPOTHESIS

MATTHEW → LUKE

MARK

As a collection of sayings, the Q document did not look much like the four New Testament Gospels, which are mostly narrative. The primary focus of these sayings was a call to a new orientation of life, one that would be grounded in recognition of God as ruler. This meant becoming a disciple of Jesus, which implies becoming like him (Luke 6:40). Just as Jesus had "nowhere to lay his head" (Luke 9:58), so his disciples were expected to leave their homes and families, abandon their jobs, and give up their possessions. Such a vision of discipleship, which scholars call *itinerant radicalism,* regards renunciation of worldly security as necessary for those who would devote themselves entirely to God.

Apparently, Q contained very few stories about Jesus. It did not even have a passion narrative, that is, an account of Jesus' death and resurrection. Those who treasured this book must have looked to the future rather than to the past for God's definitive act of salvation. While there are no references

**Figure 5**

---

Contents of Q: A Partial List

Preaching of John the Baptist (Luke 3:7-9; Matt. 3:7-10)
Temptation of Jesus (Luke 4:1-13; Matt. 4:1-11)
Beatitudes (Luke 6:20-23; Matt. 5:3-12)
Love for Enemies (Luke 6:27-36; Matt. 5:39-48; 7:12)
On Judging Others (Luke 6:37-42; Matt. 7:1-5; 10:24; 15:14)
On Bearing Fruit (Luke 6:43-45; Matt. 7:15-20)
The House Built on Rock (Luke 6:47-49; Matt. 7:24-27)
Healing of a Centurion's Servant (Luke 7:1-10; Matt. 8:5-10, 13)
John the Baptist Questions Jesus (Luke 7:18-35; Matt. 11:2-19)
The Would-Be Disciples (Luke 9:57-60; Matt. 8:19-22)
Jesus' Missionary Discourse (Luke 10:2-16; Matt. 9:37-38; 10:9-15; 11:21-23)
Thanksgiving to the Father (Luke 10:21-24; Matt. 11:25-27; 13:16-17)
The Lord's Prayer (Luke 11:2-4; Matt. 6:9-13)
Asking and Receiving (Luke 11:9-13; Matt. 7:7-11)
Return of an Evil Spirit (Luke 11:24-26; Matt. 12:43-45)
The Sign of Jonah (Luke 11:29-32; Matt. 12:38-42)
On Light (Luke 11:33-36; Matt. 5:15; 6:22-23)
Woe to the Pharisees (Luke 11:37-52; Matt. 23:4-7, 13-36)
Fear of Humans and God (Luke 12:2-12; Matt. 10:19, 26-33; 12:32)
Do Not Worry About Life (Luke 12:22-34; Matt. 6:19-21, 25-33)
Be Ready for the Master's Return (Luke 12:39-46; Matt. 24:43-51)
Divisions in the Family (Luke 12:51-53; Matt.10:34-36)
Signs of the Times (Luke 12:54-56; Matt. 16:2-3)
Settle Out of Court (Luke 12:57-59; Matt. 5:25-26)
Mustard Seed and Leaven (Luke 13:18-21; Matt. 13:31-33)
The Narrow Door (Luke 12:23-30; Matt. 7:13-14, 22-23; 8:11-12)
Lament over Jerusalem (Luke 13:34-35; Matt. 23:37-39)
Parable of the Banquet (Luke 14:15-24; Matt. 22:1-14)
Carrying the Cross (Luke 14:26-27; Matt. 10:37-38)
Parable of the Lost Sheep (Luke 15:1-7; Matt. 18:12-14)
On Serving Two Masters (Luke 16:13; Matt. 6:24)
Role of the Law and Prophets (Luke 16:16-17; Matt. 5:18; 11:13)
Rebuking and Forgiving Sin (Luke 17:1-6; Matt. 18:6-7, 15, 21-22)
The Coming of the Son of Man (Luke 17:23-27, 33-37; Matt. 24:17-18, 26-28, 37-41)
Parable of the Talents (Luke 19:11-27; Matt. 25:14-30)

---

to Jesus dying for their sins, numerous passages in the Q material speak of a second coming or parousia, a time when Jesus will return to deliver them from the afflictions of life in an evil world. This deliverance will come through a great judgment that will bring destruction upon many. In essence, the Q document appears to have been a collection of what some of Jesus' followers believed were the sayings of their coming Judge. They accepted these sayings as a guide for living in the last days and were committed both to living in accord with them and to promulgating them for others who needed to know what was required to survive the final judgment.[5]

Some scholars do not accept the Two-Source Hypothesis. A minority follow a scheme called the *Two-Gospel Hypothesis* (see figure 4), which holds that Matthew was the first Gospel written, that Luke used Matthew as a source, and that Mark produced his Gospel last, as an abridgment of the other two.[6] This theory does manage to account for the literary parallels between the Gospels without positing a hypothetical lost source, but most scholars don't think it makes sense. Matthew and Luke are much longer than Mark and are usually considered to evince a higher standard of writing, one that is more refined in terms of grammar, syntax, and the like. Most scholars find motives for expansion and refinement more explicable than motives for abridgement and colloquialization. (The Two-Gospel Hypothesis is sometimes also known as *the Griesbach hypothesis,* after the eighteenth-century scholar, Johann Jakob Griesbach, who proposed its basic precepts.[7])

If it is accepted, the Two-Source Hypothesis designates early written sources for Matthew and Luke. But what about the other Gospels, Mark and John? Did Mark's Gospel—the first of the four—also make use of early written sources? Numerous suggestions have been made in this regard (see figure 10 on p. 40), but all are disputed and nothing as grand as the Q document is proposed. As for the Gospel of John, most scholars do believe that some material was put into writing early and incorporated into the final composition at a later time. There are different theories, however, regarding these stages of editing, so that the origin, nature, and scope of what would have constituted the earliest strata is difficult to determine (for frequently cited candidates, see figure 21 on p. 115).

Whatever early written sources were used in the composition of the Gospels, much of what ended up in these books probably derived from oral tradition. Form critics study the processes through which information is transmitted orally in pre-literate cultures.[8] They recognize that small units of material often circulate independently and that these units tend to exhibit certain defining characteristics. Even today, this is often the case with jokes, which are more often told than written and which tend to be told in rather predictable ways.

As form critics study the Gospels, they try to identify places where small units of oral tradition have been incorporated into the written documents. They may do this by noting certain structural patterns or other rhetorical features typical of a particular type of material that was transmitted orally. When these units can be detected, form critics try to do three more things. First, they classify the unit according to what type of material it is (see figure 6).[9] Second, they identify the probable function that the material would have served for the people who preserved it. The technical term for this function is *Sitz im Leben,* German for "setting in life." The *Sitz im Leben* for a joke in our modern culture is usually entertainment, though it might also serve some other purpose such as social commentary. The units of oral tradition preserved by early Christians served a variety of functions, including preaching, worship, catechetics (instruction in faith), apologetics (defense), polemics (attack of critics or rivals), discipline (preserving order in the community), and, yes, entertainment. Finally, form critics attempt to reconstruct what the unit of tradition would have looked like prior to its incorporation into the written Gospel. To the extent that they are able to do this, they succeed at recovering oral sources for the Gospels. In this sense, form criticism may be considered a type of source criticism, a type that specializes in studying oral sources rather than written ones.

A major contribution that source critics and form critics make to Gospel studies may be understood in terms of the distinction between what is called *tradition* and *framework.* Scholars believe that when the four evangelists incorporated material into their Gospels, they edited the material and added their own commentary. Today, material in the Gospels that is thought to derive from a source (oral or written) is identified as tradition and material that is thought to have been added by the evangelists is called the framework.

As an example of how this works, we may consider a passage from Mark 1:21-28 (see figure 7). Form critics identify an exorcism story in these verses, and they note that exorcism stories were transmitted orally according to the following typical outline: (1) demon recognizes exorcist; (2) exorcist issues threat or command; (3) demon comes out, with signs; (4) impression upon spectators is noted. This outline corresponds almost exactly to what is reported in this passage, beginning with verse 24 and ending with the first few words of verse 27 ("They were all amazed"). Accordingly, form critics would be likely to identify these verses as the tradition that Mark received and to identify the rest of the passage (verses 21-23, the latter part of verse 27, and all of 28) as Mark's own additions to this source material. We can see why the added material is called framework, for in this case the added commentary literally forms a frame around the traditional source material.

**Figure 6**

---

Typical Forms of Material in the Gospels

1. *Sayings:* memorable quotations that may have been preserved apart from any particular context

   - *legal sayings* interpret God's will as expressed in the law (Mark 2:27)

   - *eschatological sayings* (sometimes called *prophetic* or *apocalyptic* sayings) reveal God's future and its implications for the present (Mark 9:1)

   - *proverbs* (sometimes called *gnomic* or *wisdom* sayings) express secular wisdom or "common sense" (Mark 3:24)

   - *"I" sayings* are autobiographical (Mark 2:17)

2. *Pronouncement Stories* (sometimes called *apophthegms* or *paradigms*): short narratives of incidents that provide context for memorable quotations

   - *biographical stories* recall significant moments in a person's life (Mark 11:15-17)

   - *controversy stories* recall arguments in which a person made a definitive point (Mark 12:13-17)

   - *didactic stories* recall occasions in which a person's teaching was particularly relevant (Mark 3:31-35)

3. *Parables:* longer sayings that function as extended figures of speech (similes, metaphors, allegories, and so forth). Example: the parable of the sower in Mark 4:3-8

4. *Commissioning Stories:* narrative accounts of persons or groups receiving calls to participate in the divine plan. Example: Jesus' call of Levi in Mark 2:14

5. *Miracle Stories:* narrative accounts of people displaying supernatural (that is, divine or demonic) power

   - *exorcisms* (Mark 5:1-20)

   - *healing miracles* (Mark 1:40-45)

   - *resuscitations* (Mark 5:21-24, 35-43)

*(continued)*

**Figure 6** *continued*

---

- *nature miracles* (Mark 4:35-41)

- *feeding miracles* (Mark 8:1-10)

6. *Hymns:* words to canticles or songs that may be distinguished by particular metrical patterns or by such poetic devices as alliteration, parallelism, and chiasm. Example: the Magnificat in Luke 1:46-55

7. *Genealogies:* narrative lists that trace the line of descent for persons or groups. Example: genealogy of Jesus in Matthew 1:1-17

8. *Legends:* narrative accounts of persons earning renown or glory. Example: Jesus' entry into Jerusalem (Mark 11:1-10)

9. *Myths:* narrative accounts of people interacting with supernatural beings. Example: Jesus' transfiguration (Mark 9:2-8)

*Note:* These categories are descriptive and not fixed. They may overlap; for example, all exorcism stories have a mythical component and many healing stories are also legends.

---

**Figure 7**

---

An Exorcism Story (Mark 1:21-28)

[21]They went to Capernaum; and when the sabbath came, he entered the synagogue and taught. [22]They were astounded at his teaching, for he taught them as one having authority, and not as the scribes. [23]Just then there was in their synagogue a man with an unclean spirit, [24]and **he cried out, "What have you to do with us, Jesus of Nazareth? Have you come to destroy us? I know who you are, the Holy One of God."** [25]**But Jesus rebuked him saying, "Be silent, and come out of him!"** [26]**And the unclean spirit, convulsing him and crying with a loud voice, came out of him.** [27]**They were all amazed,** and they kept on asking one another, "What is this? A new teaching—with authority! He commands even the unclean spirits, and they obey him." [28]At once his fame began to spread throughout the surrounding region of Galilee.

---

Of course, it does not always work out this neatly. Sometimes, material identified as framework may be scattered throughout the passage.

What is the point of making such a distinction? It becomes significant in three different ways. First, scholars who are interested in the early history of the Christian church find this distinction allows them to trace develop-

ments that occurred during this formative period. Traditional material offers testimony to concerns of the movement during one stage and material
ascribed to the evangelists' framework offers evidence of how these concerns
were addressed during a subsequent stage. For this type of scholarship, both
tradition and framework are equally important. Second, historical-Jesus
scholars find the distinction allows them to focus their attention on the material that is earliest and therefore most likely to represent what Jesus actually said and did. For this type of study, traditional material is far more
important than framework passages. Third, scholars who are interested in
explicating the theological views of the evangelists themselves (*redaction critics*) find the distinction allows them to isolate those passages where the evangelists' own perspectives are most evident. For this task, the framework passages are the most important.

◆

# Redaction of the Gospels

When the four evangelists set about to write what we now know as the New
Testament Gospels, they assumed what must have been enormous tasks,
fraught with responsibility. Luke says in the introduction to his work that
he first took into account the traditions he had received from others, then
investigated everything carefully himself, and finally set out to organize his
account in a way that would reveal "the truth" to his readers (1:1-4). As we
have seen, the evangelists relied heavily on oral and written source materials. At the same time, they did not simply string together miscellaneous traditions, but took strong personal interest in creating coherent narratives that
would reveal what they considered to be the true meaning of the stories
they told.

A modern analogy for composition of this sort may be found in the role
of editors, who sometimes take what has been written by others and shape
it into a work that better meets their own approval. Accordingly, the evangelists responsible for the four New Testament Gospels are often referred
to as *redactors,* and the discipline that studies the way they shaped their materials into the form of our present Gospels is called *redaction criticism* (the
word *redactor* is a somewhat archaic synonym for *editor*).

Modern newspaper editors have at least two opportunities to shape material in accord with their own standards. First, they might read all of the
copy that reporters turn in to them and make changes that they think are
appropriate. Second, they may be responsible for the layout of the paper, for

deciding where the various stories will be placed. Presumably, if one studied an editor's habits closely enough, noting what kinds of changes were made consistently and which stories got top billing, one could determine quite a bit about that editor's beliefs and values. Thus, redaction criticism usually employs two methods designed to uncover the particular ideas of each of the individual evangelists. *Emendation analysis* attempts to discern the redactor's interests by observing changes that he has made in his source material. *Composition analysis* attempts to discern those interests by noting how individual units have been ordered and arranged in the work as a whole.[10]

*Emendation analysis* presupposes the work of source and form critics discussed above. For example, since most source critics believe that Matthew used the Gospel of Mark as one of his sources, redaction critics usually begin their study of Matthew by listing all of the changes that Matthew appears to have made when he took Mark's Gospel over into his own (see figure 13, p. 63; for a similar chart on Luke's redaction of Mark see figure 18, p. 90). For example, they may note that Matthew frequently drops from his Gospel verses in Mark in which Jesus asks questions (Mark 5:9, 30; 6:38; 8:23; 9:12, 16, 21, 33; 10:3; 14:4). Why? Perhaps Matthew thought it unseemly for the Son of God to have to request information from mere mortals. If so, then this evangelist has a somewhat different view of Jesus than Mark, who obviously did not find this problematic.

As this example illustrates, emendation analysis is most helpful in the study of those portions of Matthew and Luke that are derived from Mark, since the source (Mark) is available for easy comparison. It is less helpful in the study of Matthew/Luke parallels where the source (Q) must first be reconstructed. For instance, redaction critics will note that in Luke, Jesus says, "Blessed are you who are poor" (Luke 6:20), but in Matthew he says, "Blessed are the poor in spirit" (Matt. 5:3). The difference in wording is intriguing, but how can we know for certain whether Matthew added the words "in spirit" or Luke dropped them?

Emendation analysis would seem to be least helpful in the study of Mark, John, or the M and L portions of Matthew and Luke, since in these cases no sources are available for comparison. Still, the distinction between tradition and framework material made by source and form critics allows for some application of the method even here. Let us consider once again the passage from Mark 1:21-28 containing the exorcism story (see figure 7). As we have seen, form critics believe that Mark took a simple four-part exorcism story that had been passed on to him through oral tradition and added an introduction (verses 21-22) and conclusion (verses 27b-28). Historians tend to reject this Markan framework as less authentic than the received tradition, but redaction critics regard the framework as valuable for another reason.

It provides an example of Mark's emendation of the source and so offers insight into the evangelist's own interests.

In this case, redaction critics note that the Markan framework introduces a major theme not present in the source material itself. The introduction describes the context for the exorcism as a situation in which Jesus was teaching and stresses that the authority of his teaching was apparent to all. The conclusion returns to this theme by actually referring to the exorcism as "a new teaching" and again stressing the authority of Jesus' words. Thus, Mark uses this traditional exorcism story to make a point about the authoritative word of Jesus. Redaction critics assume he does so to make the story relevant to his own community. Jesus himself is no longer present (see Mark 2:20; 14:7), but the community does still have his teaching. Mark's message to his community is that, even though Jesus himself is gone, the authoritative word of Jesus continues to operate through his teaching in ways that liberate people from what is demonic or evil.

*Composition analysis* works equally well in study of any material from Matthew, Mark, Luke, or John, since one can make observations about how a work is organized without first determining what sources were used or defining which material is derived from those sources. Redaction critics typically make general observations regarding the overall structure of each of the four Gospels. For example, the Gospel of Luke devotes ten chapters (9:51—19:40) to describing a journey that Jesus makes to Jerusalem, a trip that appears to be covered in about half a chapter elsewhere (Mark 10:32-52). Once they notice this, redaction critics seek to determine the significance of organizing the Gospel story in this way. Is it to provide an orientation that focuses more of the story on the events that occur in Jerusalem (Jesus' death and resurrection), as if to indicate that these events were Jesus' destiny toward which he had been moving all along? Or is perhaps the city itself significant? Does Luke want to call Christianity back to its Jewish roots by highlighting the significance of the Jewish capital for the life and ministry of Jesus (see also Luke 2:41-49; 24:49)?

Composition analysis is also used to examine the immediate contexts of individual passages in the Gospels. Consider the example of Matthew 18:15-20. These verses are unique to Matthew (part of the M material). We have no knowledge of any source from which they were derived and so we cannot know for sure what changes (emendations) Matthew might have made. Still, we can learn something about Matthew's interests and concerns by observing how he placed this passage in the overall framework of his Gospel. Matthew 18:15-20 offers a description of the process through which a member of the church might be accused of sin and, if unrepentant, removed from the community. But in the immediately preceding passage (18:10-14), Jesus relates the parable of the lost sheep in which he concludes "it is not the will of your Father in heaven that one of these little ones should be lost" (18:14). And in the very next passage, Matthew presents an episode in which Jesus insists that his followers should forgive each other repeatedly (18:21-22) and then tells another parable encouraging people to be as generous and merciful in their dealings with each other as God has been with them. In short, Matthew has deliberately chosen to sandwich the harsh words dealing with possible expulsion between stories emphasizing forgiveness and mercy. While recognizing that procedures for excommunication are necessary, this evangelist wanted to be sure that they would never be applied as acts of punishment or in the interests of keeping the community pure (getting rid of the "bad apple"). In context, the process outlined in Matthew 18:15-20 becomes one for identifying the lost sheep, so that the community can intensify its efforts to reach the one who is in trouble before it is too late.

As these examples illustrate, redaction criticism often exposes the intent of the evangelist in ways that have moral or religious application. For this reason, emendation and composition analysis are especially popular with clergy and other students of the Bible who are looking for didactic or homiletical insights. The methods are not, however, limited to exegesis of the Gospels as scripture. They are used by all scholars who want to uncover the distinctive perspectives of the individuals responsible for producing these four books, regardless of the attitude the scholars might take toward those perspectives.

◆

# Preservation of Manuscripts

Copies of the Gospels were made quite early. This is impressive since, in the ancient world, books had to be copied painstakingly by hand, usually by professional scribes skilled in the art. The production of even a single manuscript could be an expensive and time-consuming project.[11] Still, the Gospels appear to have been disseminated throughout the world rather quickly. If the Two-Source Hypothesis is correct, then both Matthew and Luke had separate copies of Mark's Gospel less than twenty years after it was completed. Today, we possess portions of more than forty Gospel manuscripts produced during the first two hundred years after these books were written, and we have to assume that far more copies were made that did not survive.

These early manuscripts were made of papyrus, a plant whose fibers could be stretched, dried, and woven together to form sheets similar to modern paper. Highly useful in its day, papyrus was never meant to stand the test of time, for with age it becomes so brittle that a mere touch may turn it to powder. The portions of the papyri manuscripts that we do possess are only scraps and fragments, not complete books. Still, even the smallest pieces are of great interest to scholars, who have carefully cataloged and photographed each one. The fragment known as Papyrus 52 ($p^{52}$), for instance, is no larger than a person's hand and contains only a few verses from the eighteenth chapter of John's Gospel. Still, its very existence is significant. At one time, some scholars believed that John's Gospel was written around the middle of the second century. Since $p^{52}$ itself dates from 100–125 C.E., its discovery in 1934 prompted immediate revision of those theories.

In the fourth century, the Roman emperor Constantine became a Christian, and the financial resources of the burgeoning church improved dramatically. Now, manuscripts of Christian writings could be preserved on parchment or vellum, a type of leather made from the skins of animals. Our oldest complete copies of the New Testament are two vellum manuscripts from this period called Codex Sinaiticus and Codex Vaticanus. The word *codex* indicates that the manuscript has the form of a book—pages sewn together rather than rolled up into a scroll. Many scholars believe the codex format was invented by Christians and first used in their Bible manuscripts.[12]

Over the centuries, the copying of the Gospels and other books of the Bible continued under a variety of conditions. Sometimes individuals would devote years to producing a single copy. At other times, manuscripts would be mass produced in schools called scriptoriums. Apparently some scriptoriums allowed one individual to read aloud from a manuscript while several copyists wrote what they heard (or thought they heard). Such a procedure allowed several copies of a single manuscript to be made simultaneously, but under less than desirable circumstances. Even when copyists did work from manuscripts that they had in front of them, the quality of the work could vary in accord with the individual's facility with Greek, attentiveness to the task, or degree of dedication.

The concern for accuracy was pronounced. Most copyists were monks who looked upon their work as a sacred calling. Manuscripts were supposed to be checked and, even in the scriptoriums, harsh penalties were prescribed for errors. But of course errors *were* made, such that in the manuscripts we possess (ones that supposedly passed all inspections), mistakes can be seen that range from the understandable to the ridiculous. Sometimes copyists would leave out words or misspell them so grievously that we would never know what was intended if we did not have other manuscripts for comparison. Occasionally, bored monks would write notes to each other on their parchment ("It is cold today" or "This lamp gives bad light"), which then ended up being copied by other monks right into the biblical text. Some copyists even took it upon themselves to add commentary to passages that they thought were likely to be misunderstood or to change the wording of passages to reflect their own interpretation.[13]

The study of the manuscript traditions that underlie our modern editions of the Bible is called *text criticism*.[14] Text critics compile and analyze all available manuscripts and fragments, comparing them scrupulously to note any differences. Readings that differ in any way are called *variants,* and modern text critics have developed computer databases that list every variant reading for every verse of the Bible. The more significant ones are listed in footnotes to Greek editions of the New Testament, sometimes requiring up to one-third of the page. Extremely important or difficult variants are sometimes referenced in the notes to English Bibles. Many Bibles, for example, include a note regarding the words "against you" in Matthew 18:15, since these words are missing in a variant reading found in both Codex Sinaiticus and Codex Vaticanus.

How do text critics determine which reading is best? The process involves consideration of both external and internal evidence. External evidence involves evaluation of the manuscripts themselves. Text critics recognize that an error that occurs in a manuscript is likely to be reproduced if that manuscript is itself subsequently used as a basis for making additional copies. Thus, variant readings frequently multiply, occurring not only in the manuscript where the error was first made but in all of its descendants. Accordingly, text critics have attempted to work out family trees for biblical manuscripts, designed to reveal which may be directly or indirectly dependent upon another. Ultimately, this process can become very complex, but a few of the fundamental distinctions are easy to grasp.

The most common system classifies most manuscripts into one of three major families or *text types:* Alexandrian, Western, or Byzantine. The Alexandrian text type is generally considered to be the best and the Byzantine, the worst. In other words, the family of manuscripts called Alexandrian is thought to have preserved the original reading of the New Testament with the fewest variants or errors. Ironically, the Byzantine text type is by far the largest, such that its more numerous errors have multitudinous support. This is one reason text critics say manuscript evidence must be "weighed, not counted." Byzantine variants often constitute a so-called majority reading in instances where text critics believe the majority of manuscripts are wrong.

Manuscripts belonging to all three text types are further classified as *uncials* or *minuscules*. The distinction is simple. Uncial manuscripts are printed in capital letters while minuscules are written in cursive using both capitals and lower case. The significance of this distinction is chronological. The minuscule style of writing did not develop until the ninth century, but it then quickly became standard. Thus, uncial manuscripts are older than mi nuscules and are considered to be much more valuable.

Internal evidence involves consideration of logic that would explain the development of a particular reading. In individual cases, readings in our most reliable manuscripts may be discounted if the cause of the error is explicable. For example, in the famous story of the Good Samaritan (Luke 10:30-37), Codex Sinaiticus completely omits any reference to the Levite who passes by without offering to help (verse 32). The problem, apparently, is that two sentences in a row (verses 31 and 32) end with exactly the same words (in English, "passed by on the other side"). Thus, we may assume that the copyist must have accidentally skipped from the end of verse 31 to the end of verse 32 without realizing he had left out an entire sentence.[15] Codex Sinaiticus is an uncial manuscript of the Alexandrian text type, but in this instance its reading is understood to be an erroneous variant and the readings of other manuscripts are accepted as more reliable.

Similar evaluation of internal evidence may apply in cases where the cause of error is not obvious. When faced with two readings, both of which have strong external support from manuscripts that are usually reliable, text critics must try to decide whether a development in one direction would be more logical than another. They claim that often "the more difficult reading is to be preferred,"[16] assuming that copyists would be more likely to make changes that solved problems than ones that created them. For instance, in Luke 2:41 and 43, where some manuscripts say "his parents," others read "Joseph and Mary." Text critics believe the former was the original reading and take the latter to be the variant. Why? Some copyists might have thought a reference to Jesus' "parents" contradicted the doctrine of a virgin birth and so they may have changed the wording to avoid what they thought would create a misunderstanding. If the original reading had been "Joseph and Mary" no reason for changing it to "his parents" is discernible. Or, to take another example from the opposite end of this Gospel, some manuscripts report at Luke 23:32 that Jesus was crucified with "two other criminals," while other manuscripts say he was crucified "with two others, who were criminals." The first reading seems to imply that Jesus was a criminal, a thought that might be offensive to some Christians. Since it is easy to understand why copyists might have altered this reading, it is recognized as the most difficult and therefore considered to be the original.

A similar principle of text criticism holds that "the shorter reading is often to be preferred."[17] The assumption here is that when copyists were themselves uncertain as to what the correct reading should be, they were more likely to err on the side of inclusion than exclusion. The fear of losing any word of Scripture caused them sometimes to conflate texts. We can actu-

ally see this in practice when we study the development of manuscript traditions from earlier to later times. In early manuscripts of Luke's Gospel, the
last verse sometimes reads, "they were continually in the temple *blessing*
God," and other times reads, "they were continually in the temple *praising*
God." Later on, copyists who had apparently become aware of this minor
discrepancy inevitably wrote, "they were continually in the temple *blessing
and praising* God." Modern text critics are not able to determine whether
Luke originally wrote "blessing" or "praising," but they are pretty certain
that he did not write both.

In cases such as that just cited, the work of text criticism may seem to be
obsessed with details that do not make much practical difference for interpretation. In some instances, however, text-critical questions are of considerable magnitude. In a few cases, entire passages such as Mark 16:9-20, Luke
22:43-44, and John 7:53—8:11 are missing from the best manuscripts.
Should they be taken out of modern Bibles or at least removed to the footnotes? In other cases, the meaning of a passage can be significantly altered
by the acceptance or rejection of a variant. In a very real sense, text criticism
forms the basis for all other types of Gospel research. Whether they realize
it or not, everyone who reads or studies the Gospels relies on the work of
these scholars, for it is not possible even to begin talking about what the
Gospels mean without first knowing what the Gospels say.

◆

# Translation

When people read the Gospels today, they do not normally read from any
of the numerous manuscripts that text critics have collected. Scholars may
peruse a compendium of such works through the use of a critical edition of
a Greek New Testament,[18] but most people rely on a translation of the
Greek into their own language. Numerous English versions of the Bible
are available today,[19] and these are typically cited by two- or three-letter
abbreviations (see figure 8).

The first translation of the New Testament from Greek into English was
produced by William Tyndale in 1526, and the work cost him his life. Condemned as a heretic, he was executed and burned at the stake ten years later.
Today, it is difficult to understand why merely translating the Bible into
language that people can understand would be so controversial. Before his
work was published, however, the standard biblical text for all of the Western world was a Latin translation called the Vulgate.[20] Because it went back
to the Greek text, Tyndale's Bible inevitably disagreed with the Vulgate in

ΚΑΤΑ ΜΑΡΚΟΝ

Act 12,12.25;
13,5.13; 15,37
Kol 4,10 2T 4,
11 Phm 24 1P
5,13
2-6: Mt 3,1-6
L 3,1-6 J 1,19-
23 · Ex 23,20 Ml
3,1 Mt 11,10p
L 1,76 J 3,28

Is 40,3 ⊛

Act 13,24; 19,4; ·
2,38; 22,16

Zch 13,4 Mt 11,
8p 2Rg 1,8 ·
Lv 11,21s

7s; Mt 3,11
L 3,16 J 1,26s
Act 13,25

J 16,7!

1 Ἀρχὴ τοῦ εὐαγγελίου Ἰησοῦ Χριστοῦ [υἱοῦ θεοῦ].
□2 Καθὼς γέγραπται ἐν τῷ Ἠσαΐᾳ τῷ προφήτῃ·
ἰδοὺ ἀποστέλλω τὸν ἄγγελόν μου πρὸ προσώπου σου,
ὃς κατασκευάσει τὴν ὁδόν σου·
3 φωνὴ βοῶντος ἐν τῇ ἐρήμῳ·
ἑτοιμάσατε τὴν ὁδὸν κυρίου,
εὐθείας ποιεῖτε τὰς τρίβους αὐτοῦ,
4 ἐγένετο Ἰωάννης [ὁ] βαπτίζων ἐν τῇ ἐρήμῳ καὶ κη-
ρύσσων βάπτισμα μετανοίας εἰς ἄφεσιν ἁμαρτιῶν. 5 καὶ
ἐξεπορεύετο πρὸς αὐτὸν πᾶσα ἡ Ἰουδαία χώρα καὶ οἱ
Ἱεροσολυμῖται πάντες, καὶ ἐβαπτίζοντο ὑπ' αὐτοῦ ἐν τῷ
Ἰορδάνῃ ποταμῷ ἐξομολογούμενοι τὰς ἁμαρτίας αὐτῶν.
6 καὶ ἦν ὁ Ἰωάννης ἐνδεδυμένος τρίχας καμήλου καὶ
ζώνην δερματίνην περὶ τὴν ὀσφὺν αὐτοῦ καὶ ἐσθίων ἀ-
κρίδας καὶ μέλι ἄγριον.
7 Καὶ ἐκήρυσσεν λέγων· * ἔρχεται ὁ ἰσχυρότερός
μου ὀπίσω μου, οὗ οὐκ εἰμὶ ἱκανὸς κύψας λῦσαι τὸν
ἱμάντα τῶν ὑποδημάτων αὐτοῦ. 8 ἐγὼ ἐβάπτισα ὑμᾶς
ὕδατι, αὐτὸς δὲ βαπτίσει ὑμᾶς ἐν πνεύματι ἁγίῳ.

Inscriptio: ⸉ευαγγελιον κ. M. A D L W Θ f¹³ 1 𝔐 lat ¦ το κ. M. αγ. ευαγγ. 209 al (vgᶜˡ) ¦
txt (ℵ B) pc

¶ 1,1-3 ⸂† - ℵ* Θ (28) pc samˢ; Or ¦ υιου του κυριου 1241 ¦ txt ℵ¹ B D L W pc (sed του
θ. A f¹.¹³ 𝔐) latt sy co; Irˡᵃᵗ ¦ :, et :¹. (Ir) Or Epiph ¦ [□ Lachmann cj] ¦ ⸀ 2-4 D Θ f¹
700 pc; Or Epiph ¦ τοις προφηταις A W f¹³ 𝔐 syʰ (bomˢˢ) ¦ txt ℵ B L Δ 33. 565. 892.
1241 al syᵖ·ʰᵐˢ co; Ir ¦ Τεγω ℵ A L W f¹.¹³ 𝔐 vgᶜˡ syʰ samˢ bomˢ; Or Eus ¦ txt B D Θ
28*. 565 pc lat co; Irˡᵃᵗ ¦ ⸍(Mt 11,10) εμπροσθεν σου A f¹.¹³ 𝔐 ¦ ff² ¦ vgᶜˡ syʰ samˢˢ boᵖᵗ;
Eus ¦ txt ℵ B D K L P W Θ 700* al lat syᵖ boᵖᵗ ¦ ⸀του θεου ημων (D) it ¦ T¹ (L 3,5s)
add Is 40,4-8 W (c) ¦ 4 ⸂† 1-5 B 33. (892) pc boᵐˢˢ ¦ 2-6 A W f¹.¹³ 𝔐 syʰ ᵇᵃ? ¦ 3-5 2 6
D Θ 28. 700 lat syᵛ ¦ txt ℵ L Δ pc bo ¦ 5 ⸄ 3 5 1 2 D W Θ 28. 565. 700 a ¦ 3-6 1 2 A f¹.¹³
𝔐 syʰ ¦ txt ℵ B L 33. 892. 1241 pc lat co? ¦ 6 ⸂ην δε ο (- A D W Δ pm) Ιωαννης A D
W Θ f¹.¹³ (⸍·28) 𝔐 it syʰ ¦ txt ℵ B L (33). 565 c. 892 pc lat boᵐˢˢ ¦ ⸀δερριν D a et
□ D it ¦ 7 O B (Δ 1424 t ff²); Or ¦ O¹ p) D Θ f¹³ 28*. 565 pc it ¦ 8 Τεν A (D) L W
(Θ) f¹.¹³ 𝔐 it ¦ txt ℵ B L 33. 892. 1241 pc lat co? ¦ O⸍ B L b t vg ¦ txt ℵ A D W Θ 0133 f¹.¹³
𝔐 it vgᵐˢˢ; Or

Mark 1:1-8 from the printed Greek New Testament

spots. Some took it as a direct assault on what they regarded as Holy Scripture.[21] If Tyndale's Bible was right, then their Bible was wrong.

The opposition to Tyndale serves as a reminder of the enormous power that Bible translators potentially wield. They are able to control what most people think "the Bible says" to a degree that surpasses the influence of any professor, teacher, or preacher. Such control is inevitable, despite the best intentions of the translator. Differences between language systems make it impossible ever to say in English exactly what is said in another language. For example, the Greek word that Jesus uses to refer to the Holy Spirit in John 14:16 is *paraklētos*. English Bibles refer to the Holy Spirit in this verse

Figure 8

| Some Well-known English Bible Translations | | |
| --- | --- | --- |
| *Abbreviation* | *Name* | *Date* |
| KJV | King James Version | 1611 |
| ASV | American Standard Version | 1901 |
| NAB | New American Bible | 1941 |
| RSV | Revised Standard Version | 1946; 2d ed., 1971 |
| NEB | New English Bible | 1961 |
| NASB | New American Standard Bible | 1963 |
| JB | Jerusalem Bible | 1966 |
| TEV | Today's English Version | 1966 |
| NIV | New International Version | 1973 |
| NJB | New Jerusalem Bible | 1985 |
| NAB-RNT | New American Bible | 1986 |
| | (Revised New Testament) | |
| REB | Revised English Bible | 1989 |
| NRSV | New Revised Standard Version | 1991 |
| CEV | Contemporary English Version | 1995 |
| NLT | New Living Translation | 1996 |

variously as "Advocate" (NAB-RNT, NRSV), "Comforter" (KJV), "Counselor" (NIV, RSV), and "Helper" (NASB, TEV). These terms are all somewhat synonymous, but convey different shades of meaning that might be significant for someone reflecting theologically on the role of the Holy Spirit. To translate is always to interpret, and people who read English Bibles are in fact reading interpretations of the Bible. In recognition of this, many religious bodies today insist that their clergy receive some training in the original biblical languages (Hebrew, Greek) so that they will not be completely dependent upon translations. Persons who do not have this facility are advised to consult a variety of translations when doing serious study of biblical texts and to become aware of differences significant for interpretation.

All translations strive for accuracy and clarity. With regard to the former, the first concern—aside from the qualifications of the scholars who do the work—is the quality of the manuscripts from which the translation is done. The King James Version, for instance, may be a literary masterpiece, significant historically and culturally, but among scholars, it is almost unanimously regarded as the least accurate English translation of the Bible available today. Why? Its translators did not have access to any of the uncial or papyri manuscripts that have been discovered in the last few centuries. As a result, this classic edition of the Bible is based on a handful of late, minuscule manuscripts that text critics now know to contain hundreds of errors.[22]

Beyond this, translators disagree philosophically as to what constitutes the most accurate reading. On the one hand, some strive to produce a literal translation that comes as close as possible to reproducing the original text word-for-word into English. Some versions (ASV, KJV, NASB) even italicize all words that are not actually representative of corresponding words in the original, but that were regarded as necessary to make sense in our language (Greek grammar, for example, allows pronominal subjects to be implicit, but English grammar does not). The widely used RSV attempts to produce a fairly literal translation of the Bible without adopting this extreme convention. On the other hand, some scholars favor an approach called *dynamic equivalence,* which is more concerned with thoughts and ideas than with word-for-word correspondence. The goal is to produce a translation that conveys the message of the original text in such a way as to produce the same effect on those who read it in English as would have been produced on those who read the original. This philosophy informs such popular translations as CEV, NEB, NIV, NLT, and TEV.

Scholars generally prefer the more literal translations for academic study because this work often entails detailed analysis that involves considering the meaning of every individual word. At the same time, most scholars recognize that obsessive literalism may "miss the forest for the trees." Many modern versions (including JB, NAB, NRSV) try for a balance between literal and equivalent readings. Indeed, the motto of the NRSV translation committee was "As literal as possible, as free as necessary." The tendency in recent years has been for revisions of standard versions to make freer use of equivalency than their predecessors. This would be borne out in comparisons not only of NRSV with RSV, but also of NAB-RNT with NAB, NJB with JB, and REB with NEB.

Concern for clarity is obviously necessary, since no translation will be worth much if it cannot be understood. Language is always changing, such that numerous words that were well known in 1611 when the KJV was produced require explanation today. The psalmist who "prevented the dawn" (Ps. 119:147) did not keep the sun from rising, but simply got up before daybreak ("prevent" used to mean "precede"). Even in the few decades since the RSV, language changes have occurred. The picture of John the Baptist wearing "a leather girdle" (Matt. 3:4) brings a chuckle to unruly Sunday school students, as does Paul's seeming admission, "Once I was stoned" (2 Cor. 11:25). In the NRSV, John wears a belt and Paul says, "Once I received a stoning." Likewise, people who cannot speak are now called "mute" rather than "dumb" (Mark 7:37). Unless updated, translations themselves need translating.

Sometimes, clarity and accuracy become competing concerns. A story Jesus tells in Matthew 18:23-35 describes servants who owe debts of "ten thousand talents" and "one hundred denarii." To understand the story, readers must know that the former amount is worth more than the latter. For this reason, the TEV paraphrases the amounts as "millions of dollars" and "a few dollars," while the NEB (a British translation) renders the amounts in terms of "pounds." The NAB-RNT leaves out any mention of the numbers and says simply "a large amount" and "a much smaller amount." Strict accuracy is sacrificed for the sake of making the message of the text more accessible to readers in the modern English-speaking world.

Most translators recognize that paraphrase is necessary at times to make idiomatic expressions meaningful. Even the very literal NASB decided the expression "bowels of mercy" was better translated "heart of compassion" (Col. 3:12; compare KJV), since in the Western world the heart usually symbolizes the source of love and kindness (a role ascribed to the intestines in the ancient Near East). Still, the use of paraphrase is often controversial, and most scholars prefer that it be kept to a minimum, lest something essential be lost. Ideally, academic students of the Bible will acquire sufficient knowledge of the biblical world to make sense of the Bible's expressions within their original context.

Popular paraphrases of biblical texts are produced from time to time that need to be distinguished altogether from translations. Thus, a "seaman's version of the 23rd Psalm" begins, "The Lord is my Pilot; I shall not drift," and a "Cotton Patch Version" of Paul's letters transforms the discussion of Jews and Gentiles in Corinth into one regarding whites and blacks in Atlanta.[23] The two most popular paraphrase editions in recent years have been J. B. Phillips's *New Testament* and Ken Taylor's *Living Bible*.[24] Both reproduce the biblical text in lively, evangelical language that is reader-friendly but less capricious than the examples just cited. Of the two, Phillips's version is the more scholarly, being based on Greek manuscripts, whereas Taylor developed his paraphrase from the English ASV translation. Still, both Phillips and Taylor insisted (to their credit) that their paraphrases were not intended "for study purposes."[25]

Major issues in recent Bible translation have arisen from concern for the use of inclusive language, especially with regard to gender. The examples cited in figure 9 illustrate different ways in which this concern has been addressed. In many cases, such as the first example given, the more inclusive reading is definitely a more faithful translation of what was said in the original. The Greek word that is translated variously as "men" or "people" (*anthrōpos*) means "human beings," not "males." The JB translators probably intended the word "men" to be taken in a generic sense. In any case, the inclusive-language reading presents the meaning of the original more clearly and more accurately.

Figure 9

| Inclusive Language and Bible Translations | |
|---|---|
| 1. *Matthew 4:19 (JB)* "Follow me and I will make you fishers of men." | 1. *Matthew 4:19 (NJB)* "Come after me and I will make you fishers of people." |
| 2. *Mark 8:34 (RSV)* "If any man would come after me, let him deny himself and take up his cross and follow me." | 2. *Mark 8:34 (NRSV)* "If any want to become my followers, let them deny themselves and take up their cross and follow me." |
| 3. *Matthew 28:19 (NRSV)* "Go therefore and make disciples of all nations, baptizing them in the name of the Father and of the Son and of the Holy Spirit." | 3. *Matthew 28:19 (NRSV, Inclusive Version)* "Go therefore and make disciples of all nations, baptizing them in the name of the Father-Mother and of the beloved Child and of the Holy Spirit." |

In the second example, some degree of accuracy might be sacrificed for the sake of inclusivity. The NRSV recasts Jesus' words so that masculine singular pronouns (him, his) are now rendered as plural forms (them, their). In Greek, the pronouns are singular. The question, then, is whether this minor misrepresentation of number is justified by the gender-inclusive reading that the use of plural pronouns yields. Most scholars would agree that the author of Mark's Gospel would have thought that these words of Jesus could apply to women as well as to men. Some, however, would insist that his use of singular pronouns was intentional, indicating the personal dimension of the decision Jesus says every individual must make. Thus, the gain in clarity with regard to gender inclusion must be weighed against the loss in accuracy with regard to personal reference.

The third example is the most controversial. Here, the Inclusive Version[26] adapts the text of the NRSV, changing the word "Father" to "Father-Mother" and the word "Son" to "Child." The intention is to avoid the implication that God is male or that the maleness of Jesus has christological relevance. Most scholars grant that references to God as "Father" are metaphorical and recognize that the Bible sometimes presents God as analogous to a mother as well (Isa. 46:3; 49:15; 66:13). Still, many would continue, in *this* verse (Matt. 28:19), the metaphor of Father is used, not Mother, and certainly not "Father-Mother." The editors of the Inclusive Version argue that the term "Father-Mother" is better because it can only be understood as a metaphor, while the term "Father" is often mistaken as a literal reference. At issue is whether blatantly interpretative translation is an appropriate or effective means for challenging ideas that are thought to be erroneous.

◆

# Reception

After passing through all of these stages of development, the four New Testament Gospels finally become accessible to people in our modern world. Today, we are able to hear or read in our own language the words and deeds of Jesus as they were remembered, redacted, and preserved in the four New Testament Gospels. Not surprisingly, then, many Gospel scholars are fundamentally interested in the effects that these books have on their audiences.

One approach, which goes by the German name *Wirkungsgeschichte* ("history of influence" criticism), focuses on the impact that these texts have had throughout history. These scholars often trace the different ways that stories have been understood in diverse circumstances by analyzing allusions or references to those stories in artwork, music, and literature, as well as in theological commentaries and popular sermons. The goal may be to furnish correctives that remind us of full potential for meaning, to further ecumenical understanding and broaden our horizons, or even to "clarify what we have become on the basis of these texts."[27]

Another approach, known as *narrative criticism,* draws on certain varieties of modern literary criticism to read the Gospels as coherent short stories.[28] Narrative critics would emphasize that each Gospel, as it now stands, needs to be considered in its entirety as a wholly integrated work. They would view the Gospel of Mark, for instance, not as the collection of stories about Jesus that form critics discern but as a single story about Jesus. Certain themes and motifs develop throughout the book from beginning to end. One can actually describe the "plot" for this story or speak about how individual character groups develop as the narrative progresses. Whereas form critics sometimes spoke of Mark stringing together individual pericopes "like pearls upon a string," narrative critics would prefer the analogy of weaving together diverse strands to form a single rope.[29] Narrative critics also insist that each Gospel needs to be considered on its own terms, as distinct from the others. The story of Jesus that Mark tells is different from that told by Matthew, Luke, or John, even though many of the same people, events, and themes may figure prominently in all four. Narrative critics pay close attention to the rhetoric of each Gospel, that is, to the way in which the story is told. They note literary devices and other features that indicate what sort of effect the story is expected to have on its readers.

Related to the above two disciplines is the variety of approaches called *reader-response criticism*.[30] If narrative critics attempt to discover the effect that a Gospel story is expected to have on its readers, reader-response criticism tries to analyze the effects that such a story actually does have on readers. Reader-response critics are typically interested in *polyvalence,* in the capacity for a text to generate any number of effects and to mean different things to people. The approaches encompassed by this orientation explore factors (age, gender, social location, and so forth) that contribute to this diversity of interpretation.

Some scholars are also interested in exploring the reception of the Gospels from particular ideological perspectives. Extremely influential in recent years have been varieties of *feminist criticism*.[31] Since the field of biblical studies has been dominated by men, feminist scholars might challenge traditional interpretations of texts as being androcentric or patriarchal. Or, since most of the biblical writers were apparently men, they might challenge the texts themselves as harboring a male-oriented world view. In the latter case, the task is not simply to counter misinterpretations of the text but to resist readings that legitimate oppression, regardless of whether these accord with the author's original intentions. Resistant reading[32] begins simply with a call to consciousness: texts such as the New Testament Gospels often embody a masculine perspective so thoroughly that readers adopt this point of view without knowing it. If the story is told in a way that is rhetorically effective, even women readers may find themselves identifying with the male characters in ways that assume their values are normative. One task of feminist criticism is to recognize the processes of reception so as to empower women to read the Gospels as women—even if these texts were originally intended for men.

In similar ways, critics may interpret the reception of the Gospels from other political, social, or ethnic viewpoints. African American approaches to interpretation have been prominent, especially the African American feminist approach that is sometimes called *womanist*.[33] Recent decades of New Testament scholarship have also produced studies of the Gospels informed by such diverse perspectives as Marxism, Jungian psychology, Buddhist Mahāyāna philosophy, and Latin American liberation theology.[34] Critiquing all ideologies and methodologies is the perspective of *deconstruction*[35] put forward by postmodern critics. The latter find language to be so replete with polyvalent potential that meaning is always ambiguous and transient. Thus, the very idea that criticism can ever be disinterested or objective is rejected. Postmodern scholars claim that interpretation usually reveals more about the interpreter than it does about the text.

# CHAPTER TWO

# The Gospel of Mark

The Gospel of Mark opens by introducing its readers to the figure of John the Baptist who has come to "prepare the way of the Lord" (1:2). The focus shifts quickly, however, to Jesus, who is baptized by John, receives the Holy Spirit, and is driven into the wilderness for a time of testing. After John is arrested, Jesus begins a dynamic ministry in Galilee, "proclaiming the good news of God" (1:14). He calls disciples to join him and travels throughout the countryside. He earns renown for healing people of various diseases, for casting demons or evil spirits out of afflicted persons, and for working other miracles. He also teaches his disciples and the crowds that gather, often using parables to disguise his true meaning (4:10-12). Conflicts arise as the religious authorities in the area oppose him, and his own disciples prove to be persons lacking in faith. Finally, he travels to the city of Jerusalem for a final showdown, predicting along the way that he will be killed there but will subsequently be raised from the dead. After more intense conflicts in that city, he gathers his disciples for a ritual last meal and then, having been betrayed by one of these disciples (Judas), he is put on trial and crucified. Three days later, a group of women visits his tomb, only to be told by a youth that he has been raised.

When people who already have some knowledge of the story of Jesus read the Gospel of Mark, they are often surprised by what they find. Some of the stories here are familiar, such as the miracle accounts of Jesus feeding five thousand people (6:30-44) or walking on the water (6:45-52). Likewise, the parable of the sower that Jesus tells in 4:1-20 is one of his best-known tales. In many churches, the reports of Jesus' "transfiguration" (9:2-8) and of his entry into Jerusalem on what has come to be known as Palm Sunday (11:1-10) have become lessons associated with annual festivals. Best known of all is the passion narrative, the lengthy account of Jesus' betrayal, last supper, arrest, and eventual crucifixion (chapters 14–15).

Still, there are surprises. The first surprise may be what is *not* here. Mark's Gospel contains no "Christmas stories," no references to Jesus' birth or infancy. Jesus does not preach a Sermon on the Mount. He does not teach his disciples the Beatitudes or the Golden Rule or the Lord's Prayer. He doesn't tell the story of the Good Samaritan or the prodigal son. There is no mention of his raising Lazarus from the dead. Many of our society's best-known stories about Jesus and his teaching are missing.

The greatest surprise of all, perhaps, comes at the end. When the women who visit Jesus' tomb are told that he has been raised from the dead, the youth who tells them this also says that they should go and tell his disciples. Then, Mark reports, "They went out and fled from the tomb, for terror and amazement had seized them; and they said nothing to anyone, for they were afraid" (16:8). So, what happened next? Did the women ever tell the disciples? If not, did the disciples find out about the resurrection in some other way? Did anyone ever actually see Jesus risen from the dead? Mark doesn't say. There are no "Easter stories" in this Gospel, except for the brief report that the tomb was empty and that some young person claimed a resurrection had occurred. To many readers, this doesn't seem like enough to provide a basis for faith, much less a foundation for the establishment of a major new religion. Mark's Gospel seems unfinished.

The book must have seemed that way in the early church as well, for text critics have found numerous endings for Mark's Gospel that were written at various times and places. One of these found its way into the Latin Vulgate, the fourth-century translation of the Bible that became the standard scriptural text in Western Christianity for over a millennium. The same ending appeared in a 1551 edition of a Greek New Testament in which a French printer numbered the text into chapters and verses for the first time. Thus, the passage received unofficial sanction as a designated biblical text, Mark 16:9-20. Even today, Mark 16:9-20 appears in most Bibles—in spite of the fact that scholars are certain it was not part of the original Gospel. Some modern Bibles set the verses off from the rest of the Gospel to indicate this, and some also include another of the endings for Mark composed by early Christians.

A few modern scholars think the original ending of Mark's Gospel may have been lost,[1] but most believe the book really was intended to conclude abruptly with 16:8. The surprising lack of resolution contributes to the effect the evangelist wanted the Gospel to have on his readers. They are left asking questions, wanting to know more. Beyond this, an axiom of literary criti-

Figure 10

---

Possible Sources for Mark's Gospel

- a collection of controversy stories, including those found now in Mark 2:1—3:6
- a collection or, possibly, two collections of miracle stories, including many of those now found in chapters 4–8
- an apocalyptic tract containing much of what is now in chapter 13
- an early version of the passion narrative (the story of Jesus' death and resurrection)

All of these are disputed among scholars.

---

cism holds that "unresolved conflict tends to impinge most directly upon the reader."[2] This means that when a story leaves "loose ends" or appears unfinished, readers often feel drawn into the world of that story to imagine how they would bring the tale to a satisfactory close. Thus, Mark's Gospel may conclude without a proper ending because Mark wants his readers to join in supplying that ending themselves.[3]

If Mark was the first Gospel written, what sources might he have used? Critics have offered numerous suggestions (see figure 10), which are intriguing to those who want to reconstruct the earliest layers of Christian tradition.[4] In general, though, most scholars think Mark relied more heavily on oral tradition than on materials that had previously been put into writing. The great achievement of Mark is that he appears to have been the first Christian author to weave such disparate materials into a coherent narrative. Not satisfied simply to fashion a collection of accounts (such as Q may have been), he took numerous and varied stories about Jesus and turned them into a single story, a story that from beginning to end could be called "the good news of Jesus Christ, the Son of God" (1:1).[5]

◆

## Characteristics of Mark's Gospel

We may note a few of the distinctive characteristics of this Gospel, things more typical of Mark than the other three Gospels.

1. The story is told with an *unusual urgency*. Jesus begins his ministry with an announcement that "The time is fulfilled!" (1:14). After that, things tend

to happen very quickly, such that the entire ministry of Jesus appears to transpire within a few weeks (in John's Gospel, it lasts around three years). The word *immediately* (Greek *euthys*) occurs forty-two times in Mark's Gospel, eleven times in the first chapter alone. The same word is used only once in the much longer Gospel of Luke. This sense of urgency is also felt with regard to what is still to come. Mark's Gospel seems to present an expectation that Jesus will return soon (13:30), and readers are exhorted to constant vigilance in view of this impending but unpredictable crisis (13:32-37).[6]

2. Mark's Gospel appears to *emphasize Jesus' deeds over his words*. This can be misleading, because the teaching of Jesus presented here is certainly significant.[7] Still, the material that presents Jesus' teaching takes up less space proportionately than it does in Matthew, Luke, or John, while reports of Jesus' mighty works take up more space than in the other Gospels. Mark's Gospel actually does not tell more miracle stories than the other Gospels, but the overall impression of Jesus as a miracle worker is felt more strongly here than anywhere else in the Bible.[8]

3. Mark's story of Jesus is *dominated by the relatively long passion narrative* that comes at the end.[9] The fast-paced reporting typical for most of the book slows down in the last three chapters as we are provided with a day-by-day and even hour-by-hour account of the last week of Jesus' life. In the earlier material, furthermore, Jesus makes numerous references to his eventual death. Some of these are subtle allusions (2:20; 12:6-8); others are explicit predictions (8:31; 9:31; 10:32-34). Jesus' enemies also begin plotting to kill him early in this Gospel story (3:6; as compared to 12:14 in Matthew and 19:47 in Luke). At one point, Jesus even says that giving his life is what he has come to do (Mark 10:45). Far from representing a tragic reversal, his death is the goal of his life and mission. Clearly, of all the stories Mark tells about Jesus, the story of his crucifixion is presented as the most important. Indeed, one theologian has described this entire Gospel as "a passion narrative with an extended introduction."[10]

4. In a superficial sense, this Gospel may not appear to be as well-written as the others because its *linguistic style is less refined*.[11] For example, the author makes regular use of what are called "historical present" verbs, that is, present-tense verbs that describe actions that occurred in the past (Mark 6:1 reads, literally, "He went away from there and *comes* to his own country and his disciples *follow* him"). English Bibles typically clean up these constructions. Such features remind us that the New Testament is written in *koinē* (or "common") Greek as opposed to *classical* Greek, the language of Homer, Aristotle, and Plato. All four Gospels were written in the language of the common people; Mark just seems to be a tad more "common" than the rest. Still, the author was a gifted storyteller, such that the unrefined Markan version of an event is often the most memorable. For example, the story of

the epileptic child in Mark 9:14-29 presents a more vivid characterization of the boy's father than reports of the same event in Matthew 17:14-21 and Luke 9:37-42 (see figure 11).

5. Mark's Gospel employs *effective rhetoric* that belies its apparently simple tone. Three literary devices may be noted as exemplary:[12]

(a) *Narrative anticipations* or references that prepare readers for what is to come later. In Mark 3:9, Jesus' disciples are told to "have a boat ready for him" though the boat is not actually needed until 4:1. The device provides what Keith Nickle calls "narrative glue," holding together stories that may originally have circulated independently of each other.[13]

(b) *Two-step progressions* in which a statement is repeated in a way that adds precision or clarity.[14] A simple example would be the double temporal phrases, "when it was evening, after the sun set" (1:32). More significant theological equivalents include the opening identification of Jesus as the "Christ, the Son of God" (1:1) and the climactic declaration, "The time is fulfilled, and the kingdom of God has come near" (1:15). Rhetorically, such expressions encourage readers to develop the habit of taking a second look, to see more than may at first be evident (compare the story in Mark 8:22-26).

(c) *Intercalation* or the inserting of one story within another. In Mark 6:7-13, Jesus gives his disciples special authority and sends them out on a mission. Then, in Mark 6:14-29, the narrative appears to digress to tell about the ruler Herod's reaction to Jesus and about an earlier incident in which that ruler had John the Baptist executed. Finally, in Mark 6:30, the disciples return to Jesus with a report of their mission. The point of intercalation is to prompt readers to consider two otherwise unrelated stories in light of each other. In this case, the account of John's martyrdom has a sobering effect alongside the report of the disciples' success (6:13). Mark's readers are probably expected to know that many of these "apostles" (6:30) will eventually meet with similar fates (10:39; 13:9-13). Another example of this construction is Mark 11:12-20, where the story of Jesus driving moneychangers out of the temple is inserted into a story of Jesus cursing a fig tree and making it wither. Most likely, Mark wants us to see these situations as analogous: like the fig tree, the temple is doomed because it does not "bear fruit" (see also 12:1-9).[15]

6. *The geographical focus for this book is clearly on the region of Galilee.* The first half of the Gospel tells of Jesus' ministry in Galilee, with very few references to activity elsewhere. At the beginning of chapter 10, the focus shifts abruptly to Judea, where Jesus travels to Jerusalem and is eventually killed. Even then, however, the promise attached to the news of his resurrection is that he is returning to Galilee and that his followers will see him there (16:7; compare Acts 1:3-4).

Figure 11

The Story of the Epileptic Child (Mark 9:14-29)

When they came to the disciples, they saw a great crowd around them, and some scribes arguing with them. When the whole crowd saw him, they were immediately overcome with awe, and they ran forward to greet him. He asked them, "What are you arguing about with them?" Someone from the crowd answered him, "Teacher, I brought you my son; he has a spirit that makes him unable to speak; and whenever it seizes him, it dashes him down; and he foams and grinds his teeth and becomes rigid; and I asked your disciples to cast it out, but they could not do so." He answered them, "You faithless generation, how much longer must I be among you? How much longer must I put up with you? Bring him to me." And they brought the boy to him. When the spirit saw him, immediately it convulsed the boy, and he fell on the ground and rolled about, foaming at the mouth. Jesus asked the father, "How long has this been happening to him?" And he said, "From childhood. It has often cast him into the fire and into the water, to destroy him; but if you are able to do anything, have pity on us and help us." Jesus said to him, "If you are able!—All things can be done for the one who believes." Immediately the father of the child cried out, "I believe; help my unbelief!" When Jesus saw that a crowd came running together, he rebuked the unclean spirit, saying to it, "You spirit that keeps this boy from speaking and hearing, I command you, come out of him, and never enter him again!" After crying out and convulsing him terribly, it came out, and the boy was like a corpse, so that most of them said, "He is dead." But Jesus took him by the hand and lifted him up, and he was able to stand. When he had entered the house, his disciples asked him privately, "Why could we not cast it out?" He said to them, "This kind can come out only through prayer."

*Matthew 17:14-21* (see also Luke 9:37-42) When they came to the crowd, a man came to him, knelt before him, and said, "Lord, have mercy on my son, for he is an epileptic and he suffers terribly; he often falls into the fire and often into the water. And I brought him to your disciples, but they could not cure him." Jesus answered, "You faithless and perverse generation, how much longer must I be with you? How much longer must I put up with you? Bring him here to me." And Jesus rebuked the demon, and it came out of him, and the boy was cured instantly. Then the disciples came to Jesus privately and said, "Why could we not cast it out?" He said to them, "Because of your little faith. For truly I tell you, if you have faith the size of a mustard seed, you will say to this mountain, 'Move from here to there,' and it will move; and nothing will be impossible for you."

7. Mark's Gospel appears to be *written for a gentile audience,* although it assumes familiarity with matters Christians took over from Judaism. The Gospel begins with a quotation from "the prophet Isaiah" (1:2), that is, from the writings of Jewish Scripture, yet it takes care to explain certain Jewish practices such as "the washing of cups, pots, and bronze kettles" (7:3-4). Thus we conclude that Mark's Gospel is probably written for gentile Christians, who respect the Jewish Scriptures (which they would eventually identify as "the Old Testament") even if they are ignorant of basic Jewish rituals.

8. Of the four New Testament Gospels, Mark offers *the most human portrait of Jesus.* The Christian faith would ultimately confess that Jesus was both divine and human ("fully God and fully human"), and the tension inherent in such a confession is evident in these early documents. In John's Gospel, Jesus is identified with God (1:1) and addressed as God (20:28). In Mark's Gospel, the focus is elsewhere. Like any human being, Jesus becomes tired (6:31) and hungry (11:12). He feels a wide range of human emotions, including pity (1:41), anger (3:5), wonder (6:6), compassion (6:34), indignation (10:14), and love (10:21). Most significant, perhaps, Jesus does not know everything (13:32), and his power is sometimes limited (6:5). Still, he is extraordinary in some respects: he is identified as the Son of God (1:1, 11; 9:7; 15:39), he teaches with divine authority (1:22), and by God's power he is able to work fantastic miracles.

9. Mark's Gospel is imbued with a *motif of secrecy.* Jesus describes the message of his teaching as "the secret of the kingdom of God" (4:11).[16] He even claims that this is the reason he teaches in parables—the parables are not sermon illustrations to help people grasp difficult points, but rather a sort of code language that prevents those for whom they are not intended from understanding (4:10-12). The secrecy theme extends to Jesus' deeds and person as well. Several times in this Gospel he commands those who benefit from his miracles to "say nothing to anyone" about what he has done for them (1:43-44; 5:43; 7:36; see also 9:9). He silences demons who identify him as "the Holy One of God" and orders them "not to make him known" (1:23-25, 34; 3:11-12). And when Peter identifies him as "the Messiah," he rebukes his disciples, ordering them not to tell anyone about him (8:30). This emphasis on secrecy is all the more intriguing when we observe that elsewhere in Mark's Gospel Jesus sends his disciples out as missionaries (6:7-13, 30) and speaks of them proclaiming the gospel to all nations (13:10).

10. Mark's Gospel *highlights the failures of Jesus' disciples.* The twelve disciples whom Jesus calls to "fish for people"(1:16-20; 6:7) seem to fail him at almost every turn. They are remarkably unperceptive (8:14-21) and often diametrically opposed to him in their thinking (8:33; 9:33-34; 10:37-38). Again and again, this Gospel presents them as people unable to live up to Jesus' expectations: He gives them authority over unclean spirits (6:7), but

they are unable to cast such a spirit out of a child (9:17-19). He encourages them to welcome little children in his name (9:36-37), but then they rebuke people who wish to bring children to him (10:13). He asks them to stay awake and pray with him and they fall asleep (14:32-41). Their worst failures, however, occur in the events surrounding the cross. Mark records bold statements by all twelve disciples that they are willing, if necessary, to die for him (10:38-39; 14:29-31). But when the time comes, Judas betrays him (14:43-45), the rest desert him (14:50), and Peter denies three times that he even knows who Jesus is (14:66-72).

◆

# Historical Context

## Who?

A silly but often repeated legend holds that the author of Mark's Gospel is in fact the young man in 14:51-52 who wiggles out of his tunic and runs away naked on the night Jesus is arrested. This has no scholarly basis.

What seems more likely is the ancient attribution of this book to someone named Mark.[17] But who would that be? Mark was an extremely common name in the Roman world and, though it is found several times in the New Testament, this Gospel could have been written by someone who bore that name but is never mentioned elsewhere. Nevertheless, an ancient tradition identifies the author of this Gospel with the man named Mark who is described as Peter's (metaphorical?) son in a letter attributed to Jesus' chief disciple (1 Pet. 5:13). This Mark is further identified in tradition with a person called "John Mark" in the book of Acts, a young man whose house Peter visited (Acts 12:25).

Our earliest witness to this tradition comes from the fourth-century Christian historian Eusebius who quotes from a certain Papias, who Eusebius claims wrote in the middle of the second century.[18] According to Eusebius, Papias held that this Gospel was written by a man named Mark who had not been a follower of Jesus "but, at a later date, of Peter," and who had served as the latter's "interpreter." This would explain how the author learned the stories about Jesus that he tells. Still, this view is not without its problems. For one thing, Papias's credibility is suspect since he is almost certainly wrong in what he says about Matthew's Gospel (as we shall see in our next chapter). It is possible that he is constructing a guess based on the references to a Mark who was associated with Peter. He may have been motivated to do so by a desire to make the work seem more authoritative. If it was well known in the second century that the author of this book had not actually known Jesus, Christians may have wanted to believe that he had at least known one of Jesus' closest disciples.[19]

The tradition that Peter served as a primary source for the author of this Gospel seems unlikely for other reasons, too. This Gospel tells fewer stories about Peter than the others (particularly Matthew), and the ones it does tell cast Peter in a less favorable light. Also, a number of this Gospel's most distinctive features, such as its strong gentile orientation and emphasis on the crucifixion, echo key theological themes for Paul, who we know was sometimes at odds with Peter theologically. Peter was known for his missionary work among Jews, not Gentiles (Gal. 2:7-8). Indeed, this Gospel contains material that appears to support Paul's perspective on one issue that we know caused conflict between Paul and Peter in the early church: the observance of dietary laws in Christian community (Gal. 2:11-14; see Mark 7:18-19).

In some ways, then, the author of this Gospel appears to be linked more closely to Paul than to Peter. The obvious difference is that Paul does not appear from his letters to have much interest in the earthly life or ministry of Jesus. He could not, at any event, have served as a source for this information since he had not been a follower of Jesus either. Still, three letters attributed to Paul in the New Testament also mention someone named Mark: (a) Philemon 24 speaks of a "fellow worker" of Paul; (b) Colossians 4:10 mentions a cousin of Barnabas whom Paul commends; and (c) 2 Timothy 4:11 refers to a man who is to visit Paul while the latter is imprisoned in Rome. Christian tradition usually assumes these passages are all referring to the same person, who is also usually identified as the John Mark from Acts. In the latter book, John Mark appears to know Paul better than Peter, and to be closer to Barnabas than to either of them (see Acts 15:36-39; compare 13:13).

In sum, the ancient tradition that this Gospel was written by a first-century Christian who had not been a follower of Jesus appears to be correct, and there is no good reason to doubt that the name of this person was Mark. The identification of this author with associates of Peter and/or Paul who bore that name is less certain, but not impossible. A specific connection with the John Mark who is mentioned in Acts is a bit more speculative. On the one hand, the suggestion makes sense insofar as Acts presents John Mark as one who knew Peter (12:12) but who traveled with Paul (12:25). Thus, he might have learned some stories about Jesus from the former and yet had his theological agenda shaped by the latter. On the other hand, John Mark appears to be Jewish, and most interpreters think the author of this Gospel was a Gentile.

Whoever the author was, one verse offers a clue to at least one source of information. In the story of Jesus' crucifixion, Mark reports that the Roman soldiers "compelled a passer-by, who was coming in from the country, to carry his cross" and then he identifies this person as "Simon of Cyrene, the father of Alexander and Rufus" (15:21). This information may strike the modern reader as irrelevant, since neither Simon nor his sons are ever heard from again. But, apparently, Mark's original readers knew who Alexander and Rufus were. Thus, we may assume that the author of this Gospel had access to the children of an individual who had been present at the crucifixion, and may even have been able to talk with their father, Simon of Cyrene himself. This would provide information for only a small portion of the narrative, but a portion that describes a climactic event at which Peter and the other disciples were not present. In a broader sense, the reference to Alexander and Rufus may be paradigmatic of how Mark often gathered information. Mark writes his Gospel early enough to have known people like Simon of Cyrene or their children, people who could have provided information that Mark was able to weave into a coherent narrative.

## Where?

Although most scholars believe Mark's Gospel was written for a community of predominantly gentile Christians, theories about where this community existed are diverse and speculative. Those who think the author was a companion or "interpreter" of Peter usually think the Gospel was written in Rome.[20] The person named Mark who is described as Peter's son apparently lived in that city (see 1 Pet. 5:13, where Rome is metaphorically referred to as "Babylon"). Rome is also a possible place of origin for all three of the letters that refer to a Mark who was a companion of Paul, though that can be disputed in each individual case. John Mark apparently lived in Jerusalem (Acts 12:12; 13:13), but he also traveled a great deal. An origin in Rome would fit with the gentile orientation of the book and would clarify the apparent need to explain Jewish (Palestinian) practices (7:3-4). It would also seem appropriate for the concern with persecution (13:11-13), since at this time the most terrible and violent persecutions had occurred under the emperor Nero in that city. A Roman origin does not, however, explain the Gospel's strong interest in Galilee, particularly its insistence that Galilee is the place where Jesus will be encountered after Easter (14:28; 16:7). Also, the thirteenth chapter of Mark, in which the evangelist addresses the reader directly (13:14), appears to be directed to Christians who live in Palestine, close enough to Jerusalem to be affected by what transpires there. For these reasons, many scholars believe the Gospel must be written for a community of Christians in Galilee, in the same general area where Jesus' ministry had been conducted a generation earlier.[21]

## When?

Most scholars agree that Mark's Gospel was written around the time of the Jewish War with Rome (66–70 C.E.).[22] In one verse, Mark breaks into his story to alert his reader to the direct application that a saying of Jesus may have for their lives: "When you see the desolating sacrilege set up where it ought not to be (let the reader understand), then those in Judea must flee to the mountains" (13:14). Often, scholars think Mark believed the current war had made Roman desecration of the Jerusalem Temple inevitable and that his parenthetical remark to the reader was intended to underscore the relevance of Jesus' words when this occurred. If so, his readers did not have to wait long. The temple was not only desecrated but destroyed by the Romans in 70 C.E. Some scholars think Mark is postdating the prophecy he attributes to Jesus here, writing his Gospel a little later than 70.[23]

## Why?

The most obvious reason for Mark to compose this book is given in the opening words: he wants to proclaim "the good news of Jesus Christ, the Son of God" (1:1). But why does he want to do this in writing rather than through preaching? And if he is committed to writing, why write a story about Jesus' life and mission rather than a sermon or an essay?

An answer that is often suggested is that Mark felt compelled to get the story of Jesus' life down in writing because people who knew Jesus were dying, and he did not want the tradition to be lost or forgotten. Peter, for instance, was martyred in the year 65 C.E., shortly before the Gospel was written (Paul was killed at this time also). The death of eyewitnesses probably did have some influence on the production of written Gospels (see Luke 1:1-4), but the point can be stressed too strongly. As we have suggested, Mark seems to think that the parousia is going to come soon (13:30), and his Gospel appears to be written not for posterity but for readers alive at that time.

Mark's purpose is more precise. By telling the story of Jesus as he does, he lays claim to that tradition, presenting it in what he hopes will be accepted as an authoritative form. In other words, he is not just concerned that the story of Jesus' life be remembered, but is concerned that it be remembered in a particular way. As an illustration, we may consider again the issue of dietary laws. We know that one of the biggest controversies in first-century Christianity concerned the question of whether Christians were expected to obey traditional Jewish restrictions regarding certain foods (such as pork). When Mark records the teaching of Jesus on a related topic—what constitutes true defilement—he does so in a way that indicates Jesus "declared all foods clean" (7:14-23). It would certainly be possible to report the teaching of Jesus on this subject without drawing this conclusion (see Matt. 15:10-20), since the dietary restrictions were not necessarily tied to the notion that these foods would defile. Mark has chosen to tell the story in a way that presents Jesus as supporting the view he believes is right.[24]

This does not mean that Mark is simply co-opting the traditions of Jesus to win arguments in church politics. The concerns that he wishes to address through his telling of the Jesus story are more often pastoral or theological than political. (Indeed, the debate over whether all foods are now clean is ultimately a pastoral and theological issue.) The point is not that Mark is using Jesus to advance his own agenda. Rather, he is trying to show that his agenda is based on ideas that go back to Jesus. In this regard, he may be compared to Paul. We have observed that Mark's theological ideas are often compatible with those of Paul, but the latter seldom tells stories about Jesus' life and is comfortable proclaiming his thinking as expressive of "the mind of Christ" (1 Cor. 2:16) without establishing that Jesus actually thought this way. Mark's primary motivation for writing a Gospel, then, may be to provide historical grounding for an emerging theological system and the pastoral concerns it generates. That he thinks such a system needs historical grounding is itself significant, especially when compared with the often ahistorical mythology that served as grounding for much Greco-Roman religion.

Specific concerns that Mark wants to address include the openness of Christianity to Gentiles. Mark's Gospel includes stories that address the question of whether this Jewish Messiah has anything to offer non-Jews (7:24-30). He reports incidents in which Jesus performs the same acts of ministry for Gentiles (8:1-9) that he has performed for Jews (6:30-44). By the same token, Mark does not want to sever Christianity completely from its Jewish roots, as is evident by his commitment to the Jewish writings, which he apparently believes even gentile Christians must now regard as Scripture (1:2-3). Thus we see him struggling to clarify how the Christian faith can be viewed as a legitimate expression of Jewish hope even though it has been rejected by most Jews.

Mark is also concerned to support or strengthen those whose faith is in danger. The memorable parable of the sower (Mark 4:3-9, 13-20) recognizes two principal problems that may cause those who have received the word to fall away rather than "bear fruit."[25] One is the external threat of "trouble or persecution [that] arises on account of the word" (4:17). To address this, Mark recalls numerous instances of Jesus encouraging steadfastness in the face of trial (8:34-38; 13:9-13) and, of course, describes Jesus' own passion as the supreme example of one who suffers in submissive obedience to God's will (14:32-42). The second problem highlighted in the sower parable is the internal threat posed by "the cares of the world . . . the lure of wealth, and the desire for other things" (4:19). Mark also includes stories in which Jesus describes the proper priorities his followers need to adopt (10:17-31; 12:41-44). Both of these problems, fear of persecution and misplaced priorities, are addressed through Mark's tragic portrayal of the disciples, who fall victim to both and so become negative examples whose failures are a warning to readers.

Another concern for Mark is the appearance of people he regards as "false messiahs and false prophets" (13:22). What sort of heresies he feared is unclear, but his entire Gospel is no doubt intended to serve as a defense against any whose contrary teaching would lead people astray. In keeping with this catechetical purpose, we may probably assume that Mark's narrative was also intended to meet certain liturgical needs for the Christian community, providing the church with a consistent record that could be read publicly when believers gathered for worship.[26] Precedent for such ritual reading was already set by the use of lectionaries in synagogue services. One of our earliest accounts of a Christian worship service (c. 155 C.E.) mentions readings from the Gospels as central to the liturgy.[27]

◆

# Major Themes

## The Reign of God

In Mark's Gospel, Jesus talks more about "the reign of God" than he does about anything else.[28] The concept is taken over from certain Old Testament writings (for example, Ps. 103:19; Isa. 52:7), and the phrase is used also by Paul (Rom. 14:17; 1 Cor. 4:20). In Mark, however, it receives such emphasis as to dominate the entire book. Indeed, Mark goes so far as to define what he means by "gospel" as the revelation that "the time is fulfilled and the reign of God has come near" (1:15). Followers of Jesus are expected to believe in this revelation concerning the reign of God and to alter their lives radically in light of it.

Many English Bibles translate this phrase "kingdom of God," which can be misleading. The pertinent Greek word is a cognate noun (*basileia*), that is, a noun derived from a word that can also be used as a verb (*basileuō*). The English word *reign* is also such a noun, as is the alternative translation *rule.* But the noun *kingdom* does not convey this sense of verbal action. We may say "God reigns" or "God rules," but it makes no sense to say "God kingdoms." People who rely on English Bibles may get the impression that the "kingdom of God" Jesus speaks about in Mark's Gospel is a location, a place where God lives and, possibly, a place where people may hope to live with God after they die. Actually, the phrase "reign of God" refers to the phenomenon of God reigning or ruling, and Mark presents this phenomenon as an active reality that cannot be circumscribed by space or time. One way to grasp what is meant by this significant phrase is to consider the line of the famous Lord's Prayer (though it is not found in Mark), "Your kingdom come, your will be done." Bible scholars recognize that this line employs poetic parallelism, which means, when Christians pray this they are asking for the same thing twice. God's kingdom (or reign) comes when God's will is done, for God can only truly be said to rule when what God wants to happen takes place.

Understanding what Mark means by the phrase "reign of God" aids in the interpretation of numerous passages. For example, when Jesus says, "It is easier for a camel to go through the eye of a needle than for someone who is rich to enter the kingdom [reign] of God" (10:25), he does not mean to indicate that rich people will be unlikely to go to heaven and live with God after they die. What he means is that it is easier for a camel to pass through a needle's eye than for God to rule a rich person's life. Of course, the question of whether God rules people's lives now may not be unrelated theologically to the question of what will happen in "the age to come" (10:30), but the teaching of Jesus regarding the reign of God in Mark's Gospel focuses decidedly on the first consideration.

What, then, does Jesus mean when he announces, "The time is fulfilled, and the kingdom (reign) of God has come near" (1:15)? In the theological context of Mark's Gospel, this means that the time has finally come for God's will to be accomplished. What God wants to happen is about to take place; indeed, it is already beginning to happen. This is the basic premise of Jesus' teaching in Mark's Gospel, and it is fleshed out in more detail as the narrative continues. We learn that this nearness of God's reign is a secret, not known to all (4:11). We hear that it is only the beginning of something that will eventually become very big (4:30-32). What is going to happen will transpire in a way that is mysterious (4:26-29) but powerful (9:1). Because the reign of God has now drawn near, furthermore, it is both possible and imperative for people to "enter it" (9:47; 10:15, 23-24). People do this by believing the good news that Jesus proclaims and by living their lives in ways that reflect their trust in this good news (1:14-15).

The deeds of Jesus reported in Mark's Gospel also reflect his explication of the nearness of God's reign. Jesus' healings, exorcisms, and miracles demonstrate the truth of his claim, in that God's will is thus accomplished in remarkable ways. Furthermore, these actions illustrate what it means for God's reign to draw near. It means that demons and disease and catastrophic forces of nature are vanquished. Mark wants his readers to receive the announcement that God's reign has drawn near as "good news" because God's rule in their lives will operate to defeat what is evil and to bring about what is good.

Ultimately, Mark wants to say not only that God's reign has drawn near, but that it has drawn near *in Jesus*. It is Jesus himself who brings about the accomplishment of God's will, and he does this not only through his teaching and his miracles but, most important, through his crucifixion. In some mysterious way that Mark never fully explains, Jesus' death on the cross effects the definitive accomplishment of God's saving purpose. Jesus says that the very reason he has come is "to give his life as a ransom for many" (10:45), and he rejects as Satanic anything that would deter him (8:31-33). Thus Mark believes that when Jesus dies on the cross, God's reign draws near, and the unfolding of God's purpose passes the point of no return.

## Son of Man and Son of God

Mark's Gospel is about Jesus. As its story unfolds, we are told who Jesus is, where he goes, what he does, whom he meets, and so forth. Other people come into the picture only when their life stories cross that of Jesus. At a basic level, then, understanding Mark's Gospel means understanding Mark's *Christology,* that is, his particular perspective on the enduring significance of the person and work of Jesus.

Discussions of Mark's Christology must always wrestle with the secrecy motif mentioned above. Why does Jesus try to keep his identity and actions a secret? Simple, practical explanations may be offered, for instance, that Jesus had to be circumspect about his claims to avoid being arrested before his time had come. Or, Jesus wanted to keep news of his healing powers a secret to avoid being accosted by unmanageable crowds (see 1:45). Still, Mark's level of investment with this theme suggests the need for more than just a pragmatic explanation. For one thing, none of the other Gospels seems to be this concerned with shrouding Jesus' earthly ministry in secrecy; the theme surfaces elsewhere only in passages that Matthew or Luke take over from Mark. Most scholars would agree that the secrecy theme is not simply reported as historical reminiscence of what was a practical necessity during Jesus' life. Rather, the theme is developed intentionally by Mark to further some theological agenda. But what?

In 1901 a German scholar named Wilhelm Wrede proposed a solution to this puzzle that made sense to many, but disturbed others.[29] Basically, Wrede thought that Mark invented the scheme of a "messianic secret" to facilitate a presentation of Jesus that was not historically accurate. For Wrede, Mark's Christology represented a position between two poles in early Christianity. The earliest tradition, he believed, held that Jesus became the Messiah and/or Son of God at his resurrection. Thus, the post-Easter, risen Lord Jesus whom Christians worship came to be identified as Messiah and Son of God in a way that the pre-Easter Jesus who lived and taught in Palestine had not been. For the most part, these earliest Christians did not leave writings, but Wrede found pointers to their views in occasional passages preserved in the book of Acts (2:36) or the letters of Paul (Rom. 1:4; Phil. 2:6-11). Later Christian tradition interpreted the pre-Easter Jesus in light of post-Easter theology, identifying the man who lived and taught in Galilee as the Messiah and Son of God and attributing great miracles to him as proof of these claims. This tradition Wrede recognized as standard for the four Gospels, especially the Gospel of John.

As the first Gospel written, Mark's book reflects the necessary transition from the early tradition to the later view. The secrecy theme is a device to explain why some earlier Christians had not known what otherwise would seem obvious. Unlike the other Gospel writers, Mark writes at a time when many people who knew Jesus may still be alive. As Wrede sees it, Mark wants to describe a messianic life, but memories of the actual nonmessianic life are so fresh that he cannot do this without inventing the notion that what he has to say about Jesus was a secret known only to a few. If someone says, "I was there and I don't remember Jesus ever claiming to be the Messiah or working all these miracles," Mark can respond, "He did say and do these things, but you were not one of the ones privileged to know about them."

Few scholars today would accept Wrede's provocative thesis outright, but some of his ideas continue to be influential.[30] Ongoing study in source and form criticism has demonstrated that the growth of christological ideas in the early church was more complex than Wrede allowed. (For example, most scholars would now regard the speeches in Acts as representative of a tradition later than Mark's Gospel.) Overall, Wrede seems to regard Mark as unnecessarily devious, and his assumption that Mark would be so concerned about establishing the historical credibility of his account seems anachronistic. Most likely, Mark is writing for believers who already know these stories through oral tradition. They do not have to be persuaded that these things happened, but they may (in Mark's mind) need some guidance regarding what these things mean. In light of the latter observation, many theologians believe Mark uses the so-called secrecy theme as a way of correcting what he regards as inadequate views. Thus, Mark portrays Jesus as commending silence regarding certain miracles because he does not want Jesus to be known primarily as a miracle worker. The point is not that the miracles are or should be a secret. The point is that people who go around proclaiming Christ as "a wonder worker" are preaching an inadequate Christology. The Roman world knew many stories of "divine men" who were gifted by the gods with extraordinary powers, or who learned magical arts that enabled them to do amazing things. Mark does not want Jesus to be grouped with such persons.[31]

This understanding of Mark, called "corrective Christology,"[32] focuses especially on a key text around the middle of Mark's Gospel. In Mark 8:27-30, Jesus raises the question of his own identity pointedly. "Who do people say that I am?" he asks his disciples. They give a number of responses, all of which are clearly wrong. He then continues, "But who do you say that I am?" Peter answers, "You are the Messiah!" And then Mark reports that Jesus "sternly ordered them not to tell anyone about him." According to the corrective Christology theory, the point here is not that Jesus is commanding secrecy now that his disciples know who he is, but rather that he is commanding silence because they still *don't* know who he is. Peter's identification of him as "the Messiah" is just as inadequate as the "divine man" (*theios anēr*) identifications implied by those impressed by Jesus' miracles. Why? The concept of Messiah might have been too easily connected with political aspirations. Many people would have thought of the Messiah as a deliverer who would liberate the Jewish people from Roman authorities. Writing his Gospel around the time of the Jewish war with Rome, Mark finds the traditional Christian identification of Jesus as the Messiah to be limiting and subject to misinterpretation.

If acclamations of Jesus as a divine miracle worker or even as the Messiah are inadequate, then what would Mark consider to be a proper Christology? Proponents of this view usually seize upon another title applied to Jesus in this book: *Son of Man*. This is the term that Jesus uses for himself. When he says, for instance, that "the Son of Man has authority on earth to forgive sins" (2:10) or "the Son of Man is lord . . . of the sabbath" (2:28), he means to claim that *he* has authority to forgive sins and that *he* is lord of the sabbath. The phrase "Son of Man" derives from the Old Testament, where it sometimes means simply "a human being" (Ps. 8:4) but other times refers specifically to a divine figure who is to come at the end of time (Dan. 7:13; compare Mark 8:38; 13:26; 14:62). Both senses seem appropriate for Mark's understanding of Jesus, but what is most distinctive is the additional nuance the term assumes here. According to Mark, the Son of Man is also a figure who is to be rejected, suffer, be killed, and then rise from the dead (8:31; 9:31; 10:33-34).[33]

Critics of this corrective Christology theory are especially hard on the "corrective" part. Mark himself identifies Jesus as the Messiah in the first verse of his Gospel, and toward the end when Jesus is asked point blank,

"Are you the Messiah?" he responds, "I am" (14:61-62). Mark also identifies followers of Jesus as persons who "bear the name of Christ [Messiah]" (9:41; compare 13:13). Mark may want to supplement this popular designation for Jesus with other images that present a broader focus, but to interpret the words to the disciples in Mark 8:30 as meaning Mark does not want Jesus to be identified as the Messiah seems like an overstatement. Still, the theory of corrective Christology has been widely accepted as insightful in some respects. Most scholars agree with the basic point, that Mark tells his story in ways that interpret the traditional materials he has received.

Another aspect that needs to be considered, though, is Mark's designation of Jesus as the *Son of God*. Again, this identification is first made by Mark himself in the Gospel's opening verse (1:1).[34] In the story that follows, God twice speaks dramatically from heaven and both times calls Jesus "my Son" (1:11; 9:7). Demons also recognize Jesus as the Son of God (3:11; 5:7; compare 1:24). But, curiously, no human character ever identifies Jesus as the Son of God until two climactic moments toward the end. At his trial, Jesus is asked if he is "the Son of the Blessed One" (no doubt a synonym for Son of God), and his affirmative answer earns him a death sentence (14:61-64). Later, at the moment of his death, the centurion or Roman officer in charge of his execution says, "Truly this man was God's Son!" (15:39).

Jack Kingsbury has offered yet another explanation of the secrecy motif in Mark connected to this Son of God Christology.[35] According to Kingsbury, the motif is a literary device intended to facilitate a particular reading of the story. Mark's Gospel is like a mystery, but the mystery (secret) does not concern the question, "Who is Jesus?" That answer is given to the readers in the very first verse: Jesus is the Messiah, the Son of God. Rather the mystery most pertinent to Mark's readers concerns other questions: "What does it mean to call Jesus this?" and "How do people come to know this?" These are the issues that would be relevant to a community of believers. The first question is answered in the passion narrative when readers learn that to identify Jesus as the Messiah and Son of God means to identify him as the one who is to be crucified. The answer to the second question is answered similarly in the acclamation of the centurion. Earlier in Mark's Gospel, Jesus cast out demons, forgave sins, performed extraordinary miracles, and taught the will of God, but these actions simply left people wondering who he was (1:27; 2:7; 4:41; 6:2-3). No one is able to recognize Jesus as the Son of God until he dies on the cross, though at that point the revelation becomes apparent even to an uninstructed Gentile. Mark is preaching through this story, Kingsbury avers, and the theme of his sermon is that this Jesus whom Christians know to be the Messiah and Son of God cannot be understood apart from the cross. This was a common theme in Paul's preaching also (1 Cor. 2:2).

## Discipleship and the Cross

The disciples of Jesus in Mark's Gospel serve as prime examples of persons who don't get the message of the cross. Their failings were described in 1971 in a study by Theodore Weeden.[36] According to Weeden, Mark depicts the disciples' faithlessness as developing in three stages:

(a) *Unperceptiveness.* Although the disciples seem eager in responding to Jesus' initial call (1:16-20), they do not appear to perceive who it is that they are following. They hear Jesus' words and witness his mighty acts, but do not realize that he is the authoritative agent of God. This is readily apparent in what may be called "the three boat scenes." The first time the disciples are in a boat with Jesus, a storm arises and they fear for their lives. After Jesus stills the storm, the disciples are still afraid, responding to the miracle not with faith but with a question, "Who then is this, that even the wind and the sea obey him?" (4:35-41). Later, when Jesus stills another storm, Mark reports that the disciples were "utterly astounded" because they did not understand and "their hearts were hardened" (6:45-52). Finally, when Jesus and his disciples are once again in a boat, the latter misinterpret a parabolic warning he offers against "the yeast of the Pharisees and the yeast of Herod" as a reference to literal yeast that is used in making bread. Jesus is aghast at their stupidity, and is especially annoyed that they are worried about whether there will be enough bread when he has just performed two miracles of multiplying loaves of bread to feed multitudes of people. "Do you not remember?" he implores them. "Do you not yet understand?" (8:14-21)

(b) *Misconception.* Around the middle of Mark's Gospel, Jesus' disciples finally do realize that he is the authoritative agent of God, but they draw all the wrong conclusions from this insight. Identifying him as the Messiah (8:29), they think that being his followers means that they are going to achieve success in this world and be accorded great glory and honor. Jesus repeatedly tells them they are called rather to a life of service and sacrifice and that they will meet with suffering and rejection. Their failure to grasp this point is illustrated well in their responses to Jesus' three predictions of his own passion. The first time he tells them about the suffering and death that awaits him, Peter rebukes him for thinking this way, eliciting Jesus' famous reply, "Get behind me, Satan!" (8:31-33). The next time he tries to tell them, the disciples don't understand what he is saying and, instead of asking for explanation, become embroiled in an argument over which one of them "is the greatest" (9:32-34). The third time he declares clearly that condemnation and death await him, two of the disciples respond by asking incongruously whether they can be guaranteed seats at his right and left when he comes into his glory (10:35-41). They miss his main point, that "the

Son of Man came not to be served but to serve," and its corollary, "whoever
wishes to be first among you must be slave of all" (10:43-44).

*(c) Rejection.* When the disciples finally do come to understand the nature
of Jesus' mission and its implications for their lives, they desert him. One of
Jesus' own, Judas, betrays him (14:10-11, 44-45), and when he comes with
an armed crowd to arrest Jesus the other disciples run away. Like the young
man who abandons his clothing in order to get away (14:51), their despera-
tion in separating themselves from Jesus now matches the enthusiasm with
which they left their belongings to follow him in the beginning (1:16-20).
Peter holds out a little longer than the rest but, eventually, his apostasy is
even greater than theirs. He denies three times that he even knows who
Jesus is, and then, aware that he has failed his master, breaks down and
weeps bitterly (14:66-72).

What Weeden's description of these three stages makes clear is that the
disciples are not only depicted as failures in Mark's Gospel but as persons
whose failings become progressively worse as the story develops. They go
from being people who don't understand the gospel to being people who
misconstrue it in dangerous ways to become finally apostates who reject it
altogether. Most scholars accept this description of Mark's account, but
many would have problems with Weeden's next point. He goes on to suggest that Mark wants his readers to assume that these disciples never recovered from their apostasy, and so became founders of an errant religion.
Weeden believes Mark does this because his community is representative of
a gentile branch of Christianity that is not sanctioned by the apostolic church
in Jerusalem, which claims to represent the faith as passed down by Jesus'
first followers. A variation on Weeden's thesis advanced by Werner Kelber
holds that Mark wants to minimize the significance of the loss of apostolic
witnesses as a result of Roman persecution and war.[37] In either case, the
point is that Mark wants to establish his own community as the true heir
to the Jesus tradition, while also exposing the understanding of the faith
represented by the apostles (Jesus' disciples) as inadequate.

Most scholars find the notion that Mark wants his readers to regard the
disciples of Jesus as permanent apostates intrinsically unlikely. Mark himself
seems to recognize that the disciples will eventually play a significant role
as authentic witnesses to the faith. He records words of Jesus indicating that
they will bear testimony for him and suffer for his sake (10:39; 13:9). For
that matter, Mark's Gospel also includes predictions that Jesus and his disciples will be reunited after the resurrection (14:28; 16:7). Unlike the other
Gospels, Mark never actually reports the stories in which such a reconcilia-
tion occurs (Matt. 28:16-20; Luke 24:36-53; John 20:19-29; 21:1-23), but
Mark's readers are probably expected to know that the defection of the disciples during the passion narrative was not the end of all that could be said

about them. Still, many scholars would concur with Weeden and Kelber that Mark does not report any more than he does because he wants his readers' lasting impression of these disciples to be a negative one. The disciples represent a version of Christianity that does not reckon with the cross.[38]

Mark's intention could be more pastoral than polemical. In this view, Mark is more interested in instructing his community (albeit through somewhat negative examples) than in tarnishing the image of historical persons.[39] Readers may note, for instance, that Jesus does call these disciples and so takes responsibility for them, failures that they are. In Mark's Gospel, no one volunteers to become a disciple of Jesus. Rather, people become disciples only at Jesus' initiative, as a result of his call. Furthermore, Jesus never appears to regret his choices, not even when he predicts that those he has called will betray (14:17-21), forsake (14:26-28), or deny (14:29-31) him. In short, he never gives up on them. He continues to teach them (4:33-34; 7:17-23), to correct their misunderstandings (8:34-38; 9:35-37; 10:42-45), and to empower them for the work he believes they will do (3:14-15; 6:7-13). Indeed, the message that goes out from the empty tomb is clearly that Jesus has not abandoned those who abandoned him. He wants them back (16:7). The story ends without resolution because Mark wants his readers to place themselves in the position of the disciples and to determine what they would do. At the end of this story, readers may recognize that, like the disciples, they have failed to understand the gospel of the cross and so have failed to meet the expectations of the one they call Messiah and Son of God. Even so, they may realize that they can still continue with Jesus, knowing that this relationship is (and always has been) sustained by his faithfulness, not theirs.[40]

Such a message would have specific pastoral relevance for a community in which many had suffered persecution and some had no doubt lapsed on account of it (see 4:16-17).[41] From a literary perspective, Mark's presentation of the disciples could serve as a device to challenge readers who empathize with these disciples to recognize their own failings.[42] Such a message would also have general theological relevance in terms of defining discipleship based in the cross as something that must necessarily be grounded in Christ's mercy rather than in the merits of disciples themselves. In this sense, Mark's story of the disciples becomes a narrative depiction of Paul's doctrine of justification by grace (see, for example, Rom. 5:1-11).

◆

### The Gospel of Mark As Literature: Sample Studies

*The Liberated Gospel: A Comparison of the Gospel of Mark and Greek Tragedy*
By Gilbert Bilezekian (Grand Rapids: Baker, 1977)

Tries to show that Mark contains the essential elements for tragedy as outlined by Aristotle in his *Poetics*.

*Mark As Story: An Introduction to the Narrative of a Gospel*
By David Rhoads and Donald Michie (Philadelphia: Fortress Press, 1982)
Analyzes the entire Gospel as one would a modern short story, paying attention to its rhetoric, characters, settings, and plot.

*Narrative Space and Mythic Meaning in Mark*
By Elizabeth Struthers Malbon (San Francisco: Harper and Row, 1986)
Investigates the meaning assigned to spatial locations in Mark's story, especially as these are opposed to each other: heaven vs. earth; land vs. sea; house vs. synagogue; Galilee vs. Judea.

*Irony in the Gospel of Mark: Text and Subtext*
By Jerry Camery-Hoggatt SNTSMS 72 (Cambridge: Cambridge University Press, 1992)
Explores the rhetorical strategy of dramatic irony in Mark, according to which meaning is revealed to readers while hidden from the story's central characters.

*Let the Reader Understand: Reader-Response Criticism and the Gospel of Mark*
By Robert M. Fowler (Minneapolis: Fortress Press, 1991)
Examines the rhetoric of the Gospel with an emphasis on those features that allow interpretations that are ambiguous.

*The Genesis of Secrecy: On the Interpretation of Narrative*
By Frank Kermode (Cambridge: Harvard University Press, 1979)
Contends that Mark's Gospel creates "an unfollowable world" in which it is as impossible to find true unity or coherence as it is in the world of real life.

◆

## Feminist Readings of Mark: Sample Studies

*Journeys By Heart: A Christology of Erotic Power*
By Rita Nakashima Brock (New York: Crossroad, 1988)
Interprets stories of Christian origin in Mark's Gospel from the perspective of feminist, relational theology. Brock discovers in the miracle and passion stories a source of "erotic" (that is, heart-based) power that is the basis of life and community.

"The Gospel of Mark insists that those who would travel in the territories of erotic power must risk living their new vision. This risk is the process of being on the way . . . on the journey of expectation that comes from living by heart" (p. 105).

*Women and Jesus in Mark: A Japanese Feminist Perspective*
By Hisako Kinukawa (Maryknoll, N.Y.: Orbis Books, 1994)
Examines the stories in Mark involving women who approach Jesus and contends their interactions with him are what draw out the most fully liberating implications of the Gospel.

"The women led Jesus to become a responding 'boundary breaker.' Having spent his whole life in the culture of honor/shame, which was male-oriented . . . Jesus did not take initiative until the women prepared him by stages to break down the barriers. Interactions were reciprocal and both sides received and learned something" (p. 139).

# CHAPTER THREE

# The Gospel of Matthew

When we compare the Gospel of Matthew to Mark, we notice immediately that it is almost twice as long. Indeed, Matthew has taken almost all of Mark's Gospel over into his, albeit in redacted form. In addition is the material attributed to the Q source (see figure 5) and a fairly large amount of material that is unique to Matthew (see figure 12). The label *M* is applied to the latter material only for convenience and is not meant to imply that, as with Q, this material once constituted an independent, coherent document. Rather, the M material is simply that which was collected within Matthew's own community over a period of years. As such, scholars often regard these portions of Matthew's Gospel as especially revealing of the evangelist's situation and particular concerns.[1] Even more pertinent in this regard, however, are the editorial changes that Matthew has apparently made in the Markan material (see figure 13).

Most of the passages in Matthew that derive from Q or M present sayings or parables of Jesus. The Q source does contain a narrative of Jesus' temptation by Satan (4:1-11), and the M material provides stories about the birth of Jesus at the beginning of the Gospel (1:18—2:23) and stories related to his resurrection at the end (27:52-53, 62-66; 28:11-20). Still, the basic story of Jesus' life and ministry presented in Mark's Gospel remains unchanged. The major effect of merging the Q and M material with the Markan tradition is to supplement that basic story with generous portions devoted to the teaching of Jesus. Scholars have long noted that the bulk of the Q and M material in Matthew occurs in five big chunks, called the five great discourses or speeches of Jesus. These are given names, such as:

Figure 12

---

Material Unique to Matthew

This is a partial list of what is often labeled *M* material:

| | |
|---|---|
| Genealogy of Jesus (from Abraham) | 1:2-17 |
| Birth of Jesus (with focus on Joseph) | 1:18-25 |
| Visit of the Magi | 2:1-12 |
| Flight to Egypt | 2:13-21 |
| On Fulfilling the Law | 5:17-20 |
| The Antitheses | 5:21-24, 27-29, 31, 33-38, 43 |
| On Practicing Piety | 6:1-15, 16-19 |
| Pearls Before Swine | 7:6 |
| Coming Persecutions | 10:21-23 |
| Invitation to Rest | 11:28-30 |
| Parables: Weeds, Treasure, Pearl, Net | 13:24-30, 36-52 |
| Peter Tries to Walk on Water | 14:28-31 |
| Blessing of Peter | 16:17-19 |
| Peter Pays the Temple Tax | 17:24-27 |
| Recovering the Sinful Member | 18:15-20 |
| Peter Asks about Forgiveness | 18:21-22 |
| Parable of Unforgiving Servant | 18:23-35 |
| Parable of Laborers in Vineyard | 20:1-16 |
| Parable of Two Sons | 21:28-32 |
| Prohibition of Titles | 23:2-5, 7-12 |
| Denunciations of Pharisees | 23:15-22 |
| Parable of Bridesmaids | 25:1-13 |
| Description of Last Judgment | 25:31-46 |
| Death of Judas | 27:3-10 |
| Pilate Washes His Hands | 27:24-25 |
| Resuscitation of Saints | 27:52-53 |
| Guard at the Tomb | 27:62-66; 28:11-15 |
| Great Commission | 28:16-20 |

---

| | |
|---|---|
| Chapters 5–7 | The Sermon on the Mount[2] |
| Chapter 10 | The Missionary Discourse[3] |
| Chapter 13 | The Parables of the Kingdom[4] |
| Chapter 18 | The Community Discourse[5] |
| Chapters 24–25 | The Eschatological Discourse[6] |

Of these five speeches, the first is the most famous. The Sermon on the Mount contains such well-known items as the Beatitudes (5:3-10), the Lord's Prayer (6:9-13), and the Golden Rule (7:12). It has had an enormous impact on Western civilization. Many expressions have entered our language at a

Figure 13

---

Matthew's Use of Mark

Matthew preserves almost the entire Gospel of Mark, but he edits it in accord with the following principles:

1. *Organization*
   Five miracle stories are moved to Matthew 8 9, where other miracle stories occur.

2. *Abbreviation*
   Details not immediately relevant are pruned away:

   • the demoniac's chains and behavior (Matt. 8:28; Mark 5:2-5)

   • unroofing the tiles for the paralytic (Matt. 9:2; Mark 2:2-5)

   "Extra" characters are deleted:

   • the crowd and the disciples in story of woman's healing (Matt. 9:20-22; Mark 5:24b-34)

   • the naked young man in the garden (Matt. 26:47-56; Mark 14:43-52)

3. *Stylistic Improvement*

   • Greek becomes more polished.

   • some "historical presents" are changed (130 out of 151)

   • Mark's repetitious use of words such as *and* and *immediately* is reduced

   • pronouns lacking clear antecedents are provided antecedents

4. *Accuracy*

   • Apparent inaccuracies are corrected.

   • "King Herod" (Mark 6:14) becomes "Herod the tetrarch" (Matt. 14:1)

   • Mark's reference to Abiathar as high priest in 2:26 is omitted in Matt. 12:4 (according to 1 Sam. 21:1-6, it was Ahimelech, not Abiathar)

*(continued)*

**Figure 13** *continued*

5. *Application*
   Some changes make things more relevant to Matthew's community:

   a. a Jewish-Christian community
   • omits Mark's explanation of Jewish customs (Mark 7:3-4) and the interpretation that Jesus made "all foods clean" (Mark 7:19)

   • "Kingdom of heaven" replaces "kingdom of God"

   b. an urban community
   • frequently changes "village" (*kōmē*) to "city" (*polis*)

   c. a prosperous community
   • adds "gold" and "silver" to Jesus' injunction for disciples to take no "copper" with them (Matt. 10:9; Mark 6:8)

6. *Idealization*
   The portraits of some characters are "retouched."

   a. Jesus
   • questions that imply lack of knowledge on Jesus' part are omitted (Mark 5:9, 30; 6:38; 8:23; 9:12, 16, 21, 33; 10:3; 14:14)

   • statements that imply any lack of ability or authority on Jesus' part are modified (compare Mark 6:5 to Matt. 13:58)

   • references to human emotions are dropped: pity (Mark 1:41), anger (Mark 3:5), grief (Mark 3:5), wonder (Mark 6:6), indignation (Mark 10:14), love (Mark 10:21)

   • stories that may have been thought to portray Jesus as a magician are dropped (Mark 7:31-37; 8:22-26)

   b. Jesus' disciples
   • Mark's theme that the disciples don't understand is changed so that they *do* understand after Jesus explains (compare Matt. 13:16-18 to Mark 4:13; Matt. 16:5-12 to Mark 8:14-21; Matt. 17:9-13 to Mark 9:9-13)

   *(continued)*

**Figure 13** *continued*

---

• Unseemly ambition is ascribed to James and John's mother, instead of to the disciples themselves (Matt. 20:20; Mark 10:35)

• references to the disciples worshiping Jesus and calling him Lord and Son of God are added (compare Matt. 14:33 to Mark 6:52)

c. Jesus' family
• reference to his family coming "to restrain him" is dropped (Mark 3:21)

7. *Disparagement*
The portrait of the Jewish leaders gets worse:

• a scribe whom Jesus praises (Mark 12:28-34) becomes an opponent who puts Jesus to the test (Matt. 22:34- 40)

• Jairus (Mark 5:22) and Joseph of Arimathea (Mark 15:43) are no longer identified as Jewish leaders (Matt. 9:18; 27:57)

---

popular level, such that even people who are not Bible readers have heard about "the salt of the earth" (5:13), "turning the other cheek" (5:39), and "wolves in sheep's clothing" (7:15). Thomas Jefferson, who repudiated most elements of Christian faith, identified the Sermon on the Mount along with the Ten Commandments as expressive of the moral principles on which the United States of America should be founded.[7]

In 1930 a scholar by the name of Benjamin Bacon proposed an outline for the entire Gospel of Matthew based on the pattern of these five great speeches (see figure 14).[8] In an ingenious way, this outline recognizes that narrative material preceding each of the speeches often deals with the same theme addressed in the subsequent discourse. Bacon suggested that the pattern of organization is itself significant, intended to represent a Christian Pentateuch or "Five Books of Jesus" analogous to the "Five Books of Moses" that comprise the Jewish Torah.[9] His outline has been extremely influential and is still used by many Matthew scholars today, but few would agree with his designation of the passion and resurrection narrative as an "epilogue." Literary critics invariably identify the death and resurrection of Jesus in Matthew as the climax of the narrative's plot, as the goal toward which most of the action is directed throughout the book. In this regard, many scholars prefer the simpler, more direct outline for the Gospel proposed by Jack Kingsbury (see figure 14).[10] Theologians note that Kingsbury's approach is more christological (tracing the book's presentation of Jesus) while Bacon's is more ecclesiological (outlining its content according to church-related themes). Indeed, Bacon described the Gospel of Matthew as "an early Christian catechism" while Kingsbury has called it "a story about Jesus."[11]

◆

## Characteristics of Matthew's Gospel

We may note a number of distinctive attributes of this Gospel that help to set it apart from the other three.

1. Matthew's Gospel displays a *penchant for organizational patterns,*[12] including numerical ones. We have already noted the five great speeches of Jesus and the possible connection these could have to the five books of Moses. Elsewhere in the Gospel, Matthew includes exactly twelve *fulfillment citations,* that is, passages that claim what is reported "happened to fulfill what was written in the prophets" (1:22-23; 2:5-6, 15, 17-18, 23; 4:14-16; 8:17; 12:17-21; 13:14-15, 35; 21:4-5; 27:9-10). The number twelve is often symbolic of Israel, since in the Hebrew Scriptures the nation of Israel consists of twelve tribes. Another obvious example of such organizational patterns is found in the genealogy of Jesus (1:1-17), which is divided into three sets of fourteen generations apiece. What is the significance of the number fourteen? In the Hebrew language, letters of the alphabet also serve as numerals, and those who knew Hebrew in the first century often added up the numerical value of all the letters in a person's name (a practice called *gematria*). The letters in the Hebrew name David add up to fourteen, and since tradition held that the Messiah would be a descendant of David, that number apparently took on messianic overtones for Matthew's community.

2. For some reason, Matthew seems to be fond of pairs, so that his Gospel exhibits what is called a *doubling motif.*[13] Appropriately, this motif has two elements: First, when Matthew's Gospel is compared to Mark's, some minor characters appear to be doubled. Mark 5:1-14 contains a story about Jesus casting a legion of demons out of a man and into a herd of pigs (New Testament students jokingly refer to it as the story of "deviled ham"). The same story is found in Matthew 8:28-33, but now the legion of demons must be cast out of two men. Similarly, Mark 10:46-52 reports the healing of a blind man while Matthew 20:29-34 records the healing of two blind men. Most remarkable, perhaps, is the Palm Sunday story of Jesus' entry into Jerusalem. In Matthew's version, Jesus sits on two animals as he rides into the city (21:6-7). Is this just an overly literal fulfillment of the prophecy cited in 21:5 (Zech. 9:9), or is it a doubling of the one animal found in Mark 11:7? The

Figure 14

---

The Structure of Matthew: Two Outlines

**Benjamin Bacon's Outline**

Preamble: Infancy Narrative (chapters 1–2)

Book 1: Discipleship (3–7)
  A. Narrative (3–4)
  B. Sermon on the Mount (5–7)

Book 2: Apostleship (8–10)
  A. Narrative (8–9)
  B. Missionary Discourse (10)

Book 3: Hiding of the Revelation (11–13)
  A. Narrative (11–12)
  B. Parable Discourse (13)

Book 4: Church Administration (14–18)
  A. Narrative (14–17)
  B. Community Discourse (18)

Book 5: Judgment (19–25)
  A. Narrative (19–23)
  B. Eschatological Discourse (24–25)

Epilogue: Passion and Resurrection (26–28)

**Jack Kingsbury's Outline**

Part 1: The Presentation of Jesus (1:1—4:16)

Part 2: Ministry of Jesus to Israel (4:17—11:1) and Israel's Repudiation of Jesus (11:2—16:20)

Part 3: Journey of Jesus to Jerusalem and His Suffering, Death, and Resurrection (16:21—28:20) second element of Matthew's doubling motif involves repetition of sayings or entire pericopes within the Gospel itself. Jesus' words on divorce are reported twice (5:31-32; 19:9) as are stories of the religious leaders seeking a sign from him (12:38-42; 16:1-4) and accusing him of operating with the power of Beelzebul (9:32-34; 12:22-24).

3. The *disciple Peter receives special prominence* in this Gospel, in that Matthew contains a number of stories concerning Peter that are not found anywhere else. These include a curious tale about Peter finding a coin in a fish's mouth to pay taxes for himself and Jesus (17:24-27) and the well-known account in 18:21-22 of Peter asking Jesus how many times it is appropriate to forgive someone ("As many as seven times?" Answer: "Not seven times, but seventy times seven"). Matthew also expands stories from Mark's Gospel with new information about Peter. The story of Jesus walking on the water (Mark 6:47-52) now concludes with an account of Peter trying (with limited success) to walk on the water (Matt. 14:28-31). Most significant, Matthew has attached to the Markan story of Peter acknowledging that Jesus is the Messiah (Mark 8:27-29) an extended blessing in which Jesus declares, "You are Peter, and on this rock I will build my church" (Matt. 16:17-20). The latter passage has been interpreted by Roman Catholicism as supporting a doctrine of the papacy, since every Pope is believed to be heir (via "apostolic succession") to this privileged position bestowed first upon Peter.[14]

4. Matthew's Gospel is the only one of the four to display *Jesus talking explicitly about the "church"* that is to continue after he is gone.[15] Two passages use the word *church* outright. One is Matthew 16:17-20, which we have just mentioned, where Jesus tells Peter, "on this rock I will build my church." Another is Matthew 18:15-18, where Jesus speaks of the church as though it already exists during his ministry, outlining a process by which disciples who have complaints against each other may bring their disputes to the church for resolution. According to Matthew's Gospel, then, the church did not simply come into being after Easter as followers of Jesus struggled to understand what had transpired. Matthew portrays Jesus as starting the church during his life on earth. This church is not just a social movement but an institution, with rules and procedures for defining membership and conducting business.

5. Many passages in Matthew's Gospel display a *strong Jewish orientation*. Although the book ends with a commission to "make disciples of all nations" (28:19), Jesus' disciples are explicitly commanded during his earthly life to "Go nowhere among the Gentiles (nations)" (10:5). Similarly, Jesus insists that he has been "sent only to the lost sheep of the house of Israel" (15:24). At times, he appears to respect the Jewish authorities, paying the temple tax so as not to offend them (17:24-27). In one passage, he goes so far as to acknowledge that "the scribes and Pharisees sit on Moses' seat," which

means his followers should "do whatever they teach you and follow it" (23:2-3). All of these verses are unique to Matthew—they either derive from the M material or represent redactional changes Matthew has made in his sources.

6. At the same time, many passages in Matthew also display what some regard as an *anti-Jewish orientation*. Certainly Jesus regards the religious leaders of the Jewish people with more hostility here than in the other Gospels.[16] He repeatedly calls them a "brood of vipers" (12:34; 23:33), viewing them as "evil" (9:4; 12:34; 16:4) and indicating that they represent the devil, not God (15:13; cf. 13:24-30, 36-43). Furthermore, Jesus tells these leaders that "the kingdom of God will be taken away from you and given to a people that produces the fruits of the kingdom" (21:43) and, when praising the faith of a Gentile, he says that people from many nations will enter the kingdom of heaven while "the heirs of the kingdom will be thrown into the outer darkness" (8:12). Some interpreters believe these verses suggest an ultimate rejection by God of the Jewish people as a whole in favor of righteous and faithful Gentiles. In one chilling verse, Matthew presents "the (Jewish) people, as a whole" calling for Jesus' death and saying, "His blood be on us and on our children!" (27:25). Throughout the centuries, this verse has been quoted by anti-Semitic groups who wished to label Jewish people "Christ-killers" and portray them as accursed by God.

7. Matthew's Gospel shows *particular interest in "the law,"* that is, in the commandments and moral codes of the Jewish Scriptures that Christians call the Old Testament.[17] In keeping with the two points above, however, the perspective on the law does not always appear to be consistent. On the one hand, Jesus declares that he has come not to abolish the law but to fulfill it (5:17). He insists that "until heaven and earth pass away, not one letter, not one stroke of a letter, will pass from the law" (5:18). In keeping with this, Matthew omits Mark's interpretive comment that Jesus "declared all foods clean" (Mark 7:19; cf. Matt. 15:17) and adds a comment that Christians undergoing tribulation should pray that they will not have to flee on a sabbath (Matt. 24:20; cf. Mark 13:18). Apparently, as far as Matthew is concerned, dietary and sabbath laws are still in effect, as much for Christians as for Jews. On the other hand, some texts in Matthew's Gospel appear to present Jesus as setting aside what Moses or other traditional exponents of the law have said (5:21-48; 19:3-9) in favor of his own teaching. Notably, the Great Commission to make disciples of all nations is to be fulfilled by teaching people to obey not the law but the commandments of Jesus (28:20).

8. The *fulfillment of prophecy* is an important theme in Matthew, as indicated by the twelve fulfillment citation passages mentioned above.[18] Indeed, Jesus says he has come to fulfill the prophets as well as the law (5:17), and Matthew appears to regard his entire life as previewed or predicted in the

Scriptures. He finds references in those writings to Jesus' conception (1:22-23), birth (2:4-6), upbringing (2:23), ministry (12:17-21), and passion (26:54). Scholars sometimes struggle to explain Matthew's precise construal of these prophecies: the citation in 2:5-6 appears to add words to the text of Micah 5:2, and the passage presumably quoted in 2:23 cannot be found. In any event, Matthew is also conscious of prophecies that refer to the time after the earthly life of Jesus, including new prophecies given by Jesus himself. These include specific predictions regarding the destruction of the Jerusalem Temple (24:1-2), which is probably a past event by now for Matthew and his community, and sweeping projections regarding the end of the world (24:3—25:46). While much of this is derived from Mark and Q, Matthew incorporates unique material as well, generally enhancing concern for the final judgment (7:21-23; 25:1-13, 31-46).

9. Matthew's Gospel seems to present an *apocalyptic vision of the world* beyond that evident for the other Synoptic Gospels.[19] In this instance, "apocalyptic" refers to a dualistic perspective that clearly divides everything into spheres of divine or demonic influence. This may be presented most clearly in a parable unique to this Gospel in 13:24-30, 36-43. Here, the world is likened to a field in which wheat and weeds grow side by side. The wheat are the "children of the kingdom," while the weeds are "children of the evil one, and the enemy who sowed them is the devil" (13:38-39). Mark and Luke believe that Satan has spiritual agents—demons—analogous to God's angels, but Matthew goes so far as to suggest that some human beings were put in this world by Satan. We cannot be sure, of course, that this evangelist would want such descriptions to be taken literally, but the metaphors used in this parable do seem to exert a controlling influence over the story. Elsewhere, for instance, Jesus identifies some of the religious leaders of Israel as "plant[s] that my heavenly Father has not planted" (15:12-13). Thus, they are not persons to be challenged with a summons to repentance (as in Mark and Luke) but are simply to be left alone (15:14), left to be uprooted in time and "sentenced to hell" (23:33). The effect of this apparently harsh characterization is to cast much of the story into a symbolic sphere that allows it to work on more than one level. Seemingly trivial disputes between Jesus and the Pharisees become representative of the ultimate conflict of good and evil, the cosmic clash between God and Satan.

10. The *presence of God* is an overriding theological motif throughout much of this Gospel.[20] From the virginal conception of Jesus on, Matthew insists that "God is with us" (1:23), and numerous passages that are unique to this Gospel explore ways in which God's presence is manifest in the world. These include traditional affirmations of God's presence in the temple (23:21) and more innovative declarations of God's presence in Jesus and his followers (10:40). Matthew also assumes that while the divine pres-

ence in our world is assured (18:20; 28:20), it may assume unlikely guises so
as to go unrecognized by the righteous and the wicked alike (25:31-46).

---

◆

---

# Historical Context

## Who?

Popular Christian tradition ascribes this Gospel to the tax collector named
Matthew who, according to this book, became one of Jesus' twelve disciples
(9:9; 10:3). The story of this person's call is also reported in the Gospel of
Mark, although his name is given there as Levi and there is no indication
that he ever became one of the twelve (Mark 2:14; 3:16-19).

The earliest witness to this tradition is probably the somewhat mysterious
Papias, mentioned in the last chapter. According to the fourth-century historian Eusebius, Papias wrote around the middle of the second century, claiming that the disciple Matthew "collected the sayings [or records] in the Hebrew language and each one interpreted [or translated] them as he was
able."[21] Scholars don't know what to make of this enigmatic remark. The
church has usually assumed that Papias is referring to the book that we now
know as the Gospel of Matthew, describing it as a collection of materials
compiled by Matthew the disciple of Jesus. But our Gospel of Matthew contains only materials written in Greek, not Hebrew. Some scholars have
thought that Papias may be referring to some earlier stage in the tradition—
the disciple Matthew might have collected sayings of Jesus that were eventually incorporated into our Gospels even if he was not responsible for putting
any of those Gospels together in their final form.[22] A few have even suggested that Papias might be referring to what we now call the Q source,
though that of course is speculation. Evaluation of the Papias tradition is
complicated even more by the fact that we know so little about this person:
his credentials, his resources, his basis for making these claims, or his motivation in making them. We don't even know for certain that Eusebius is
correct in his dating of the citation.

The bottom line is that very few scholars believe this Gospel was written
or compiled by Matthew the disciple of Jesus. The Gospel itself makes no
such connection, and the church's tradition to this effect seems to be relatively late and confused. Most scholars think that this Gospel uses Mark as
a principal source. If its author had the advantage of actually having been

an eyewitness to the events that Mark reports, we would expect him to offer greater detail, filling in the blanks left by Mark's sketchy accounts. But this is not the case. The Gospel of Matthew adds very little of a historical nature to Mark's report of Jesus' ministry. What it *does* do is develop theologically the reports found in Mark in ways that would render them more meaningful to Christians of a later era. Thus, most scholars believe this Gospel reflects the concerns of second-generation Christianity, coming from a time when all of the original disciples were probably dead.

Acknowledging that the book is anonymous, scholars try to describe its author, who for the sake of convenience is still called "Matthew," in generic rather than specific terms. Almost all regard him as Jewish,[23] which immediately sets this Gospel apart from that of Mark, who most scholars believe was a gentile Christian. In fact, this evangelist shows some evidence of professional education as a Jewish leader or scholar. His biblical quotations are not all drawn from the Septuagint (the Greek translation of the Hebrew scriptures) but sometimes appear to represent his own translations from the Hebrew. His style of writing and approach to argumentation have suggested to some that he might be a converted rabbi or former Pharisee.[24] Far from exhibiting the perspective one would stereotypically attribute to a first-century tax collector (an outcast and traitor to the Jewish nation), the evangelist known as Matthew is preeminently concerned with the same issue that motivates Jesus' opponents in this story: the correct interpretation of the Scriptures and, in particular, the law. Therefore, many scholars have noted that the reference in this Gospel that best describes what its author was like is found, not in 9:9, but in 13:52: a "scribe who has been trained for the kingdom of heaven." Like the scribe in this parable of Jesus, Matthew the evangelist struggles to bring "out of his treasure what is new and what is old." He wants to proclaim the good news of what he believes God has now done in Christ in a way that preserves and interprets the tradition of what God has done in the past.

A great debate rages among scholars concerning the question of whether Matthew and his community still see themselves as belonging to Judaism. Some describe the evangelist as *intra muros* or "within the walls" of Judaism.[25] According to this view, Matthew regards the emerging Christian movement as a sect of Judaism, analogous to the Pharisees or Sadducees. This evangelist and his community are more accurately described as "Christian Jewish" than as "Jewish Christian."[26] He is not a convert from Judaism to Christianity but rather has made a less radical move from Pharisaic Judaism to Christian (or messianic) Judaism. Proponents of this view point to some of the passages cited above (17:24-27; 23:2-3) in which Jesus shows respect for the institutions and leaders of Judaism. Notably, Jesus predicts that his followers will be persecuted *in* synagogues (10:17; 23:34) but in this

Gospel never refers to them being excluded *from* synagogues (compare Luke
6:22; John 9:22; 12:42; 16:2).

Another view holds that Matthew and his community are already *extra
muros* or "outside the walls" of Judaism.[27] A definitive break has been made,
such that Matthew now regards "the Jews" (28:15) as a group to which he
does not belong. He and his community are committed to making disciples
primarily from "the nations," that is, Gentiles (28:19). Some proponents of
this view assume the break was not voluntary. In the decades after the disas-
trous war with Rome, Jewish authorities met in the city of Jamnia in western Judea to clarify legal and doctrinal issues that would serve to define
normative Judaism to the present day. Possibly, Matthew and other Christian groups were excommunicated in some official or authoritative way.[28]

This debate is not easily resolved. A great many passages in Matthew
evince sufficient ambiguity to be read either way. References to *"their* synagogues" (4:23; 9:35; 10:17; 12:9; 13:54) imply some distinction (*theirs* not *ours*),
but who is the "they"? Does Matthew mean to distinguish Jewish synagogues from Christian churches, or does he mean to distinguish the synagogues of the Pharisees from those of Christian Jews? At any rate, scholars
agree that Matthew and his community are caught somewhere in the transi-
tional process from Jewish sect to Christian religion. Graham Stanton sees
the issue as complicated in that Matthew may have been writing for a number of communities struggling with self-definition in the aftermath of the
Jewish War.[29] Amy-Jill Levine introduces another dynamic by suggesting
that the distinction between Jew and Gentile has been transcended in Matthew's community by a new distinction between privileged and marginalized.[30] Anthony Saldarini suggests that the precise relationship of Matthew
and his community to Judaism may have been just as debatable in the first
century as it is today. He believes that Matthew himself regarded his community as a sect within the bounds of Judaism, while other Jews had come
to think of them as sufficiently deviant to constitute a separate entity.[31]

## Where?

Redactional changes that Matthew is believed to have made in material derived from Mark indicate that he shaped his Gospel for a fairly prosperous,
urban community (see figure 13).[32] In addition, the Gospel must have been
produced in an area that contained numbers of both Jews and Gentiles, since
its author is concerned about both relations with Judaism and fulfillment of
a mission to "all nations" (28:19). Numerous cities in the Roman Empire
would meet these criteria, so we cannot possibly determine the exact location
with certainty. Reasonable guesses include Alexandria, Caesarea Martima,
and Antioch. The latter has gained popularity in recent years, partly because

Matthew's Gospel is first quoted by Ignatius, the Bishop of Antioch, in 115 c.e. and may also have been used as a source for the early Christian writing called the *Didache*, which was produced in the Syrian region around Antioch in about 100 c.e. The possibility of the Gospel being composed in Antioch is also intriguing because we know that both Peter and Paul ministered here and quarreled over a question related to the continuing validity of the law (Gal. 2:11-14). What's more, although we have only Paul's account of this incident, the community in Antioch appears to have sided with Peter against Paul (Gal. 2:13). Numerous scholars have noted that Matthew's Gospel does favor Peter more than any other and appears to challenge the more extreme positions regarding the law expressed by Paul (compare Matt. 5:17 with Rom. 10:4). Accordingly, scholars sometimes speak of Antioch as providing the appropriate theological context for this Gospel's origin, even if we cannot be certain that it provided the geographical context as well.[33]

## When?

If Matthew used the Gospel of Mark as a source, then he must have composed his work sometime after 70 c.e., a fact that might receive additional support from what appears to be an allusion to the Roman destruction of Jerusalem in one of Jesus' parables (22:7). Ignatius's quotation of Matthew indicates the book was already regarded as authoritative by 115 c.e., and the likely reliance of the *Didache* on Matthew means the Gospel probably had to be written before the end of the first century. Other factors come into play as researchers attempt to fine-tune their projected dates for the book, but the great majority of Matthean scholars place the work within the decade of 80–90 c.e. An earlier date is preferred by a minority of scholars, including some supporters of the Two-Gospel Hypothesis who reject the thesis that Matthew used Mark as a source (see figure 4).[34]

## Why?

Matthew's community had many of the same concerns as the community for which Mark's Gospel was written. They faced trouble from without and from within.[35] From without, they had met or expected to meet with persecution at the hands of both Jews (5:11; 10:17, 23; 21:35; 23:34) and Gentiles (10:18, 22; 24:9). From within, they were confronted with problems of heresy (7:25; 24:11), apostasy (13:21-22; 24:12), and betrayal (24:10). But Matthew's community also struggled with issues that may not have been major concerns for Mark. The Jewish background or influence was felt more heavily, so that issues related to the continuing validity of the law and the fulfillment of the Hebrew Scriptures were more pressing. It has even been said that Matthew was written specifically as "a Christian response to Jamnia," that is, to the Jewish councils held in that city during the latter decades of the first century.[16]

Still, if we assume that Matthew did have a copy of Mark's Gospel and a copy of the Q source, then we must ask why he did not simply present these to his community, alongside his own collection of additional materials? The community would then have had three independent books about Jesus, each significant in its own right, but with very little overlap between them. The evangelist we call Matthew did not do this. Instead, he edited all of these materials, integrating them together into a single coherent document. We must assume then that Matthew regarded the Gospel of Mark (as well as Q and M) as not only incomplete but also inadequate. He probably intended for his Gospel to replace that of Mark, not stand alongside it as in our modern Bibles. Otherwise, we would expect some defense or explanation for changes it makes, such as when the friendly scribe in Mark 12:28-34 is transformed into an enemy who wants to test Jesus in Matthew 22:34-40.

The production of a book such as the Gospel of Matthew was a difficult, time-consuming, and expensive proposition. Matthew would not have been likely to undertake such an effort simply to render Mark's Gospel more relevant to his social setting. Rather, Matthew appears to have regarded Mark's Gospel as theologically inadequate in at least three ways: (1) Mark does not present Christ as currently present among his followers, and thus the locus of God's continuing presence in the world is ambiguous; (2) Mark offers little insight with regard to the discernment of God's will for contemporary situations; and (3) Mark's portrait of discipleship does not address the possibility of progress and so provides little hope or incentive for improvement. All three of these points may be gathered under one umbrella observation: from Matthew's perspective, the Gospel of Mark contains no effective doctrine of the church. Addressing this concern may have been Matthew's major incentive for producing a replacement Gospel.

◆

# Major Themes

## The Abiding Presence of God

We have already identified the presence of God as a significant motif in Matthew's Gospel, but a more detailed examination of how this motif is developed may provide a key for understanding the book's principal contributions to theology and faith. This theme is related to that of the "reign of God" discussed with regard to Mark's Gospel in chapter 2. Though Matthew prefers the phrase "kingdom [or reign] of heaven," he takes over into his Gospel virtually all of the material in Mark related to this theme. Thus, Matthew also affirms that God's rule has both present and future dimensions: people experience the benefits of God's rule already (12:28) even though the full consummation of that rule is still to come (6:9-10). Matthew, however, develops these thoughts in ways that go beyond anything we find in Mark.

The first thing Matthew wants to say is that God is present in Jesus. Such an affirmation goes a subtle shade beyond Mark's insistence that God *acts* through Jesus. For Matthew, the reality of God's presence is tied to the very existence of Jesus. When Jesus is born, Matthew can say, "God is with us" (1:23). Matthew believes, of course, that God has been present with the people of Israel in the past, before Jesus was born, but the presence of God manifested now in Jesus is nevertheless unprecedented and superlative. God may have dwelt in the Jerusalem Temple, but the coming of Jesus represents "something greater than the temple" (12:6). God is present with people now in a way that God has never been present before.

Just how far Matthew is willing to take this becomes evident when we trace the theme of worship in this Gospel.[37] On nine different occasions Matthew portrays people worshiping Jesus, always in a sense that meets with approval (2:11; 8:2; 9:18; 14:33; 15:25; 20:20; 21:16; 28:9, 17). The Greek word used in most of these verses (all but 21:16) is *proskyneō*. It can refer to an act of extreme respect or obeisance that one human may show to another, but in Matthew it seems to mean something more. Jesus himself declares in Matthew 4:10 that people should worship (*proskyneō*) no one except "the Lord God." Yet when people worship Jesus, they are not rebuked. As far as Matthew is concerned, God is present in Jesus to such an extent that worshiping him counts as worshiping the Lord God. We can see here a significant step in the development of Christian doctrine. Mark's Gospel presents Jesus as the Son of God through whom God's reign draws near and God's will for salvation is accomplished, but Mark offers no hint that his community would therefore worship Jesus or pray to him. Matthew's Gospel appears to have made that move, though many years would pass before Christians would work out the dogma to justify it, as evidenced in such formulations as the Nicene Creed (c. 325 C.E.) and the Chalcedonian Definition (451 C.E.). In other words, Matthew locates the presence of God in Jesus on a pragmatic rather than theoretical level, treating Jesus effectively as divine without attempting to articulate any rationale for doing so.[38]

Matthew does more than this. He also emphasizes the continuing presence of Jesus in the world after Easter. The last verse of the Gospel records Jesus saying, "I am with you always, to the end of the age" (28:20). The

Gospel of Mark describes the time between Jesus' resurrection and his second coming as a difficult time of absence (Mark 2:20; 14:7). Matthew recognizes the literal or physical absence of Jesus during this period also (Matt. 9:15; 26:11) but reduces its significance by insisting that Jesus remains present nonetheless. Specifically, Jesus promises that he will always be with those who baptize people in the name of the Father, Son, and Holy Spirit and who teach them to obey his commandments (28:19-20). Likewise, in Matthew 18:20, Jesus says that where two or three gather for prayer in his name he will be "among them." The obvious expectation, then, is that the presence of Jesus will continue to be manifested within the community of his followers, the community that Matthew calls "the church" (16:18; 18:17). Even the well-known story of the separation of sheep and goats in Matthew 25:31-46 probably reflects this thinking. Jesus says that whatever is done for one of the least of those who belong to his family is done for him. For Matthew, the "family" of Jesus is probably the church (cf. 12:50). As representatives of this church go out into the world to "make disciples of all nations" (28:19), Matthew wants them to know that these nations will be held accountable at the end of time for how they treat Jesus' family (25:32). Those who are kind to his followers will be rewarded (10:42; 25:34-40) and those who are not will be punished (10:11-15; 25:1-46).[39]

In theological scholarship, the question of God's continuing presence is sometimes related to discussions of what is called *salvation history*, which tries to undertand how God is thought to have related to humanity in different periods of time. Some Matthean scholars would hold that this Gospel envisions three distinct epochs: a time of Israel, a time of Jesus, and a time of the church.[40] A distinction between the first two is not controversial. Matthew certainly believes that the coming of Jesus inaugurated a new era. The question is whether Matthew's Gospel presents the church as living in a time that is definitively different from the period of Jesus. The claim is that Matthew presents the time of Jesus' earthly life as a period in which salvation was typically restricted to Israel (10:5-6; 15:24), and God's people were expected to keep the entire law of Moses (5:18). During the time of the church, however, salvation is for all nations (28:19) and only the commandments of Jesus remain binding (28:20).

Others suggest that Matthew really only envisions two epochs of salvation history, since Jesus remains present in the church in all the ways mentioned above.[41] In fact, Matthew also speaks of the church as though it is present already during the earthly career of Jesus (18:17; cf. 16:18). Thus, Matthew puts the church into what is called "the time of Jesus" and also puts Jesus into what is called "the time of the church," confusing these categories so that no neat distinction can be made. Discontinuity with regard to ecclesiological matters is trivialized by the transcending continuity of God's abiding presence expressed in Matthew's christological understanding.

Figure 15

---

A Passage from the Talmud

Matthew's Gospel portrays Jewish scribes as dour and petty. Their own
writings display humor and a frank intolerance of casuistry.

> The Mishnah states: If a fledgling bird is found within fifty cubits of a dove-
> cote, it belongs to the owner of the dovecote. If it is found outside the limits
> of fifty cubits, it belongs to the person who finds it. Rabbi Jeremiah asked: If
> one foot of the fledgling bird is within the limit of fifty cubits, and one foot
> is outside it, what is the law? It was for this question that Rabbi Jeremiah
> was thrown out of the House of Study. (*Bava Batra* 23b)

---

We cannot easily resolve this debate, especially since it is cast in language
that Matthew's Gospel itself does not use. What we can affirm is that Matthew believes the church now represents the continuing presence of Jesus
on earth in a way analogous to that in which Jesus represented the presence
of God.[42] In Matthew 10:40, Jesus tells his disciples, "Whoever welcomes
you welcomes me, and whoever welcomes me welcomes the one who sent
me." This is a bold claim: responses to the followers of Jesus are ultimately
responses to God. If Matthew truly believes this, then his *ecclesiology* (understanding of the church) is as important for interpreting his Gospel as his
*Christology* (understanding of Christ); indeed, the two concepts appear to
be inseparable.

## Jewish Law and Christian Faith

Jesus explicitly refers to "the church" twice in Matthew's Gospel, and in
both of these passages he tells those who constitute the church, "Whatever
you bind on earth will be bound in heaven, and whatever you loose on earth
will be loosed in heaven" (16:19; 18:18). In the historical setting for this Gospel, the terms "bind" and "loose" were used in rabbinic interpretations of
the law to designate whether or not a specific scriptural admonition was
applicable for a given circumstance.[43] For example, some rabbis might insist
that the law forbidding work on the Sabbath was binding with regard to
travel on the Sabbath, since travel is a form of work. By the same token,
they might also decide that this law should be loosed with regard to certain
types of travel or with regard to travel for certain purposes. Such discussions
were widespread among Pharisaic Judaism around the time that Matthew's
Gospel was written. The Talmud contains hundreds of decisions regarding
application of the law to all aspects of daily life (but as the humorous passage
quoted in figure 15 illustrates, the Jewish teachers engaged in this work
knew there were limits to how far a matter should be pressed).

Throughout Matthew's Gospel, Jesus contests such decisions. He claims that they "make void the word of God" for the sake of their tradition (15:6). But at the same time, Jesus himself acts like a rabbi, declaring whether or not laws are binding. He insists that the commandment forbidding adultery *does apply* to lustful thoughts, because anyone "who looks at a woman with lust has already committed adultery with her in his heart" (5:28). Then, he declares that the law forbidding work on the sabbath *does not apply* to healing the sick on that day because "it is lawful to do good on the sabbath" (12:12). In such passages, Jesus sounds very much like a Pharisee himself, even though, ironically, the Pharisees are condemned throughout this Gospel as persons whose teaching is dangerous (15:14; 16:12; 23:15). At issue is not the practice of binding and loosing as such, but the manner in which this is carried out. Matthew's Gospel invariably presents Jesus as the good example of one who binds and looses the law in accord with God's will. By the same token, the Pharisees are made to serve as bad examples of people who do not know God's will and therefore bind what should be loosed and loose what should be bound.

Why does Matthew do this? A simple explanation would be that he wants to assert the authority of his emerging Christian community over against groups that make competing claims. Matthew not only portrays Jesus as the one who has divine authority to bind and loose the law, but also presents Jesus as explicitly extending this authority to Peter and the other disciples (16:19; 18:18). When Jesus promises that what the church binds and looses will be bound and loosed in heaven, the clear implication is that God will hold people accountable for following the ethical decisions of this church. Matthew seems to be saying to someone, "We have the authority to determine God's will and you don't!" As we have seen, some scholars would regard this as an inter-Jewish rivalry (Christian Jews have the authority and Pharisaic Jews don't), while others would see it as a definitive element of the break with Judaism (Christians have the authority and Jews don't). Many scholars would also grant that struggles internal to Christianity may be in view here: communities in line with the tradition of Peter and the other disciples have a claim to authority that other Christian communities (such as those founded by Paul?) lack.

We must be careful, however, not to construe Matthew's intention so narrowly as to miss the central theological claims of his Gospel or to lose sight of its most enduring contributions. Although Matthew's theological claims have political implications, he is certainly interested in the claims for their own sake and not simply as theoretical means to political ends. Matthew grounds the church's authority to interpret God's will in eschatological and christological propositions. Eschatologically, he believes that "the kingdom of heaven has come near" (4:17), that God's reign is in the process of being established so that God's will can now be discerned and followed in ways not previously possible. Christologically, he believes that Jesus, the Son of God, manifested God's presence on earth and that he continues to do so through his enduring presence among his followers. The church has the authority to declare God's will not because it exhibits more insight or greater faithfulness to God than others but because Jesus Christ, God's Son, has chosen to be present in the church and to exercise his authority on earth through this community. Whatever we think of these propositions, we should not sell Matthew short by implying that he simply constructed them to support a political agenda. More likely, he articulates these ideas because he believes they are true. Matthew and his community are prepared to confess this position even when their claims go unrecognized and, in fact, bring terrible persecution and suffering upon the church. They believe these claims belong to the content of "the gospel," the good news about what God has done and is doing through Christ.

Aside from these theological propositions, one of the most enduring contributions of Matthew's Gospel has been the insight it offers concerning interpretation of ethical mandates for existential situations. Jesus not only declares that he and his followers have the authority to interpret God's will, but also articulates a number of principles that guide him and his followers in doing so. Best known may be the Golden Rule: "In everything do to others as you would have them do to you; *for this is the law and the prophets*" (7:12). The latter part of this verse indicates that the rule is not simply good advice, but a hermeneutical principle for determining how laws are to be interpreted. The same is true for the double love commandment that Matthew takes over from Mark. Jesus says people are to love God with all their being and love their neighbor as themselves because "on these two commandments hang all the law and the prophets" (22:40). Since these two commandments are themselves found in the Hebrew Scriptures (Deut. 6:5; Lev. 19:18), Jesus' prioritization of them as "the greatest" commandments (22:36) implies a recognition that some scriptural mandates are foundational and ought to serve as the basis for interpretation of those that are not. A similar philosophy informs his use of Hosea 6:6, which he cites twice to the Pharisees: they "condemn the guiltless" with their legal interpretations because they do not realize that God prefers mercy to sacrifice (12:7; compare 9:13). Elsewhere, Jesus tells these Pharisees that while insisting on obedience in trivial matters, they "have neglected the weightier matters of the law: justice and mercy and faith" (23:23).

We noted above that the attitude toward the law displayed in Matthew is somewhat ambiguous, and principles such as these help to explain why. Matthew may believe that the entire Jewish law remains in full force for followers of Jesus, but he recognizes that this law must be interpreted to discern the true will of God. The realization that certain concerns (love, mercy, justice, faith) are primary holds the key to discerning how the law must be taught and obeyed in ways that will be truly pleasing to God. At times, Jesus does appear to set aside legal prescriptions as no longer relevant (5:38-39), but Matthew probably considers these to be instances, not of abolishing the law, but of fulfilling it through an interpretation that brings out its true intent (5:17). Overall, Jesus binds laws more often than he looses them, demanding that his followers adopt standards of righteousness that exceed those of the scribes and Pharisees (5:20). Still, the claim is that Jesus' stricter interpretations of the law constitute a paradoxically light burden compared to the heavy burdens laid on people by the Pharisees' misguided judgments (11:28-30; 23:4). Why? Matthew believes that strict interpretations that are grounded in the divine preference for mercy, love, justice, and faith are bearable, while loose interpretations that are casuistic, arbitrary, and unreflective of those qualities are not.[44]

Historians are quick to point out that Matthew's presentation of the Pharisees is one-sided. We know, for instance, that a famous Pharisee, Rabbi Hillel, actually articulated a principle similar to Matthew's Golden Rule decades before Jesus. And in Mark's Gospel, the priority of the double love commandment is accepted by a Pharisaic scribe, whom Jesus says is "not far from the kingdom of God" (12:28-34). Still, Matthew's stories of Jesus and the Pharisees have become classic anecdotes illustrative of ethical principles embraced by persons of diverse backgrounds and faiths. For many, these stories offer timeless lessons in moral discernment that transcend the first-century power struggles evident in the rhetoric with which they are told.

## People of Little Faith

Four times in this Gospel, Jesus addresses his disciples as "you of little faith" (6:30; 8:26; 14:31; 16:8; see also 17:20). The expression apparently derives from the Q source, since it is found also in Luke 12:28, but in Matthew it becomes a stereotypical description of those who constitute the church, which as we have seen is invested with great authority. By contrast, Matthew's narrative mentions two persons who have "great faith"—a centurion (8:10) and a Canaanite woman (15:28)—but Jesus does not call either of these to become his disciples or commission them for ministry as his followers in the world. His disciples are, definitively, people of little faith.

This characterization emphasizes the inadequacy of Jesus' followers and, accordingly, their dependence upon him. This theme, we recall, is also present in Mark's Gospel, which strongly emphasizes the failings of Jesus' disciples. As in Mark, so also here Jesus declares that he has "come to call not the righteous but sinners" (Matt. 9:13; cf. Mark 2:17). For Matthew, then, the church is to be composed of people whom Jesus has saved from their sins (1:21), specifically by shedding his blood for the forgiveness of their sins (26:28). Indeed, forgiveness becomes one of the hallmarks of this community. Because Jesus' followers are by definition inadequate people and because they often fail at fulfilling even their best intentions (26:41), they need to be forgiven repeatedly and, in turn, need to forgive others repeatedly as well (18:21-35).

As people of little faith, Jesus' disciples struggle not only with sin but also with doubt. Matthew's Gospel twice describes the disciples of Jesus as doubting (14:33; 28:17) and, curiously, these are also the only two passages in which they are ever said to worship him (14:32; 28:17). These two concepts—worship and doubt—are clearly not antithetical or incompatible in Matthew's vision of the church. The first of the two instances is significant in that Peter, Matthew's favorite disciple, the "rock" on which the church is to be built (16:18), is singled out as a person of little faith, a man who doubts. The second instance is also significant in that it occurs within the resurrection narrative immediately preceding the Great Commission with which the Gospel concludes. Having failed Jesus miserably, denying and deserting him in his darkest hour, the disciples have had to be recovered for Jesus by a group of women who proved more faithful than they (27:55, 61; 28:1-10). But even now, at the end of the story, worship and doubt still coincide within the community of disciples. Still, this does not prevent Jesus from sending them out to "make disciples of all nations" (28:19). Apparently, even doubters, people of little faith, are able to baptize others in the name of the Father, Son, and Holy Spirit, and to teach them to obey all that Jesus has commanded (28:19-20).

Thus, Matthew's presentation of the disciples as "people of little faith" goes beyond Mark's characterization of them as failures. In Mark's gospel, Jesus questions whether his disciples have any faith at all. The difference between "no faith" (Mark 4:40) and "little faith" (Matt. 8:26) is significant for Matthew, because elsewhere in this Gospel Jesus affirms that only the tiniest amount of faith is needed (17:20). The epithet "people of little faith," then, is not as insulting as it may at first sound. It indicates two things: (a) these disciples do have *some* faith, indeed, enough to do whatever God calls them to do, and (b) these disciples have *only* a little faith and therefore have only begun to experience the implications of the gospel at a basic level. If people of little faith are able to move mountains (17:20), what might Jesus' followers accomplish if their faith were to grow? Indeed, growth is a significant theme in Matthew. In this Gospel, the disciples benefit from the teaching of Jesus, coming to understand what was initially unclear (13:51; 16:12). Unlike the disciples in Mark, they do not get worse as the story progresses. Although they apparently remain people of little faith to the end, they also show some signs of improvement.

Matthew's intention here is undeniably pastoral. He wants to edify his readers, to encourage them to believe that although they are accepted into the church as inadequate sinners, their continued participation in that community will indeed have an effect on them. Christian theology sometimes labels these concepts *justification* (initial acceptance) and *sanctification* (subsequent transformation), and theologians usually regard Matthew as a resource primarily for the latter, since he develops this dimension more obviously than Mark. Matthew's Gospel presents incredibly high expectations for the followers of Jesus: they are to attain a higher level of righteousness than that evidenced by the religious leaders of Israel (5:19-20); in fact, they are to be perfect, just as God is perfect (5:48). As such, Matthew's Gospel also presents high expectations regarding the impact that Jesus' followers are to have on their society: they are to be the "salt of the earth" (5:13) and the "light of the world" (5:14); they are to overcome "the gates of Hades" (16:18), that is, the stronghold of the devil and the realm of death.[45]

In short, we see in this Gospel signs of further theological development that would transform the new faith into the sort of movement that sociologists would classify as "a religion." A doctrine of the church is emerging, one that attempts to take seriously both the implications of the faith (Christology and eschatology) and the existential context in which that faith is confessed. The former offers grand promises: as God's reign draws near through Christ and his followers, nothing will be impossible (17:20; 19:26; 21:21-22). The latter offers harsh reality: trials and persecution afflict those whose spirit is willing but whose flesh is weak (13:20-22; 26:41). Matthew attempts to respect both promise and predicament by presenting the church as a community of called sinners (9:13), of worshiping doubters (28:17), of disciples whose inadequate faith is paradoxically sufficient. Thus he is able simultaneously to insist upon the certainty of forgiveness and the necessity of improvement.

◆

## The Gospel of Matthew As Literature: Sample Studies

*Matthew as Story*
By Jack Dean Kingsbury; 2d ed. (Philadelphia: Fortress Press, 1988)
Traces the intertwining story lines of Jesus, his disciples, and his antagonists in an analysis that understands Matthew's plot in terms of conflict development between these principal characters.

*Matthew's Inclusive Story: A Study in the Narrative Rhetoric of the First Gospel*
By David B. Howell; SNTSS 42 (Sheffield: Sheffield Academic Press, 1990)

Explores the ways that Matthew's narrative seeks to draw its readers into its narrative world and accept Jesus as their model for discipleship.

*Matthew: Storyteller, Interpreter, Evangelist*
By Warren Carter (Peabody: Hendrickson, 1996)
Seeks to combine literary and historical concerns by developing a strategy that enables modern readers to experience Matthew's story as its author would intend today.

*The Gospel According to Matthew: A Structural Commentary on Matthew's Faith*
By Daniel Patte (Philadelphia: Fortress Press, 1987)
Examines every verse of Matthew, using the literary approach of "structuralism" to uncover narrative and semantic oppositions that reveal the evangelist's deepest convictions.

◆

## Feminist Readings of Matthew: Sample Studies

*Toward a Feminist-Critical Reading of the Gospel According to Matthew*
By Elaine Mary Wainwright (Berlin: de Gruyter, 1991)
An analysis of the entire Gospel of Matthew that seeks to highlight or restore attention to the roles played by women both in the stories of the Gospel itself and in the community that preserved and shaped the Gospel.

"Both text and context must be analyzed to determine the extent to which they disclose or conceal the feminist principles of liberation and inclusion" (p. 34).

"Matthew: Gender and Reading" in *Semeia* 28 (1983): 3–27
By Janice Capel Anderson
Explores the symbolic significance of gender as it relates to the reading process, exposing the androcentric perspective from which the Gospel was written and raising questions about how female readers may respond to this.

"In following the guidance of the narrator and Jesus, the actual reader may be led to judge some of the patriarchal assumptions implicit in their ideological viewpoints" (p. 23).

# CHAPTER FOUR

# The Gospel of Luke

The Gospel of Luke is similar to Matthew in that it combines both Mark and Q with traditions that are unique. Two differences, however, are immediately obvious:

(1) Whereas Matthew takes most of Mark's Gospel over into his own, Luke uses only a little more than half of Mark. In fact, Luke omits all of the material that is found in Mark 6:45—8:26 and in Mark 9:41—10:12. Scholars refer to these lapses respectively as *the big omission* and *the little omission*. Some have theorized that perhaps Luke possessed a defective copy of Mark's Gospel that was missing these sections, but most assume he skips over this material intentionally.

(2) Whereas the material unique to Matthew (*M*) represents less than a third of that Gospel, the material unique to Luke (*L*) accounts for a full half of his completed Gospel (see figure 16). This material, furthermore, contains many of the most-beloved stories in the Bible, such as the Christmas story of the baby in the manger and the tales of Jesus' encounters with Mary and Martha, Zacchaeus, and the two men on the road to Emmaus. Several of Jesus' best-known parables are found here also, including the Good Samaritan, the prodigal son, the rich man and Lazarus, and the Pharisee and the tax collector. Scholars of literature often remark that stories contained in this L material are of a superior literary quality than is usually evident in the Gospels. This evangelist, they speculate, was a gifted storyteller, and he may be at his best when he is least reliant on tradition.[1]

As regards the overall structure of this Gospel, Luke appears to have alternated between material from Mark and Q in the following way:[2]

Figure 16

Material Unique to Luke

This is a partial list of what is often labeled *L* material:

| | |
|---|---|
| Dedication to Theophilus | 1:1-4 |
| Promised Birth of John | 1:5-25 |
| Announcement of Jesus' Birth to Mary | 1:26-38 |
| Mary's Visit to Elizabeth | 1:39-56 |
| Birth of John the Baptist | 1:57-80 |
| Birth of Jesus (with shepherds, manger) | 2:1-20 |
| Presentation in the Temple | 2:21-38 |
| Childhood Visit to Jerusalem | 2:41-52 |
| John's Reply to Questions | 3:10-14 |
| Genealogy of Jesus (to Adam) | 3:23-38 |
| Good News to the Poor | 4:14-23, 25-30 |
| Miraculous Catch of Fish | 5:1-11 |
| Widow's Son at Nain | 7:11-17 |
| Encounter with Homeless Woman | 7:36-50 |
| The Ministering Women | 8:1-3 |
| Rejection by Samaritan Village | 9:51-56 |
| Return of the Seventy | 10:17-20 |
| Parable of Good Samaritan | 10:29-37 |
| Mary and Martha | 10:38-42 |
| Parable of Friend at Midnight | 11:5-8 |
| Parable of Rich Fool | 12:13-21 |
| Parable of Barren Tree | 13:1-9 |
| Healing of Woman on Sabbath | 13:10-17 |
| Healing of Man with Dropsy | 14:1-6 |
| Lessons for Table Guests and Hosts | 14:7-14 |
| Counting the Cost | 14:28-33 |
| Parable of Lost Coin | 15:8-10 |
| Parable of Lost Son | 15:11-32 |
| Parable of Dishonest Steward | 16:1-12 |
| Parable of Rich Man and Lazarus | 16:19-31 |
| Cleansing of Ten Lepers | 17:11-19 |
| Parable of Widow and Judge | 18:1-8 |
| Parable of Pharisee and Tax Collector | 18:9-14 |
| Story of Zacchaeus | 19:1-10 |
| Jesus Weeps over Jerusalem | 19:41-44 |
| The Reason for Peter's Denial | 22:31-32 |
| The Two Swords | 22:35-38 |
| Jesus before Herod | 23:6-12 |
| Pilate Declares Jesus Innocent | 23:13-16 |
| Sayings Associated with Jesus' Death | 23:28-31, 34, 43, 46 |
| Appearance on the Road to Emmaus | 24:13-35 |
| Appearance to the Disciples | 24:36-49 |
| The Ascension | 24:50-53 |

| 3:1—6:1 | draws primarily from Mark |
| 6:20—8:3 | draws primarily from Q |
| 8:4—9:50 | draws primarily from Mark |
| 9:51—18:14 | draws primarily from Q |
| 18:15—24:11 | draws primarily from Mark |

The two Q sections are often called *the little interpolation* and *the big interpolation* because from our perspective they appear to be insertions into the Markan Gospel. The little interpolation (6:20—8:3) contains Jesus' Sermon on the Plain (6:20-49), which parallels Matthew's more developed Sermon on the Mount (Matt. 5:1—7:27). The big interpolation makes up the bulk of what is often called Luke's Travel Narrative (9:51—19:44), the account of Jesus' journey to Jerusalem.[3] Luke's unique L material is integrated throughout the Gospel, but is especially prevalent in the Travel Narrative section (where it is intertwined with Q material) and at the Gospel's beginning and ending (see figure 16).

The first two chapters of Luke's Gospel are composed entirely of L material.[4] What is found here is not only without parallel in the rest of the New Testament but is also distinctive even within Luke's own work. The style of the Greek language differs from the rest of Luke's Gospel, resembling more closely the Greek of the Septuagint (the Greek translation of the Hebrew Scriptures that Christians came to call the Old Testament). Also, these two chapters contain liturgical hymns, which are often identified today by Latin titles: the Magnificat (1:46-56), the Benedictus (1:67-79), the Gloria in Excelsis (2:14), and the Nunc Dimittis (2:29-32).[5] Such hymns are not found anywhere else in Luke's narrative. These differences are substantial enough to have led scholars in the past to speculate that Luke 1–2 may have been written by another author and attached to the Gospel at a later date.[6] Today, however, this thesis is rejected, and Luke 1–2 is more likely to be viewed as "an overture" to the Gospel narrative, setting out its principal themes in ways that are deliberately memorable and distinctive.[7]

Finally, we must note that Luke differs from the other Gospels in one other respect, which is possibly the most significant of all. Luke is the only such book that has a sequel, the book of Acts, which provides a vivid account of the early church intended to supplement or continue the story of Jesus presented in the Gospel. Since the evangelist responsible for this Gospel is also the author of Acts (see Acts 1:1), most scholars regard the book of Acts as another rich resource for discovering the theological interests and concerns that helped to shape the Gospel. Some have noted what they believe to be elaborate parallels between the Gospel and the book of Acts, as though Luke wrote these two books in a way that invites comparison (see figure 17).[8] For such reasons, many scholars do not even speak of Luke and

**Figure 17**

Parallels between Luke's Gospel and Acts

| *Luke's Gospel* | *Acts* |
|---|---|
| Preface to Theophilus (1:1-4) | Preface to Theophilus (1:1-5) |
| Spirit descends on Jesus as he prays (3:21-22) | Spirit comes to apostles as they pray (2:1-13) |
| Sermon declares prophecy fulfilled (4:16-30) | Sermon declares prophecy fulfilled (2:14-40) |
| Jesus heals a lame man (5:17-26) | Peter heals lame man (3:1-10) |
| Religious leaders attack Jesus (5:29—6:11) | Religious leaders attack apostles (4:1—8:3) |
| Centurion invites Jesus to his house (7:1-10) | Centurion invites Peter to his house (10:1-23) |
| Jesus raises widow's son from death (7:11-17) | Peter raises widow from death (9:36-43) |
| Missionary journeys to Gentiles (10:1-12) | Missionary journeys to Gentiles (13:1—19:20) |
| Jesus travels to Jerusalem (9:51—19:28) | Paul travels to Jerusalem (19:21—21:17) |
| Jesus is received favorably (19:37) | Paul is received favorably (21:17-20) |
| Jesus is devoted to the temple (19:45-48) | Paul is devoted to the temple (21:26) |
| Sadducees oppose Jesus, but scribes support him (20:27-39) | Sadducees oppose Paul, but Pharisees support him (23:6-9) |
| Jesus breaks bread and give thanks (22:19) | Paul breaks bread and gives thanks (27:35) |
| Jesus is seized by an angry mob (22:54) | Paul is seized by an angry mob (21:30) |
| Jesus slapped by high priest's aides (22:63-64) | Paul slapped at high priest's command (23:2) |
| Jesus is tried four times and declared innocent three times (22:66—23:13) | Paul is tried four times and declared innocent three times (23:1—26:32) |
| Jesus is rejected by the Jews (23:18) | Paul is rejected by the Jews (21:36) |
| Jesus regarded favorably by centurion (23:47) | Paul regarded favorably by centurion (27:43) |
| Final confirmation that Scriptures have been fulfilled (24:45-47) | Final confirmation that Scriptures have been fulfilled (28:23-28) |

Acts as separate works but prefer to treat Luke-Acts as a single two-volume entity.[9]

As with the Gospel of Matthew, scholars attempt to discern the particular focus of Luke's work by paying close attention to the unique material (in this case, L and Acts) and by studying the redactional changes that Luke has made in his sources, especially Mark (see figure 18). Many of the latter changes are similar to those made by Matthew (figure 13), because Luke worked at about the same time and faced similar issues. Careful attention to Luke's scheme, however, reveals that his perspective differs from that of both Matthew and Mark in key respects.

◆

## Characteristics of Luke's Gospel

Let us now consider some distinctive features of Luke's Gospel:

1. The Gospel of Luke begins with a preface addressed to a person named Theophilus (1:1-4), as does Acts (1:1-5). Luke is the *only Gospel to identify its audience* at all, much less with such specificity. In some respects, however, the identification is more puzzling than helpful. Scholars do not know of anyone in the first century who bore this name; in fact, there is no record of Theophilus ever being used as a proper name at all. The word itself means "lover of God," prompting some to wonder whether Luke uses it in a fictitious sense: his books are addressed to anyone who loves God. If there was a literal Theophilus, most scholars believe he probably served as the patron for Luke's project, perhaps providing financial support for the research and writing. In that case, the address would be more of a dedication. Certainly, Luke intended for his Gospel and the book of Acts to be read by more than just one person.

2. Luke is explicit in *designating the historical context* for the story he tells. The beginning of John the Baptist's ministry is reported in this way: "In the fifteenth year of the reign of Emperor Tiberius, when Pontius Pilate was governor of Judea, and Herod was ruler of Galilee, and his brother Philip ruler of the region of Ituraea and Trachonitis, and Lysanias ruler of Abilene, during the high priesthood of Annas and Caiaphas, the word of God came to John son of Zechariah" (Luke 3:1-2). This is quite a contrast from Mark's simple report that "John the baptizer appeared" (Mark 1:4). Luke introduces his story of the birth of Jesus in a similar way (Luke 2:1-2; see also 1:5). The implication that Luke wants to be considered a historian is compatible with recognition that his book of Acts is, in some sense, the first attempt to write church history.

**Figure 18**

---

Luke's Use of Mark

Luke preserves only a little more than half of the Gospel of Mark, and he edits what he does preserve in accord with the following principles:

1. Abbreviation
   Luke omits from Mark's stories what he apparently considers to be insignificant or inappropriate:

   - a comment on the incompetence of physicians (Luke 8:42-48; Mark 5:25-34)

   - conversation between Jesus and father of demoniac child (Luke 9:37-43; Mark 9:21-24)

   - the naked young man in the garden (Luke 22:47-53; Mark 14:43-52)

2. Stylistic Improvement
   Greek becomes more polished.

   - "historical presents" are changed (150 out of 151; he missed Mark 5:35 at Luke 8:49)

   - Mark's repetitious use of words such as *and* and *immediately* is reduced

   - pronouns lacking clear antecedents are provided antecedents

   - use of syntactical constructions such as genitive absolutes and articular infinitives is increased (these portend a "higher class" of Greek)

3. Application
   Some changes reflect an attempt to appeal to a wider audience.

   - Aramaic expressions are eliminated ("Talitha cum" in Mark 5:41 at Luke 8:54)

   - notations providing broad historical/cultural context are introduced (compare Luke 3:1-3 to Mark 1:4)

4. Idealization
   The portraits of some characters are "retouched."
   a. Jesus

(continued)

---

**Figure 18** *continued*

---

- statements that imply any lack of ability or authority on Jesus' part are omitted (comment in Mark 6:5 not found in Luke 4:16-30)

- references to human emotions are dropped: pity (Mark 1:41), anger (Mark 3:5), grief (Mark 3:5); wonder (Mark 6:6); indignation (Mark 10:14); love (Mark 10:21)

- stories in which Jesus acts in an emotional way are also omitted (cursing of fig tree, Mark 11:12-14, 20-25) or modified (cleansing of temple, Luke 19:45-46; Mark 11:15-17)

- stories that may have been thought to portray Jesus as a magician are dropped (Mark 7:31-37; 8:22-26)

b. Jesus' disciples

- stories of Jesus rebuking Peter (Mark 8:33), of James and John's presumptuous request (Mark 10:35-40), and of disciples' flight at Jesus' arrest (Mark 14:27, 50) are eliminated

- Peter's denial (Luke 22:31-34; Mark 14:29-31) and disciples' sleep in Gethsemane (Luke 22:45-46; Mark 14:37-41) are muted and explained

c. Jesus' family

- reference to his family coming "to restrain him" is dropped (Mark 3:21)

- description of "true family" is reworded so as to include his earthly family (Luke 8:19-21; Mark 3:31-35)

---

3. *Jerusalem receives special attention* as a geographical focus in Luke's Gospel. In the opening chapters, Luke relates two stories of Jesus visiting Jerusalem as a child (2:22-40, 41-51) and indicates that the visits were actually annual (2:41). Then, in the center of the Gospel, ten entire chapters are taken up with a journey to Jerusalem (9:51—19:44). Throughout this Travel Narrative, Luke repeatedly reminds the reader that Jerusalem is the destination (9:51, 53; 13:22, 33; 17:11; 18:31; 19:11, 28, 41). Thus, much of the teaching material drawn from the Q and L traditions takes on whatever subtle connotations an orientation toward this city might bear. When Jesus finally reaches Jerusalem, he weeps over it (19:41-44), revealing both his great love

for the city and his frustration over its rejection of him. Most significant, perhaps, Luke places all of the resurrection appearances of Jesus in and around Jerusalem (24:1-43; compare Matt. 28:16-20) and even presents Jesus as telling his disciples not to leave that city until a future date (24:49; see also Acts 1:4). Mark's Gospel, we recall, speaks of postresurrection reunions only in Galilee (Mark 14:28; 16:7). This focus on Jerusalem continues in Acts, where that city is identified as the starting point for the church's ministry (Acts 1:8) and serves as the site of the churchwide council in Acts 15.

4. Luke's Gospel *emphasizes worship and prayer.* In fact, the Gospel begins (1:8) and ends (24:53) with scenes of worship, and even the death of Jesus on the cross is presented as an occasion for praising God (23:47). We have also noted the abundance of liturgical material found in the first two chapters. In addition, Jesus prays more often in this Gospel, and he has more to say on the topic of prayer than in the other three Gospels combined. Specifically, prayer is mentioned in relation to such significant occasions as Jesus' baptism (3:21) and transfiguration (9:28). Jesus' prayers determine the lives of his disciples: he prays before he chooses them (6:12), before he questions them about his identity (9:18), and before he predicts Peter's denial (22:32). Only in this Gospel do Jesus' disciples ask him to teach them to pray (11:1), and he does so not only by teaching them the Lord's Prayer (Luke 11:2-4)— found also in Matthew (Matt. 6:9-13)—but also through frequent encouragements to prayer (18:1; 21:36; 22:40) and through parables about prayer, not found anywhere else (11:5-8; 18:1-8, 9-14).

5. Luke's Gospel also seems to display an *unusual interest in food.* Readers note (sometimes humorously) that in Luke's Gospel, Jesus appears to be always eating. In fact, the book mentions nineteen meals, thirteen of which are peculiar to Luke. Jesus also talks about food a great deal, telling parables about banquets (14:7-11, 12-14, 15-24; 15:25-32; 16:19-30) and speaking about discipleship in terms that, on the surface, appear to be lessons in table etiquette (7:44-46; 14:7-14; 22:27). Jesus is also criticized for eating too much (7:34) and with the wrong people (5:30; 15:1-2).

What is going on? In the first chapter of this Gospel, the coming of Jesus is described poetically as meaning that God "has filled the hungry with good things" (1:53). Food may be a metaphor for life, and the sharing of food may symbolize the sharing of life.[10] In this sense, the food motif in Luke may resemble the imagery we will encounter in the Gospel of John, where Jesus describes himself as "the bread of Life" (John 6:35, 51). But Luke could also have a more mundane, practical agenda. From his own book of Acts, we learn that Christian fellowship and worship in the first century often occurred within the setting of a meal. Thus, followers of Jesus are described as gathering for "the breaking of bread" (Acts 2:42, 46), meaning they ate together in a context that included teaching, worship, and, probably, observance of the eucharistic ritual Jesus had told them to do "in remembrance" of him (Luke 22:19). If meals were indeed frequent settings for worship, then Luke may have discovered that stories referring to meals were especially relevant for sharing with the community that gathers at these events. The sermonic potential becomes evident for a story such as Luke 7:36-50, where Jesus' host is offended when their meal is interrupted by an outcast woman. Read around tables in first-century worship services, the message becomes, "Are we willing to allow outcasts to participate in our meals, that is, to join our worshiping community?"

6. Luke's Gospel *emphasizes Jesus' ministry to those who are oppressed, excluded, or otherwise at a disadvantage in society.* At one point, Jesus actually describes his mission as being "to bring good news to the poor" (4:18). Concern for the poor is demonstrated in many other verses as well, often in ways that imply a corresponding hostility toward the rich.[11] God will provide the hungry with good things, but will send the rich away empty (1:53). The poor are blessed (6:20-21), but the rich are doomed (6:24-25). Jesus illustrates this graphically in parables where the rich are depicted as fools (12:16-21) or, worse, as persons destined to suffer eternal agony while the poor receive their comfort (16:19-31). Still, Luke's evident concern for the excluded sometimes brings him to sympathize with the rich as well. Jesus brings salvation to the house of Zacchaeus, who is rich but also a despised tax collector (19:2, 6). Luke also adds other new stories revealing Jesus' acceptance of tax collectors (15:1-2; 18:9-14) to those that he inherited from Mark (5:27-32) and Q (7:34).[12] And Luke's Gospel is the only one of the Synoptics that contains any stories demonstrating concern for Samaritans. The Samaritans were generally despised by Jewish people, but Luke's unique material includes two stories in which Samaritans serve as good examples of what God's people should be (10:29-37; 17:11-19) and one story in which Jesus rebukes hostility toward Samaritans even when they do not behave admirably (9:51-56). In short, people who suffer genuine economic hardship may head the list of the disadvantaged for whom Luke is concerned, but ultimately that concern is broad-based, recognizing that people may be placed at a disadvantage for a variety of reasons.

7. *Women figure more prominently in Luke than in the other Synoptic Gospels.* The infancy narrative in the opening chapters focuses on the role of Mary rather than on that of Joseph, as in Matthew (Luke 1:26-56; Matt. 1:18-25), and only in Luke do we hear about such women as Elizabeth (1:24-25, 41-55) and Anna (2:36-38). Other stories found only in Luke describe Jesus' miracle involving a widow's son (7:11-17), his forgiveness of a homeless woman (7:36-50), and his visit to the home of two women named Mary and Martha (10:38-42). Luke alone tells us that Jesus' ministry was supported financially by a group of women (8:1-3). Modern scholarship divides over its evaluation of Luke's attitude toward women.[13] Granting his attempt to include women in the story, some scholars nevertheless believe that he does so

in a patronizing way. Women do not exercise leadership but serve Jesus in supportive ways; they often enter the story as victims in need of assistance rather than as persons empowered to help others. The Mary and Martha story may be read as encouraging subservience (10:38-42), and Luke's comment that a report of Jesus' resurrection by a group of women was dismissed as "an idle tale" (24:11) may be taken to imply that women lack authority to proclaim the gospel persuasively.

Other scholars think such judgments are overly harsh and anachronistic. They argue that Luke's concern for women is a legitimate example of the overall concern for the oppressed discussed above. Luke is not a feminist by modern standards and does not envision a complete restructuring of societal gender roles. Still, he recognizes that women are inevitably placed at a disadvantage in the patriarchal world he knows and, given this, demonstrates concern for their plight and repulsion for attitudes that maintain it. Jesus' words in Luke 11:27-28 are often cited as expressive of an enlightened view: when someone implies that Jesus' mother must be blessed to have a son as great as Jesus, he responds, "Blessed rather are those who hear the word of God and obey it!" Thus, he rejects the popular notion that the worth of women is linked to the sons they produce for society and insists that women be evaluated on the merits of their own faithfulness.

8. Luke's Gospel *emphasizes the work of the Holy Spirit* in a way that the other Synoptic Gospels do not. Although a great deal is said about the Spirit in the Gospel of John, Matthew and Mark have only a few references (Mark 1:8-12; 3:29; Matt. 3:11, 16; 4:1; 12:28-32). In Luke, people are filled with the Spirit (1:15, 41, 67) and inspired by the Spirit (2:25-27). Jesus himself is conceived by the Spirit (1:35) and anointed with the Spirit (3:22; 4:1, 14, 18). Where Jesus promises in Matthew that God will give "good things" to those who ask (Matt. 7:11), he specifies in Luke that God will give the Holy Spirit (Luke 11:13). This emphasis prepares readers for Luke's second book (see 24:39), in which some would say the Holy Spirit becomes the main character.[14]

9. *Promise and fulfillment* is another theme receiving emphasis in this Gospel. We noted in the last chapter that Matthew is concerned with demonstrating that Jesus' life and ministry fulfilled specific prophecies found in the Old Testament. This is true to some extent in Luke as well (24:25-27, 45-47), but here the focus is more on a general fulfillment of God's overall plan.[15] Luke often declares that things happen simply because it is necessary for them to happen (13:33; 24:7). This reminds some of the Greek concept of fate, but for Luke the necessity is tied to the divine will revealed through Scripture. At least two points seem to be significant theologically. First, Luke wants to emphasize that everything is developing as it ought. New developments such as the gentile mission do not constitute diversions but

were part of God's plan all along. Luke does not seem interested, for example, in asking *why* it is necessary for Christians to suffer (Acts 9:16; 14:22). He is content to know and affirm that this necessity, too, has been taken into account. Second, Luke wants to call attention to the past faithfulness of God to instill hope and trust in promises yet to be fulfilled, including the return of Jesus (Acts 1:11) and, possibly, the redemption of Israel (Luke 2:38; Acts 1:6-7). By repeatedly indicating how God has kept promises made in the past, Luke shows that God can be counted on to keep all promises remaining for the future.[16]

10. *Salvation* is also an important theme in Luke's Gospel. This should come as no surprise, since concern for salvation is at the heart of the Christian faith and is addressed throughout most of the New Testament writings. But actually, Luke is the only one of the Synoptic Gospels in which Jesus is called "Savior" (Luke 2:11; see John 4:42). It is also the only Gospel in which Jesus specifically says that he has come "to seek out and to save the lost" (19:10). Furthermore, Luke seems to have some distinctive ideas regarding the content of salvation, which will be discussed below. For now, we will note only the striking fact that salvation is not linked to Jesus' death on the cross in the same ways that it is elsewhere. He omits Mark's reference to Jesus giving his life "as a ransom for many" (Mark 10:45), and his Gospel contains nothing similar to Matthew's image of Jesus' blood being "poured out for many for the forgiveness of sins" (Matt. 26:28). Many scholars have thought that the passion narrative in Luke reads more like a report of a pious martyrdom than a theological account of atonement for sin. Others note, however, that it is only in Luke that Jesus actually succeeds in saving someone while on the cross, welcoming a penitent thief into paradise (23:42-43). Although Luke might not think of Jesus' death as a sacrifice for sin, he does insist that this death is necessary (9:22, 44; 24:7, 26, 44) and, thus, related in some mysterious way to God's plan of salvation.[17]

◆

# Historical Context

## Who?

Although this third Gospel is anonymous, a long-standing church tradition attributes it to "Luke the physician," a companion of Paul (Col. 4:14; Phlm. 24; 2 Tim. 4:11). The earliest witness to this tradition comes from a document known as the Muratorian Canon (170–80 C.E.), where the authorship is regarded as well established. We have seen with regard to Matthew and Mark that modern scholarship tends to regard these ancient traditions with skepticism, and that is the case here as well. Still, the traditional authorship for Luke has found wider acceptance than traditions regarding the authors of any of our other Gospels. For many, this tradition has an intrinsic likelihood because it does not seem like the sort of story that anyone would have been motivated to invent. With all three of the other Gospels, church tradition attempts to link the document to one of Jesus' disciples: one to Matthew the tax collector, another to Mark the interpreter of Peter, and a third (as we will discuss in the next chapter) to John the son of Zebedee. Such traditions present the authors as persons with direct access to the events that they report and therefore help to ensure the reliability of their accounts. In this case, however, the claim is simply that the author was a second-generation Christian who knew Paul, a famous missionary but not an eyewitness to any of the events reported in the Gospel.

The greatest support for the tradition, however, comes from the book of Acts, where this same author writes about Paul and uses the pronoun "we" to describe the movements of Paul's party (Acts 16:10-17; 20:5-15; 21:1-18; 27:1—28:16). Some have dismissed these as the mere use of a literary device, according to which the author invites us, the readers, to experience Paul's story as though "we" were there. Others suggest the pronoun is a carryover from a source (a diary or travel log) that the evangelist may have used without having been present with Paul himself. Most scholars admit, however, that the "we passages" are best explained as indicators that the author of Acts and, therefore, also of Luke's Gospel, really was present with Paul on those occasions where the pronoun occurs.[18]

The issue is complicated on another front. Most Pauline scholars do not believe that the presentation of Paul in Acts is representative of the picture of Paul gained from his own letters.[19] The argument is that the author of Acts shows no knowledge of Paul's epistles, little understanding of his theology, and only slight appreciation for his main concerns (the righteousness of God, freedom from the law, justification by grace). For example, in Acts, Paul can speak of Jesus' crucifixion without ever mentioning its significance for salvation (Acts 13:27-30; compare Rom. 5:6-11; 2 Cor. 5:14-21). Thus, even scholars who agree that this evangelist claims to have been a companion of Paul (in the "we" passages) may question whether that claim is authentic. The dominant view, however, is that misrepresentation of Pauline thought does not in itself discredit the tradition of Lukan authorship. The claim is that the author was a *companion* of Paul, not his *disciple*.[20] As such, he could have been an independent thinker with his own theological agenda. In writing Acts, he may have edited his own recollections of Pauline preaching the same way he edited the written accounts of Jesus' preaching he had in the Gospel of Mark. Selective reporting would have allowed him to emphasize the themes that were most significant to him.

The question of authorship may also be approached generically, based on what the writings themselves reveal. Quite apart from any traditions, we may discern from the Gospel's preface (1:1-4) that the evangelist was not an eyewitness to the life and ministry of Jesus but relied on accounts of others. He also claims to have done research, "investigating everything carefully from the very first" (1:3). Literary studies reveal that this evangelist was probably well educated and possessed a broad range of knowledge. Scholars have found evidence of familiarity with Greco-Roman literature (Virgil, Homer) and philosophy (Stoics, Epicureans, and Cynics) in his writings. Luke actually presents Paul as quoting from the philosopher Epimenides and the poet Aratus in Acts 17:28. Thus the evangelist has often been thought to be a Gentile (Luke the physician was apparently a Gentile; see Col. 4:11, 14). At the same time, however, both the Gospel and Acts are filled with references and allusions to the Old Testament that often go much deeper than the simple citations found in Matthew. Some recent studies have tended to view him not as a Gentile but as a Hellenistic Jew, that is, a Jew who had probably received a classical education and had come to be enculturated within the Greco-Roman milieu.[21]

Many have said that this evangelist has a better knowledge of both Greek philosophy and Hebrew Scripture than any of the other Gospel writers. This breadth of knowledge makes specific identification (Jew or Gentile) difficult but is significant in its own right. A lesson may be learned here from the history of scholarship. About a century ago, some scholars tried to prove that Luke the physician was the author of these books by pointing to the abundant use of medical terms. Then Henry Cadbury, who was ultimately to become one of the most prominent Lukan scholars of this century, put an end to such foolishness with a dissertation that demonstrated that the evangelist had an equal grasp of legal terminology and nautical language, though no one proposes that he must therefore have been a lawyer or a ship's captain.[22] Indeed, Luke has the richest vocabulary of any writer in the Bible. His two books use almost eight hundred words that are not found anywhere else in the New Testament, a feature that makes them somewhat infamous to beginning Greek students. Medical terms don't prove Luke was a physician any more than familiarity with Greek poetry proves he was a Gentile or knowledge of the Old Testament proves he was a Jew. What is certain is that this evangelist was able to communicate effectively across cultural and linguistic barriers in the diverse world of the Roman Empire.

In sum, the author of Luke's Gospel was a well-educated second-generation Christian, either a Hellenistic Jew or a Gentile with deep knowledge of Jewish Scripture. Although he admitted that he had never known

Jesus, he claimed that he had known Paul, while maintaining a theological agenda distinct from that of the famous missionary. Beyond this is only speculation. It is said that Henry Cadbury's students used to joke that their mentor earned his doctorate by taking Luke's away. But Cadbury did not *disprove* the tradition that the evangelist is the physician mentioned in Paul's writings; he merely discredited attempts by others to establish that tradition illegitimately. Many scholars today would agree that the tradition is compatible with the description of the author stated above. So, they may reason, if traditions are innocent until proven guilty, this one should be allowed to stand. No one can prove that the evangelist we conventionally refer to as Luke was in fact "the beloved physician" (Col. 4:14), but many scholars today will grant that this is at least a good guess.

## Where?

Scholars have no clue as to where this Gospel might have been composed, except that most assume it was written outside of Palestine, since Luke's knowledge of the geography there is imprecise (17:11). By the same token, the provenance of this Gospel is considered less significant than for the others because Luke does not appear to be writing for a specific community in a particular locale. More likely, as the dedication to Theophilus may indicate, he is writing for people everywhere, hoping that his book will be accorded a place in churches and libraries throughout the empire.

## When?

As with the Gospel of Matthew, Luke's Gospel is usually dated after 70 C.E. because it is thought to be dependent upon the Gospel of Mark and because scattered references seem to reflect knowledge of the destruction of Jerusalem that occurred in that year (13:34-35; 19:41-44; 21:20-24). There is no certain evidence of the Gospel's existence until quotations begin to appear around the middle of the second century, but almost everyone agrees that a date closer to 70 is more likely than one later than 100. For one thing, Luke does not seem to be aware of Matthew's Gospel. Also the book of Acts, which is later than the Gospel (see Acts 1:1), displays no knowledge of Paul's letters, which had certainly been collected and circulated by the beginning of the second century (Ignatius, the bishop of Antioch, takes knowledge of these for granted in 110 C.E.). Most scholars guess that both Luke and Acts were composed in the decade between 80 and 90, around the same time as Matthew's Gospel but, apparently, in a different sector.

# Why?

Luke is the only one of the Synoptic evangelists to state clearly his purpose for writing (1:1-4): he wants his readers (like Theophilus) to "know the truth" concerning the things about which they have been instructed. They may know this truth, furthermore, because what he writes is "an orderly account" based on careful investigation of traditions handed down by eyewitnesses and servants of the word. Such language, as well as the existence of Acts, has led Christians to identify Luke as "the historian" among the four evangelists. Some scholars object to this designation when they think it denigrates Luke's role as a theologian, but the protest can become an overreaction. Certainly Luke is interested in doing more than just recording facts. Still, he wants his readers to believe that he *is* recording facts. As we have seen, Luke is more concerned than any of the other evangelists in providing historical context and perspective for his narrative. Writing history may be a means to a theological end, but at a basic level Luke wants to establish his account of these events as the definitive version of what happened.[23]

Beyond this, Luke's purposes may have been manifold. As we have indicated, he appears to write for a broad audience and so may be offering material that addresses most of the issues facing Christianity during his time. Theologically, Luke is often thought to be responding to the crisis of faith Christians faced concerning "a delay of the parousia," that is, a recognition that Jesus had not returned as early as had been expected.[24] Luke is also concerned with establishing the gentile mission as the outworking of God's plan and in exploring why Israel has not accepted God's salvation through Christ.[25] Some scholars think he challenges what he regards as false teaching within the church, such as gnostic notions that regarded matter as inherently evil and so denied the full humanity or bodily resurrection of Christ.[26] Politically, Luke may hope to establish Christianity as a legitimate religion so as to reduce the terrible persecutions inflicted upon the church by the Roman government.[27] And, pastorally, he certainly hopes to guide Christians whose faith may falter in the face of all these quandaries, heresies, and tribulations.[28]

◆

# Major Themes

## Models for Understanding Jesus

Because Luke is writing for a culturally diverse audience, he tries to present Jesus in ways that might appeal to people with a wide variety of backgrounds. Scholars have identified an apparent attempt to seize upon numerous images and to apply them to Jesus with little concern for the potential confusion such superimpositions might produce.[29]

We have, first, models drawn from the Hebraic world of the Old Testament. These Scriptures often speak of the future, promising that God will continue to aid people by sending agents of divine help, and Luke wants to link all of these to Jesus. Five examples stand out:

*(a) Messiah.*[30] Numerous Old Testament texts could be related to the notion that God would raise up a Messiah, an ideal king within the line of David who would restore the fallen fortunes of Israel (2 Sam. 7:5-16, Psalm 89). We know from Paul's letters that Christians identified Jesus as the Messiah very early, to the point of making the title part of his proper name, Jesus the Christ, or simply, Jesus Christ (the word *Christ* is Greek for *Messiah*). The identification was found in at least one of Luke's sources, the Gospel of Mark (Mark 1:1), though as we have seen, some scholars think Mark believed the title was inadequate and needed to be corrected. Luke takes it over with no such ambiguity: Jesus is the Messiah of God (9:20).

*(b) Son of Man.*[31] The book of Daniel describes the coming of a heavenly figure called "the Son of Man" (Dan. 7:13-14). Both the Gospel of Mark and the Q source used this designation for Jesus, but Luke develops it in a way that goes beyond either of his sources. Whereas they described Jesus as the Son of Man with reference to either his past earthly ministry (Mark 2:10-12) or future second coming (Mark 13:26), Luke emphasizes that Jesus is the Son of Man who is *currently* "seated at the right hand of the power of God" (Luke 22:69; compare Acts 7:56).

*(c) Mosaic Prophet.*[32] Deuteronomy presents Moses as promising that "the Lord your God will raise up for you a prophet like me from among your own people" (Deut. 18:15). Luke describes Jesus' career in ways that recall elements from the Moses story, even referring to the work that he accomplishes at one point as an "exodus" (9:31; NRSV translates the Greek word *exodos* "departure"). This leads, in Acts, to explicit identification of Jesus as the prophet like Moses spoken of in Deuteronomy (Acts 3:22; 7:37). Some scholars, we may recall, have suggested that Matthew also presents Jesus as

a new Moses, but that Gospel never refers to Deuteronomy 18:15 despite its penchant for demonstrating that various prophecies are fulfilled by Jesus.

(d) *Suffering Servant.* Isaiah speaks of a suffering "servant" through whom God will establish justice (Isa. 42:1-4; 49:1-6; 50:4-11; 52:13—53:12). The imagery associated with these passages may have influenced Mark's account of Jesus' passion but, again, in Luke the identification is made explicit. Jesus himself testifies that "this scripture must be fulfilled in me" (22:37, referring to Isa. 53:12) and in Acts, Isaiah's prophecies of a suffering servant are a starting point for proclaiming "the good news about Jesus" (Acts 8:30-35). Notably, Matthew also identifies Jesus as fulfilling Isaiah's prophecies of a suffering servant, albeit with reference to his ministry rather than to his death (Matt. 8:17; compare Isa. 53:4; Matt. 12:17-21; compare Isa. 42:1-4). The theme is also picked up in other New Testament writings, such as Hebrews 9:28, 1 Peter 2:22-25, and, less obviously, Romans 15:21.

(e) *Elijah.* Malachi predicts that the prophet Elijah will return "before the great and terrible day of the Lord comes" (Mal. 4:5). Early Christian tradition seems to have linked this saying to the role of John the Baptist (Mark 9:11-13; Matt. 11:13-14; 17:10-13). Luke is aware of this tradition also (Luke 1:17), but many scholars believe Luke wants to present Jesus as the one who ultimately fulfills the hopes associated with the return of Elijah. Luke describes Jesus' raising of a widow's son in terms that recall Elijah's similar deed (Luke 7:11-17; 1 Kgs. 17:17-24). Most important, Luke presents Jesus as ascending into heaven, just as Elijah did, endowing his successors with a rich measure of his spirit (Luke 24:50-51; Acts 1:6-11; 2 Kgs. 2:9-12).[33] Notably, Luke omits from his Gospel the sayings in Mark in which Jesus appears to link Elijah with John (Mark 9:11-13).

In the first century, all of these passages from the Hebrew Scriptures were understood differently by different groups (as they still are today). At issue would be such questions as whether the promises had already been fulfilled or whether they were to be fulfilled literally. Still, no Jewish group of which we have knowledge assumed that all these promises referred to the same person. At Qumran (the community where the Dead Sea Scrolls were found), the Essenes had subdivided messianic prophecies in such a way that they were expecting two Messiahs. The focusing of diverse scriptural traditions onto a single individual was an innovation of the Christian faith. Luke, himself, does not appear to have been the innovator, but his writings serve as the best example in the New Testament of this comprehensive approach to Christology. Jesus is the Messiah, the Son of Man, the prophet like Moses, the suffering Servant, *and* the returned Elijah. He is all these things and more because things are written about him "in *all* the scriptures" (Luke 24:27; compare 24:44).

Even more intriguing to some are the models for Jesus that Luke appears to draw from the Greco-Roman world. Here, he does appear to be innovative, seizing upon images that may make Jesus understandable to readers who have little familiarity with Jewish traditions or Old Testament Scriptures. Three such images have caught the attention of scholars:

(a) *Philosopher.*[34] Luke-Acts is sometimes compared to an early third-century work by Diogenes Laertius called *Lives of Eminent Philosophers.* This work presents brief biographies of wandering philosophers, many of whom undertake journeys similar to Jesus' journey to Jerusalem in Luke 9:51—19:44. The journeys are usually taken in response to divine commands and, indeed, Laertius appears to regard the philosophers themselves as divine in some sense. Furthermore, a key concern in these writings is to present the philosophers as founders of schools, that is, of communities that continue to venerate the founder and to be sustained by him. This could help to explain why Luke attaches Acts to his account of Jesus' life. Laertius considered narrative regarding a philosopher's successors to be integral to the biography of a philosopher, because the presence of such successors demonstrates the continuing worth of the philosophy. If such biographies were popular in Luke's time, readers of Luke-Acts would be likely to regard Jesus as similar in some respects to a wandering Greco-Roman philosopher who established a school of followers. For Laertius, we should note, philosophy was not so much abstract speculation as a way of living, something learned through imitation of the philosopher's lifestyle as much as by remembering his precepts. Luke certainly presents Jesus as one who teaches his disciples a new way of living, calling them to become like their teacher (6:40).

(b) *Immortal.*[35] In Greek and Roman mythology, the Immortals were divine beings (like Dionysius or Hercules) begotten through the union of a god with a human being. Typically, they lived on earth among other humans but performed extraordinary feats that gave evidence of their link to the gods. Initially, the Immortals could be distinguished from gods (such as Zeus) who were eternal, but often at some point in their career they underwent a transformation involving a visible ascent into heaven, where they essentially joined the heavenly pantheon. Even then, however, the Immortals retained interest in the affairs of humanity. They sometimes appeared to their friends on earth, and they could be persuaded to intervene on behalf of disciples who sought their aid. Luke's writings, while respecting Jewish monotheism, tell the story of Jesus in ways that sound themes familiar from mythology. First, although it seems a far cry from the crude Hellenistic tales of gods mating with humans, Luke's story of the virgin birth does present Jesus as the offspring of some type of encounter between the Most High God and a human woman (1:35). Jesus does perform remarkable feats of power. And, he ascends into heaven but continues at times to intervene on behalf of his followers on earth (Acts 9:1-9). Granting that there are differences, these similarities are no doubt sufficient to have inspired first-century readers to compare Luke's Jesus to figures known from Greek and Roman mythology.

(c) *Benefactor.*[36] In the Roman world, emperors and other public figures were sometimes referred to as Benefactors, whose existence was a blessing to society. Such persons were regarded as gifts from providence and were sometimes themselves thought to be divine. They were distinguished for word and deed, for both saying and doing what was right. Chief among their contributions were the bestowal of peace and the granting of clemency or mercy to enemies. Benefactors were often presented as persons who had suffered hardships or even endured death on behalf of others. Luke emphasizes all these elements in his portrait of Jesus: the congruence of word and deed (24:19; Acts 1:1), the bestowal of peace (1:79; 2:14, 29), the forgiveness of enemies (23:34; 24:47), and the endurance of trials (22:28). Furthermore, Luke seems to borrow some of the language associated with Roman benefactors for his story of Jesus. One Roman inscription calls Nero "the Savior and Benefactor of the world" and another describes the coming of Augustus as good news for the world that will benefit all people. As we have indicated, Luke is the only one of the Synoptic Gospels to apply the title Savior to Jesus, and Luke is also the Gospel that presents the coming of Jesus as good news for the whole earth (2:10, 14). In Acts 10:38, Luke even describes Jesus as one who, literally, "went about as a benefactor" (NRSV, "went about doing good").

Why would Luke rely on imagery drawn from the "pagan world" for his presentation of Jesus? On the one hand, he might have been trying to assert the claims of Christianity polemically against those of Greco-Roman religion. In other words, he may have wanted his readers to regard Jesus as the only true philosopher whose way of life they should follow, as the one true divine figure who would heed their intercessions, and as the only one truly worthy of being called "Savior and Benefactor of the world." On the other hand, Luke might have been seeking common ground, hoping to portray Jesus in language that Greeks and Romans could understand. Thus, his entire two-volume work could be analogous to the sermon he depicts Paul preaching at Athens in Acts 17:22-31. On that occasion, Paul does not denounce the Athenians as idolaters but, appearing to accept their polytheism, declares his intention as being simply to inform them of another god, hitherto unknown to them.

Luke's use of so many diverse models for understanding Jesus has theological significance beyond the particular implications for his own Christology. The use of such models is always controversial, tending inevitably toward syncretism at the same time that it enables cultural transcendence. Throughout the centuries, Christians have proposed and revised metaphors and images for understanding the person and work of Jesus, arguing frequently over the relative values of tradition and innovation. The New Testament itself contains a wealth of such imagery which has retained varied levels of appeal. Sacrificial imagery of Jesus as the "Lamb of God" (John 1:29) has been especially popular in Protestant churches, while the equally biblical presentation of Jesus as the high priest (Heb. 5:1-9) has been more deeply appreciated in Roman Catholic and Eastern Orthodox communions. Metaphorical identification of Jesus as the good shepherd (John 10:11) has continued to be very popular even in cultures where shepherding is no longer practiced, while descriptions of Jesus as a bridegroom (Mark 2:19; John 3:29) seem to have less relevance for many in our modern world.

The search for such images did not cease after the New Testament was written. In the fourteenth century, the mystic Julian of Norwich liked to call Jesus "Mother" because Jesus is the one from whom we are born anew (John 3:3) and by whom we are nurtured. In the Ankan culture of Africa, Jesus is still often called "Ancestor" to emphasize the preeminence of his standards over all others. In Korea, he may be known as the "Great Ying-Yang," the one whose divine-human nature represents a perfect complementarity of opposites.[37] In all of these cases, Christians may be doing what Luke sought to do: describe Jesus with imagery that, while admittedly imprecise, conveys truth concerning a certain aspect of who he is believed to be. Luke, notably, presents no hierarchy of images that allow one to be rated above the rest. Less interested than the other Gospels in describing the correct or best view, he seems more committed to finding a multitude of perspectives that offer glimpses of the truth. Taken together, these glimpses provide a complex and somewhat confusing portrait of Jesus that would have offered most of Luke's readers something that was familiar—mixed, perhaps, with much that was not.

## Salvation Happens Now

We noted above that Luke is the only one of the Synoptic Gospels that calls Jesus "Savior," and we also noted that Luke is distinctive in that he never links salvation definitively to Jesus' death on the cross. These two observations may be related. In Matthew and in Mark, salvation is primarily something that God accomplishes through Jesus' death on the cross. It would be anachronistic, then, to call Jesus "Savior" during the story of his life and ministry. He doesn't actually "save" anybody until the end of the story when he dies on the cross. In Luke's Gospel, however, Jesus saves people throughout the story.

We may illustrate the difference in these concepts by comparing two passages from the infancy narratives of Matthew and Luke. In Matthew's Gospel, an angel announces that Jesus "will save his people from their sins" (1:21). The future reference implies that the infant Jesus is destined to someday become a Savior, and as Matthew's story continues we see that this destiny is fulfilled at the cross when Jesus "gives his life as a ransom" (Matt. 20:28) and sheds his blood "for the forgiveness of sins" (Matt. 26:28). In Luke's infancy narrative, by contrast, an angel announces, "To you is born this day . . . a Savior" (Luke 2:11). Jesus is already a Savior from the day of his birth. Thus we arrive at the widely held perception that in Luke-Acts salvation is tied less to Jesus' death than to his *life*. As Jesus lives out his life on earth, he continues to bring salvation to those he encounters, claiming that the very reason he has come is "to seek out and to save" (19:10).

The content of this salvation is also distinctive. For many people today, the religious concept of salvation has an undeniably future orientation. To "be saved" may mean to be assured that one will receive a favorable review at the final judgment and so be permitted to live forever in heaven after one dies. It is this concept of salvation that is typically tied most closely, in Christian doctrine, to Jesus' death. Various theories of atonement attempt to explain how Jesus' death opened the way to eternal life for those who believe in him. These theories do not draw heavily on the writings of Luke.

In all of the Gospels, salvation has both present and future dimensions, but in Luke a decided shift can be observed toward the former.[38] Luke does affirm the Christian hope for eternal life in "the age to come" (18:30), but in general he lays more emphasis on life that is possible here and now. We see this in the several verses, all unique to this Gospel, that make use of the word *today* (see figure 19).

In Luke, salvation may mean different things to different people. To a blind man, it means reception of sight (18:42) and to a leper it means being

**Figure 19**

| Salvation Happens Now |
| --- |
| The Gospel of Luke emphasizes the present consequences of God's saving action.<br>"Today . . . a Savior is born" (2:11)<br>"Today . . . this scripture is fulfilled" (4:21)<br>"Today . . . we have seen strange things" (5:26)<br>"Today . . . I must stay at your house" (19:5)<br>"Today . . . salvation has come to this house" (19:9)<br>"Today . . . you will be with me in Paradise" (23:43) |

made clean (17:19). To others it may mean the reception of such blessings as peace (2:14) or forgiveness (7:48) or the removal of various infirmities (6:10; 8:48). Salvation for Luke is essentially *liberation*. Jesus the Savior claims that he has come "to proclaim release to the captives" and "to let the oppressed go free." In Luke's story, Jesus saves people by liberating them from whatever it is that prevents their lives from being as God wishes their lives to be. In this regard, Luke makes no distinction among what might be construed as physical, spiritual, or social aspects of salvation. Forgiving sins, healing disease, and feeding the hungry are all saving acts. In Luke's theology, God is concerned with all aspects of human life such that salvation may involve righting any part of life that is not as it should be.[39]

Luke 19:1-10 relates a story that may illustrate this concept. Jesus visits the home of a wealthy tax collector named Zacchaeus, who declares that he will give half of his wealth to the poor and generously repay anyone whom he might have defrauded. Jesus responds to this declaration by saying, "Today salvation has come to this house." What does he mean? The main point cannot be that Zacchaeus is going to go to heaven when he dies. As the word *today* indicates, the focus is not on the man's eternal destiny but on the immediate quality of his earthly life. Elsewhere in Luke, riches are presented as a false master that enslaves people (16:13) and prevents them from living life as God intends (for example, from being rich toward God, 12:21; from hearing Moses and the prophets, 16:28-30; or from following Jesus, 18:22-23). For Zacchaeus, then, salvation means being set free from this slavery to mammon; his (partial) renunciation of wealth demonstrates that devotion to possessions will not rule his life.

If salvation for Luke is the result of a liberating encounter with Jesus, then how can people experience salvation in a world where Jesus is no longer present? In one extremely influential study, the German theologian Hans Conzelmann argued that Luke "historicizes" salvation, relegating it to the sacred past in a way that makes it essentially unavailable today.[40] In developing this argument, Conzelmann suggested that Luke discerned three distinct periods of salvation history: the time of Israel, the time of Jesus, and the time of the church. The latter period will endure until the parousia, and the apparent delay of this parousia has made it necessary for Luke to struggle theologically to define the role of the church in the interim. Conzelmann's thesis has not fared well in recent scholarship.[41] The trend has been to argue that Luke discerns only two periods of salvation history: a time of promise and a time of fulfillment.[42] The latter period would include Conzelmann's time of Jesus and time of the church.

The discussion ultimately turns on how one understands the ascension. Those who support Conzelmann's thinking regard this event as the departure of Jesus or even "a parousia in reverse," inaugurating a period of absence.[43] Most recent scholars, however, have claimed that Luke presents the ascension as Jesus' exaltation or enthronement.[44] Thus, according to Luke, Jesus is not absent—except in the relatively insignificant sense of no longer being on earth in bodily form. Standing now at the right hand of God in heaven (Acts 7:56), Jesus continues to bring God's salvation to people on earth.

Thus, in Acts, liberating encounters with Jesus remain possible. In some mysterious way, God continues to send Jesus to people even while Jesus remains in heaven (Acts 3:20-21). This happens through the continuing activity of the Holy Spirit, who can also be called "the Spirit of Jesus" (Acts 16:7). It also happens when works of salvation, such as healing (Acts 3:6; 16:18) or forgiveness of sins (Acts 10:43), are performed in Jesus' name (Acts 2:21; 4:12). Indeed, when Peter ministers the gift of healing to a paralyzed man, he is able to say with confidence, "Jesus Christ heals you!" (Acts 9:34). The content of Christian preaching may be summarized as "the message of salvation" (Acts 11:14; 13:26) because such preaching is believed to convey the reality and power of Jesus' presence to transform lives as God intends.[45]

Theologically, Luke's concept of salvation draws from both the Jewish world of the Hebrew Scriptures and the Hellenistic milieu of the Greco-Roman empire. The Jewish world typically associated salvation with deliverance from enemies, while Greco-Roman society thought of it more as the bestowal of various blessings. Luke does not choose between these options but manages to incorporate both the introduction of positive features and the removal of negative ones into his paradigm of salvation. As the Messiah of Israel, Jesus initiates a new exodus that leads people out of bondage to such enemies as sin, disease, death, and the devil. As Lord of all nations, he behaves like a supreme benefactor, granting such divine gifts as peace, health, and forgiveness.

## Success, Growth, and Triumph

We have seen that in Mark's Gospel, Jesus' disciples are presented essentially as failures to whom Jesus nevertheless remains faithful. Luke redacts this portrait to present an altogether different picture. He completely omits passages in which Jesus offers his harshest critiques of these disciples, including the one in which Jesus refers to Peter as "Satan" (Mark 8:31-33; compare Luke 9:22; also compare Mark 8:14-21 to Luke 12:1). Most telling, he completely omits any reference to Jesus' disciples deserting him when he is arrested (Mark 14:27, 50) and in fact portrays Jesus as telling them, "You are those who have stood by me in my trials" (Luke 22:28). In other cases, he explains the disciples' apparent failures in ways that soften any indictment of them. Peter's denial of Jesus is part of a necessary test that will eventually help him to strengthen others (22:31-33; compare Mark 14:29-31). And when disciples whom Jesus has asked to pray with him fall asleep instead, Luke is quick to tell us it was because they were overcome with grief (Luke 22:45; compare Mark 14:41).

Jesus' disciples are not without their problems in Luke's story. They engage in petty rivalry over rank, arguing about which one of them is the greatest (9:46; 22:24). They entertain premature messianic expectations (19:11; Acts 1:6) and use authority abusively to exclude others (Luke 9:49-50; 18:15-16).[46] What many have noted, however, is that these are the sort of problems associated with powerful or successful people. In Matthew, the disciples are definitively people "of little faith" (8:26), and in Mark they are sometimes people with no faith at all (4:40), but in Luke the disciples' problems do not stem from any lack of faith. Their devotion to Jesus and confidence in him remain unshaken, even if the implications of this devotion for their relations with others have not been fully realized.

Two texts illustrate this well. First, let us consider a story that is unique to Luke's Gospel, found in 9:51-55. When a Samaritan village refuses to welcome Jesus and his group, two of the disciples ask Jesus, "Lord, do you want us to command fire to come down from heaven and consume them?" Jesus rebukes them for thinking this way, but the most remarkable part of the story is that the disciples actually believed they had the power to do such a thing. This is a very different characterization than we witnessed in Mark's Gospel, where the disciples were for the most part ineffectual and tended to doubt that God's power could be manifest through Jesus, much less themselves. In Luke, the disciples are, if anything, overconfident and need to learn that the divine power and authority entrusted to them is to be used for service.

A second passage that deserves a closer look includes Jesus' words to Simon Peter regarding his denial, found in Luke 22:31-34. Although the story of this denial is found in all four Gospels, the words of Jesus presented here are peculiar to Luke. Jesus informs Peter that Satan is going to sift the disciples like wheat, that is, put them to a test, but that Jesus has prayed for Peter so that his faith will not fail. Apparently, then, Luke does not consider what happens subsequently to represent a failure of faith. How can this be, when Peter denies three times that he knows Jesus (22:54-62)? Peter does not actually renounce his allegiance to Jesus; he merely pretends that he does not know him. Luke may regard this as an act of cowardice, as a lie that Peter tells to save his skin, but he does not regard it as a failure of *faith*. Peter does not waver in his earlier confession that Jesus is "the Messiah of God" (9:20). Once again, then, Luke seems to locate the disciples' problems on a horizontal axis rather than a vertical one. The integrity of the disciples' faith in

God or relationship with Jesus is never in question for Luke, though he presents these disciples as sometimes failing to practice their faith appropriately in the world of human society.

Some theologians regard this apparent distinction between faith and practice as problematic. Perhaps Luke wants to assure his readers that, whatever failings the disciples of Jesus may have had, they can be regarded as faithful witnesses to the confessional tradition on which the faith of the church is based.[47] In any case, Luke's theology has been cited as exemplary of "early catholicism," partly because it appears to conceive of faith as adherence to a confessional tradition rather than as a relational orientation that necessarily includes all aspects of life ("horizontal" and "vertical").[48] Such a conception may also derive from the Greco-Roman environment in which Luke is striving to proclaim the Christian message. This Hellenistic world tended to categorize different aspects of the human personality while the Hebraic milieu insisted on the essential unity of humanity. The Greek concept remains dominant in the Western world today, as is evident in modern specializations that focus on physical, emotional, or spiritual matters.

Another theological problem emerges when Acts is considered along with Luke's Gospel. Here, the already positive portrait of the disciples is taken to an incredible extreme. Peter, Paul, and others become Spirit-filled agents of God who are almost duplicates of Jesus. They perform miracles similar to his, healing the sick (Acts 5:12-16; 19:11-12) and raising the dead (Acts 9:36-43; 20:7-12). All of the problems Jesus' disciples exhibited in the Gospel seem to vanish. Now, his followers are committed to service (Acts 1:17, 25), willing to suffer (Acts 5:41), and courageous in the face of persecution (Acts 4:18-20). Indeed, the martyr Stephen meets his death with words that recall almost exactly those of Jesus on the cross (Acts 7:59-60; compare Luke 23:34, 46). Furthermore, the sermons and speeches of Jesus' followers in Acts are presented with the same authoritative weight given to the words of Jesus in the Gospel. Luke's readers are seldom, if ever, expected to regard what these first Christians say as anything less than the word of God. In the Gospel, Jesus had told his disciples that "everyone who is fully qualified will be like the teacher" (6:40). Now, in Acts, this appears to have been fulfilled.

This presentation of successful discipleship is part of a broader theme in Luke-Acts, one that presents the story of the church as marked by growth and triumph. Repeatedly in Acts, the ongoing success of the church's mission is stressed in summaries that mark its progress: 1:14; 2:41; 4:4; 5:14; 6:7; 9:31; 11:21, 24; 12:24; 14:1; 16:5; 19:20; 28:30-31. Christians succeed not only in being faithful disciples themselves but also in "turning the world upside down" (Acts 17:6), that is, in having a transforming effect on society. Numerous stories present the church as triumphant over all forms of evil, wiping out poverty (Acts 4:32-37) and healing diseases (Acts 5:12-16). The devil has fallen (Luke 10:17-18) and the world now seems to belong to Christ and to Christians.[49]

Such a portrait is often criticized as naive and unrealistic. Theologically, Luke is accused of replacing the "theology of the cross" prominent in Paul's understanding of the gospel with a "theology of glory."[50] The former notion regards the mission of the church as being fulfilled paradoxically through suffering and rejection, for God's power is revealed through human weakness (1 Cor. 1:26—2:5; 2 Cor. 12:10). The latter construes the destiny of the church in terms of victory and success. Defenders of Luke point out that he does portray Jesus' followers as suffering (albeit joyfully) in Acts (5:41; 16:22-25) and that he is realistic in admitting that the attempts to evangelize Jews have largely met with failure (Acts 13:44-46; 18:5-6; 28:23-28).[51] The overwhelmingly positive image of discipleship may seem idealistic, but it is probably intended to be inspiring. Luke wants to show his readers what God accomplishes through the lives of ordinary people to heighten their expectations of what God might accomplish through them. Luke wants his readers to believe that the possibility of God's will being accomplished in their lives and in the world is greater than they imagine.

◆

## The Gospel of Luke As Literature: Sample Studies

*The Narrative Unity of Luke-Acts. Vol. I: The Gospel according to Luke*
By Robert C. Tannehill; FF (Philadelphia: Fortress Press, 1986)
A comprehensive study of the character of Jesus in Luke, particularly as he relates to others, including John the Baptist, the oppressed, the crowd, the authorities, and his disciples.

*On Character Building: The Reader and the Rhetoric of Characterization in Luke-Acts*
By John A. Darr; LCBI (Louisville: Westminster/John Knox Press, 1992)
A study in the interaction of readers and texts that examines how readers construct characters in Luke's writings and, in the process, undergo a certain character building of their own.

*Reading Luke-Acts: Dynamics of Biblical Narrative*
William S. Kurz (Louisville: Westminster/John Knox, 1993)
Application of modern literary criticism to passages that have caused interpreters problems, with an emphasis on the role that the narrator plays in guiding the act of reading.

*Mark and Luke in Poststructuralist Perspectives: Jesus Begins To Write*
By Stephen D. Moore (New Haven: Yale University Press)
Applies a postmodern reading strategy to Luke (and Mark), bringing apparently dissimilar materials to bear on the text in ways that challenge traditional concepts of meaning and language.

◆

## Feminist Readings of Luke: Sample Studies

*Choosing the Better Part? Women in the Gospel of Luke*
By Barbara E. Reid (Collegeville, Minn: Liturgical Press, 1996)
A commentary on the manner in which women are portrayed as characters in Luke's stories, with an aim to engage the liberating potential of stories that admittedly do not depict the participation of women and men as equals.

"Scholars rightly alert the modern reader to the danger of too simply exalting Luke as a 'friend of women.' . . . In order for this Gospel to reveal God's liberating word to a Church of equal disciples, a process of recontextualization and reinterpretation is needed" (pp. 3–4).

*The Double Message: Patterns of Gender in Luke-Acts*
By Turid Karlsen Seim (Nashville: Abingdon Press, 1994)
Contends that Luke recalls stories in his Gospel that attribute strong, positive roles to women even though he appears to accept strict social boundaries for women's activity that legitimate the masculine preferences attributed to the church in Acts.

"The double message nurtures a dangerous remembrance." Locating traditions in the past "does not bring them to silence. What was, is not to be forgotten" (p. 260).

# CHAPTER FIVE

# The Gospel of John

Clement of Alexandria described the Gospel of John as "a spiritual Gospel," recognizing even in the early third century that this book is noticeably different from the three Synoptic Gospels. Some of the key differences can be detected by observing what is unique to this Gospel, what is missing, and what is told differently (see figure 20).

Scholars estimate that about 90 percent of the material in John's Gospel is unparalleled in Matthew, Mark, or Luke. Included in this unique material are many well-known Bible stories, including the account of Jesus changing water into wine (2:1-11) and the story of him washing the feet of his disciples (13:1-20). Like Luke, John also demonstrates a knack for including memorable minor characters in his narrative. Nicodemus, Lazarus, and Thomas (the "doubting disciple") are all examples of persons who through their brief appearances in this book attained prominence in subsequent religious devotion and reflection. Also like Luke, John's Gospel gives prominence to women characters: Mary Magdalene, an unnamed Samaritan woman whom Jesus meets at a well, Mary and Martha (the sisters of Lazarus), and others.[1]

For those who are well acquainted with the other Gospels, omissions from John's account are remarkable. Exorcisms are so prominent in Matthew, Mark, and Luke—how can John report the ministry of Jesus without mentioning them? Or, how can he give in-depth summaries of Jesus' teaching without relating a single parable? John manages to do these things in a way that, had we not read the other Gospels, such elements would never be missed. Indeed, such features only appear as "omissions" when John is evaluated from a Synoptic perspective. Eventually, we need to get past com-

Figure 20

---

John and the Synoptic Gospels

1. Examples of Material Unique to John

| | |
|---|---|
| 2:1-12 | Miracle at Cana (water into wine) |
| 3:1-21 | Conversations with Nicodemus |
| 4:7-26 | Samaritan Woman at the Well |
| 5:1-18 | Healing of Man at Pool of Beth-zatha |
| 7:53—8:11 | Woman Caught in the Act of Adultery |
| 9:1-41 | Healing of the Man Born Blind |
| 11:1-44 | Raising of Lazarus |
| 13:1-20 | Washing the Disciples' Feet |
| 17:1-26 | The "High Priestly" Prayer |
| 20:24-29 | Resurrection Appearance to "Doubting Thomas" |

2. Examples of Material Absent from John

No stories of Jesus' birth, baptism, or temptation
No transfiguration
No parables
No exorcisms
No predictions of Jerusalem's downfall (but see 2:19-22)
No references to repentance
No institution of the Eucharist
No references to a parousia (unless maybe 14:3; 21:22-23)

3. Examples of Material Notably Different in John from the Synoptics

References to three Passovers indicates ministry lasts three years (2:13; 6:4; 11:55)
Temple cleansing comes at beginning of ministry (2:13-22; Mark 11:15-19)
Jesus' ministry overlaps with that of John the Baptist (3:22-24; Mark 1:14)
Call of disciples includes Philip and Nathanael (1:35-51; Mark 1:16-20; 2:13-14)
Feeding of five thousand features a boy with a basket (6:1-15; Mark 6:30-44)
Anointing at Bethany is by Mary, sister of Martha (12:1-8; Mark 14:3-9)
Jesus dies on the day before the Passover meal (18:28; see 13:1) rather than on the day after (Matt. 26:17; Mark 14:12; Luke 22:7)
Crucifixion story contains three unique sayings (19:17-37; Mark 15:21-39; Luke 23:33-47)
Miraculous catch of fish after Easter (21:1-8; Luke 5:4-11)

paring John with the other Gospels to understand this book on its own terms.[2] But the differences may serve as early clues to alert us that we really are entering a very different literary and theological world.[3]

Scholars debate the question of whether the author and community responsible for John's Gospel had any knowledge of the other three Gospels.[4] Obviously, if he intended to write an additional book to set alongside one or more of the others, this would explain why he concentrates on material not found elsewhere. Yet this would not explain some of the differences in material that overlaps. If John's readers already had a copy of Matthew, Mark, or Luke, why would he tell the story of Jesus overturning tables in the Temple (2:13-17) when that story was already present in all three of the other Gospels? More to the point, why would he place his report of this incident at the *beginning* of Jesus' ministry when the other three place it near the end? If his readers knew the other Gospels, wouldn't they want some explanation for such a change? Also, many scholars call attention to John's postscript in 20:30-31. Here, he admits that Jesus did many other things that he has not related but claims the things that he reports have been "written so that you may come to believe that Jesus is the Messiah, the Son of God, and that through believing you may have life in his name." Some take this to mean that John regards his Gospel alone as sufficient to convey all that is essential for believers. If so, John may have known about other Gospels without necessarily thinking his readers needed to know about them.

If the question of whether John and/or his readers knew the other Gospels cannot be answered with certainty, theories regarding other sources for this Gospel are even more tenuous.[5] Many sources have been proposed (see figure 21), and of these one has proved particularly intriguing. At certain points in John's Gospel, miracles of Jesus are referred to as enumerated "signs": the transformation of water into wine is called "the first of his signs" (2:11) and the healing of an official's son is referred to as "the second sign" (4:54). Thus, many scholars have assumed that a major source for John's Gospel may have been a collection of miracle stories that would have concluded with what is now John 20:30-31 ("Now Jesus did many other signs . . .").[6] Numerous studies have tried to detect differences in vocabulary, style, or ideology with regard to this material, and some scholars have even published reconstructions of this source.[7] A few, in fact, regard the collection as an early Gospel in its own right, claiming that portions of John's passion and resurrection narrative also derive from it. If such a document did exist, it could have been either the first edition of what eventually grew into the Gospel of John as we have it, or it could have been a work of independent origin that a redactor combined with other materials in much the same way Matthew and Luke combined Q with the Gospel of Mark.

Figure 21

---

Possible Sources for John's Gospel

- a "Signs Gospel" that recorded seven or eight miracle stories (2:1-12; 4:46-54; 5:1-9; 6:1-13; 9:1-7; 11:1-44; 21:1-8; maybe 6:15-25) and may have included an account of the passion and resurrection
- a collection of remembrances of one called "the beloved disciple," dealing mostly with the last week of Jesus' life
- a body of material underlying the great discourses of Jesus, possibly sermons by the beloved disciple or another prominent member of the community

The formation of traditions such as these prior to the final editing of John's Gospel is widely accepted among scholars, but the nature and extent of these sources are greatly disputed.

---

Figure 22

---

A Gospel Composed in Stages

One theory for the composition of John's Gospel:

| | |
|---|---|
| *First*: | Gospel materials consist of an oral, unorganized collection of reports of Jesus' words and deeds; |
| *second,* | preaching and teaching over several decades shapes material into distinctive units; |
| *third,* | units are organized consecutively into first draft of a written Gospel; |
| *fourth,* | subsequent editions are redacted to meet objections to the first; and |
| *fifth,* | final editing and addition of chapters 15–17 and 21 take place. |

---

Although none of the proposed sources can be established with certainty, most scholars would agree that John's Gospel in the form we now have it passed through stages of editing (see figure 22).[8] There are moments when the text makes little sense as is. In John 8:31, Jesus is said to be speaking to "the Jews who had believed in him," but in 8:37 he is presented as telling these people, "You look for an opportunity to kill me, because there is no place in you for my word." Again, in John 11:2, Mary is introduced to the readers as "the one who anointed the Lord," but in our versions of this Gospel, she does not actually do this until later (12:3). Most scholars think such anomalies are best explained as editorial glitches, revealing that some of the material may once have been presented in a different order than what we now possess. Another sign of such an editorial process may be the manuscript problems associated with the story of the adulterous woman, in which Jesus issues his famous challenge to her accusers, "Let anyone among you who is without sin be the first to throw a stone at her." In modern Bibles, the story is listed as John 7:53—8:11, but in some manuscripts it is found after John 7:36 or at the very end of the Gospel, following John 21:25. In at least one case it is actually found in Luke's Gospel, and in many manuscripts it is missing altogether. Text critics aren't sure what to make of such evidence. Perhaps, the well-known story was added to John's Gospel by Christians of a later generation, or perhaps it simply got separated from the rest of the Gospel during the cycles of editorial revision, with the result that no one was quite sure where it belonged anymore.

Finally, we should note that the last chapter of John's Gospel (chapter 21) appears to be an addendum to the book as a whole. Whatever one makes of theories regarding a Signs Gospel, the last few verses of chapter 20 read like a conclusion, indicating that nothing more needs to be said. At the very least, then, someone must have added the twenty-first chapter at a later time and perhaps made other editorial changes in the book. A major purpose of this addendum is the debunking of a rumor that someone called "the disciple whom Jesus loved" would not die (21:20-23). Accordingly, one prominent theory is that John 21 was added to the rest of the Gospel after this person had in fact died, to correct the false expectations of those who had thought this would not happen.

---

◆

## Characteristics of John's Gospel

As we have noted, the Gospel of John is unique in many ways. Here are a few noticeable features:

1. This Gospel begins with a *hymnic prologue* that presents Jesus as the preexistent Word made flesh (John 1:1-18).[9] This reference to Jesus as "the Word" is almost unique in the Bible (see Rev. 19:13), and it has been interpreted in light of both Greek philosophy and Hebrew prophetic tradition regarding the word of God.[10] Most remarkable is the notion that Jesus, or at least this Word that ultimately becomes Jesus, was present "in the beginning with God" and indeed "was God" (1:1). As we have seen, Mark's Gospel begins its story with Jesus' baptism, and both Matthew and Luke begin

Figure 23

---

The Christological Moment

What moment in Jesus' life is most significant christologically?
At what point is he to be acclaimed something more than human?
The Gospels (and Q) seem to answer this differently:

| | |
|---|---|
| The Q Source | at his parousia (Matt. 24:37-39; Luke 17:26-30) |
| Mark | at his baptism (Mark 1:9-11) |
| Matthew/Luke | at his birth (Matt. 1:20-25; Luke 1:30-35) |
| John | in the beginning (John 1:1-2) |

The documents are listed here from earliest to latest.

Thus scholars note that as time passed what was perceived to be the essential "christological moment" moved earlier.

---

with announcements of his conception. Only John insists that the central figure of the Christian faith has been both present and divine from the very beginning (see figure 23). As a result, John's Gospel in general and the prologue in particular have provided a foundation for the Christian doctrine of incarnation, that is, the belief that in Jesus, God became a human being. John does not articulate this doctrine as such, but he does provide materials for its development.[11] If John appears to attribute divinity to Jesus, furthermore, he also insists more explicitly than any of the other evangelists on the actual humanity of Jesus—the Word did become *flesh* (compare 1 John 2:19; 2 John 7).[12] Thus, this Gospel also lays the foundations for the Christian doctrine of "the two natures of Christ," that is, the confession that Christ was and remains both fully divine *and* fully human.[13]

2. John's Gospel makes *numerous references to a mysterious figure called "the disciple whom Jesus loved"* (see figure 24). Some scholars have taken this to be a literary device: the beloved disciple was not an actual person but serves as an imaginary character in John's story with whom readers can identify.[14] Most scholars, however, take the references as historical: the beloved disciple was an actual person, but who was he? Among numerous theories, two have been prominent. From the second century on, popular Christian tradition has identified the disciple whom Jesus loved with John the son of Zebedee, who is a fairly significant disciple in the other Gospels but is not mentioned by name here (but see 21:2). The beloved disciple, however, does not come into the story until fairly late, and John the son of Zebedee was present with Jesus from the beginning of his ministry. In fact, this Gospel does not report any of the events that concern John the son of Zebedee in the Synoptic Gospels. Accordingly, some suggest the beloved disciple is Lazarus, whom Jesus

Figure 24

---

The Disciple Whom Jesus Loved

John's Gospel claims to be based on the testimony of someone called "the beloved disciple" (21:23-24). The disciple is mentioned at the following points in the narrative:

| | |
|---|---|
| 13:23 | Leans on Jesus' chest at last supper |
| 13:24-25 | Intermediary between Peter and Jesus |
| 18:15-16 | Gains admittance for Peter to Pilate's court |
| 19:26-27 | Entrusted with care of Jesus' mother |
| 20:4 | Outruns Peter to the tomb on Easter morning |
| 20:8 | First to believe in the resurrection |
| 21:7 | Identifies the risen Jesus for Peter |
| 21:21-23 | Fate should not be a matter of concern for Peter |

---

raises from the dead in chapter 11.[15] Lazarus is explicitly described as one whom Jesus loved in 11:36, and all of the Gospel's references to "the disciple whom Jesus loved" are subsequent to this identification. Also, if the beloved disciple had been one whom the Christian community regarded as having been raised from the dead, this might have contributed to the rumor that he would not die (21:23). Still, Lazarus is never called a disciple, and nothing here or elsewhere indicates why he would be among that group on such occasions as Jesus' last supper (13:23). Other candidates have also been suggested, including John Mark and, lately, Thomas.[16]

3. John's Gospel makes *abundant use of symbolism*. Early on Jesus is called "the Lamb of God" (1:29, 36). As the story progresses, Jesus identifies himself seven times with metaphorical "I am" sayings (see figure 25).[17] The entire Gospel story is imbued with dualistic imagery of light and darkness (1:5; 3:19; 8:12; 12:35, 46) and with references to what is above and below (3:31; 8:23).[18] Much Johannine interpretation focuses on attempts to understand these symbols and, for that matter, to determine what is a symbol in the first place.[19] Particularly controversial has been the question of "sacramental symbols." Numerous references to water (3:5; 4:10-15; 5:2-7; 7:37-39; 9:7; 13:3-10; 19:34) are sometimes linked to Christian baptism, just as references to bread (6:5-13, 28-58; 21:9-13), wine (2:1-10), or blood (6:53-56; 19:34) may be taken as symbolic of the eucharistic meal. John's Gospel, however, contains no account of Jesus being baptized or instituting the eucharistic meal, which seems to signal that the community initially (at least) had a decidedly nonsacramental theology.[20] Many other symbols are simply obscure. Why does John note that Jesus' disciples caught exactly 153 fish (21:11)? Most

Figure 25

Seven Metaphorical "I Am" Sayings

Jesus says,

"I am the bread of life" (6:35; see 6:51)
"I am the light of the world" (8:12; 9:5)
"I am the gate" (10:7, 9)
"I am the good shepherd" (10:11, 14)
"I am the resurrection and the life" (11:25)
"I am the way, and the truth, and the life" (14:6)
"I am the vine" (15:1, 5)

Even the words "I am" may be symbolic, recalling God's self-designation in Deuteronomy 32:39 or Isaiah 46:4.

scholars think the number is probably symbolic, but no one is absolutely sure what symbolic meaning such a number would have had.

4. A *motif of misunderstanding* recurs throughout John's narrative, according to which various characters in the Gospel fail to understand what Jesus says.[21] This motif is related to the prominence of symbolism just noted, for symbolic language is typically what characters fail to understand. On another level, it may be related to a prominence of irony, wherein characters can fail to understand the full implications even of their own speech or actions (11:50).[22]

When Jesus says, "Destroy this temple, and in three days I will raise it up," his audience assumes he is talking about the Temple in Jerusalem. But John tells his readers that Jesus "was speaking of the temple of his body" (2:19-21). The Gospel is replete with such misunderstandings: Nicodemus thinks he must reenter the womb of his mother in order to be born anew (3:4). When Lazarus dies and Jesus tells his disciples that he has "fallen asleep," they think he is getting some healthy rest (11:12). When he says, "The bread that I will give for the life of the world is my flesh," people think he is advocating some bizarre form of cannibalism (6:51-52). Similarly, he confuses his disciples by speaking of his desire to do God's will as his "food" (4:31-34), and he stymies the crowds by describing his divine destiny as going where they cannot (7:33-36; 8:21-22). Other misbegotten attempts to make literal sense out of symbolic speech may be found in 4:1-15; 6:32-35; 8:51-53, 56-58. Most scholars recognize the purpose of this motif as being to sensitize readers to look for multiple or deeper meaning throughout the narrative, to look for possible instances of symbolism even where no obvious misunderstanding has occurred. The unwrapped bandages of Lazarus (11:44), the seamless robe of Christ (19:23), the unbroken net of fishes (21:6, 8, 11)—do these references also have significance that is more than literal?

5. The *content and style of Jesus' teaching are noticeably different in John's Gospel* from the Synoptics. As for content, Jesus does not talk much about the kingdom of God, Mosaic law, or specific moral behavior expected of his followers. Instead, he talks primarily about himself, about who he is and about what his coming means for the world. As for style, Jesus does not use parables or aphorisms that relate matters of faith to daily life, but delivers relatively long, philosophical discourses on such abstract notions as "truth" and "freedom." Examples of such discourses may be found in 5:19-47; 6:25-70; 7:14-52; 8:12-59; 10:1-18, 22-39; 12:23-36; 14:1—16:33. The greatest attention has been focused on the latter block of material: chapters 14–16 (or, sometimes, 13–17) are often analyzed as a grand "farewell discourse" of Jesus or as a series of such discourses. They contain distinctive christological images, teaching on the role of the Spirit, and Jesus' call for his followers to "abide" in him. These chapters may be given a position of prominence in Johannine studies analogous to that accorded the Sermon on the Mount in studies of Matthew's Gospel.[23]

6. John's Gospel *emphasizes the role of the Spirit,* which is referred to distinctively as "the Paraclete" (14:26; 15:26; 16:7; English Bibles often translate this name as "Advocate" or "Helper"). The Spirit is promised by Jesus (7:37-39; 14:16-17), who tells his followers that his leaving is actually to their advantage since it allows him to send the Spirit to them (16:7). John's Gospel shares this emphasis on the Spirit with the writings of Luke. John even records a story of Jesus giving the Holy Spirit to his disciples after his resurrection (20:22), a story that makes for an interesting comparison with the more dramatic account of the Spirit's outpouring in Acts 2:1-4. In general, however, Luke presents the Spirit as a source of power for mission and ministry (Acts 1:8), while John focuses more on the Spirit as one who teaches and reveals truth (14:25-26; 16:13).[24]

7. As we noted already, John's Gospel sometimes *refers to Jesus' miracles as "signs"* (2:11, 23; 3:2; 4:54; 6:2, 14; 7:31; 9:16; 12:18; 20:30). This is striking even apart from questions of source analysis, because in the Synoptic Gospels Jesus refuses to work signs (Matt. 12:38-39, Luke 11:29-32) and even links the working of signs to the activity of false prophets (Mark 13:22). In John, signs lead people to true faith (20:30-31). At the same time, John's Gospel also betrays some reservations regarding faith that is based on signs (4:48). As indicated above, the perspective presenting a positive relationship between signs and faith may derive from a source that this evangelist used, but in any case the Gospel as it now stands offers an ambiguous evaluation

of miracles as an inducement to faith. On the one hand, people are encouraged to believe on account of the works that they see Jesus perform (9:16; 10:38). On the other hand, a special blessing is pronounced upon all "who have not seen and yet have come to believe" (20:29).[25]

8. John's Gospel *presents Jesus' crucifixion as his exaltation.* Whereas each of the other Gospels portrays Jesus predicting his suffering and death three times (in Mark, 8:31-32; 9:31; 10:33-34), John presents Jesus as saying three times that he will be "lifted up" (3:14; 8:28; 12:32-34). When Jesus was crucified, the cross to which he was nailed was literally lifted up from the earth, but John's use of this term carries the double meaning of implying that he is exalted or glorified through his death. John's story of the passion reflects this perspective. Although Jesus' death certainly involves suffering, he is depicted as one who remains in control of the events throughout. All along, he has maintained that no one can take his life from him, but that he will lay it down of his own accord, knowing he can take it up again (10:17-18). Now, Jesus declares and demonstrates that no one has any power over him, not Satan (14:30), nor soldiers (18:6), nor Pilate who sentences him (19:10-11). When Jesus finally dies on the cross, he does not cry out in agony, "My God, my God, why have you forsaken me?" (Mark 15:34), but simply declares, "It is finished," indicating that the work he has come to do is now successfully completed. Thus, he is glorified (John 17:5).[26]

9. John's Gospel *typically identifies Jesus' opponents as "the Jews,"* a designation not found in the other Gospels except for Matthew 28:15. Such an identification strikes many as anachronistic since, historically, Jesus and his disciples were all Jewish. John acknowledges this fact (4:9), but still uses the term "Jews" in a way that suggests Christianity and Judaism have become distinct religious movements.[27] People must choose whether they are disciples of Jesus or Moses (9:28), and confessing faith in Jesus provides grounds for being expelled from the synagogue (9:22; 12:42; 16:2). John does maintain that "salvation is from the Jews" (4:22), but he also depicts Jews as people who do not believe their own scriptures (5:39-47), who disavow allegiance to God (19:15), and who indeed are not children of Abraham but children of the devil (8:44). In our modern day, many believe John's repeated use of the term "Jews," describing people who are portrayed negatively, contributes to anti-Semitism. Some translators now advocate using a different term, such as "Judeans," to indicate that it was a particular group of Jewish people in a particular time and place whom John depicts as the enemies of Jesus and his followers.[28]

10. John's Gospel *emphasizes love for one another as the great new commandment of Jesus and as the distinctive mark of his followers* (13:34-35). In fact, this Gospel and the New Testament letter called 1 John uplift this standard of communal love more than any other books in the Bible. Throughout history,

John's Gospel has been treasured in Christian piety because of its poetic and persuasive presentation of this ethic: "This is my commandment, that you love one another as I have loved you" (15:12; see also 15:17; 1 John 3:23; 4:21). Somewhat remarkable, then, is the absence in this Gospel of any call for Jesus' followers to love their neighbors (Mark 12:31; Lev. 19:18) or their enemies (Matt. 5:44; Luke 6:27). How a community grounded in a commandment to love can also exhibit the sort of hostility noted in the references to Jews above is a frequent subject for theological reflection on this book.[29]

◆

# Historical Context

## Who?

Popular Christianity often attributes five New Testament books to John the son of Zebedee, one of Jesus' twelve disciples:[30] the Gospel of John, which claims to have been written in part by "the disciple whom Jesus loved" (21:20, 24); the epistle called 1 John, which is anonymous; the letters called 2 John and 3 John, written by someone who calls himself "the elder" (2 John 1; 3 John 1); and the book of Revelation, which is written by someone named John (Rev. 1:1, 4).

Of these five works, then, only the book of Revelation actually claims Johannine authorship for itself. Legends abound as to how, of the original apostles, only John escaped martyrdom and died an old man in exile on the island of Patmos, where he received the angelic vision recorded in this apocalyptic book. Even in the early church, however, many disputed that the author of this book was John the Apostle, the son of Zebedee who had been one of Jesus' disciples. For one thing, in the Synoptic Gospels, Jesus seems to predict that John the son of Zebedee *will* suffer martyrdom. The reference is admittedly ambiguous. What he actually says is that John and his brother James will "drink the cup" that Jesus himself must drink (Mark 10:38). Most interpreters take this reference to the cup Jesus must drink as a metaphor for suffering unto death (Mark 14:36), not merely exile—this is certainly what it meant with regard to James (Acts 12:1-2). Thus it is likely that John the son of Zebedee had died as a martyr by the time Mark's Gospel was written, and probably before the book of Revelation was written as well. The man who wrote the book of Revelation (often called John the Seer) was most likely a Christian who is otherwise unknown to us.

Figure 26

---

Three Persons Named John

*John the Apostle*—the son of Zebedee. He and his brother James were called to be among Jesus' first disciples (Mark 1:19-20). He ministered alongside Peter (Acts 3–4) and came to be known as a pillar of the church (Gal. 2:9). Some people believe he may be "the disciple whom Jesus loved" whose testimony is incorporated into the Gospel of John (John 21:24).

*John the Elder*—author of epistles? Although he is never mentioned in the New Testament, we hear of this person in other writings from the early church, including Eusebius. He is probably the "elder" responsible for at least two of the Johannine epistles (2 John 1; 3 John 1). Some scholars think he also wrote the first of these letters (1 John) and may have served as a redactor of the Gospel at a late or final stage.

*John the Seer*—visionary author of Revelation. We know nothing about this person except what he tells us, that he wrote the book of Revelation while in exile on the island of Patmos (Rev. 1:1, 9). Though he is often confused with the two persons mentioned above, there is no good reason to identify him with either of them.

---

To say this, however, is not ultimately determinative for decisions regarding the Gospel and the epistles. Most scholars believe that, contrary to tradition, they probably had a separate origin from the book of Revelation. Although the latter book has some features in common with the Gospel of John (such as the use of symbolic language), it is distinctive in style, language, and perspective, and it addresses different concerns. Most notably, the Gospel of John displays practically no interest in the parousia or the end of the world, which are dominant themes for Revelation. The three epistles, however, are similar to the Gospel both theologically and linguistically, and most scholars do believe that these four works at least derive from the same community. Thus even if John the Apostle (the son of Zebedee) is not to be identified with the author of Revelation, he could still be the beloved disciple associated with the community that produced the Gospel and the epistles.

Still, we must complicate matters further by noting that the beloved disciple associated with the Gospel is probably not the same person as the elder associated with the last two epistles. The fourth-century historian Eusebius says that the elder's name was in fact John, but he distinguishes this person from the apostle. Apparently, then, the first-century world knew *three* prominent Christians who bore the name John (see figure 26).

One possibility is that John the Apostle had nothing to do with this Gospel, but John the Elder who wrote the epistles also had a prominent role in editing the traditions handed down by Jesus' beloved disciple, whoever that might have been. Thus the book would first have become known as "the Gospel of John" due to its association with John the *Elder* and only later come to be regarded as the work of John the *Apostle* (as did the book of Revelation) through confusion of names. It is also possible, of course, that the beloved disciple *was* the apostle, John the son of Zebedee. If so, then this book could have been associated with both John the Apostle (at its inception) *and* John the Elder (at its completion).[31] In that case, perhaps it should be called the Gospel of Johns!

Recognizing that the process of composition was complicated, many scholars are more comfortable speaking of "a Johannine school" than of a particular individual author.[32] If the beloved disciple was an early member of this school, furthermore, then his precise identity may ultimately be less significant than the mere fact that this book can lay claim to eyewitness testimony. This Gospel sometimes notes minor historical details missing from other accounts. This happens particularly in the passion narrative, which is where the references to the beloved disciple seem to be found. For example, all four New Testament Gospels report that on the night Jesus was arrested one of his disciples drew a sword and cut off the ear of a high priest's slave. Only John, however, seems to know that the man who did this was Peter, and that the name of the man he attacked was Malchus (John 18:10; compare Matt. 26:51; Mark 14:47; Luke 22:50).

Aside from providing such information, however, the book does not offer a more historical presentation of Jesus than the Synoptics. On the contrary, most historical critics regard John as the most overtly interpretative of the four.[33] Aside from the problem of trying to determine which portions of the Gospel derive from the beloved disciple, they call attention to the Gospel's own characterization of this beloved disciple's words as "testimony" (John 21:24). The word carries the sense of evangelistic witness or preaching. The beloved disciple's role in the Johannine community was quite different from the role Simon of Cyrene may have played for the church that produced Mark's Gospel. In chapter 2 we noted that, since Mark and his readers apparently knew Simon's sons (Mark 15:21), Simon may have served as a source for some of the information presented in Mark's passion account. But the beloved disciple did more than supply the Johannine community with factual information regarding what had happened. The reverence with which he is regarded indicates that he probably exercised a pastoral role as a leader of the community, guiding them in their theological interpretation of the events. Indeed, some scholars believe that the speeches Jesus gives in this Gospel were originally sermons the beloved disciple gave about Jesus (see figure 21). This would explain their distinctive style and, more important, it would explain why Jesus himself is the principal topic of the speeches. The implication of such a theory is that, for this community, the teaching of the beloved disciple *about* Jesus became more relevant than the original teaching of Jesus himself.

## Where?

Early church tradition holds that the Gospel of John was composed in Ephesus, and to this day tourists can be shown the site where the book was written. Scholars, of course, are skeptical of such traditions. They note, for instance, that when Ignatius writes to Ephesus in the early second century, he makes much of Paul's former residence there but does not mention previous ministry by any of Jesus' disciples or refer to any community in the city that is likely to have produced this book. Since the island of Patmos is off the coast of Ephesus, some speculate that John's Gospel came to be associated with this city through the erroneous assumption that its author was the person who also wrote Revelation.

Scholars are generally more interested in defining the type of locale that might have given rise to this Gospel than in determining the precise geographical location. The book's philosophical orientation in general and treatment of the Logos theme in particular (1:1-18) are signs of an especially Hellenistic milieu. At the same time, its presentation of Jews as primary opponents suggests a city with a large and fairly powerful Jewish population. Also, the Gospel must have developed within a community that was to some extent independent of other Christian movements.

Syria is often suggested as a likely locale for the Johannine community: this region was not too far removed from Palestine and the strong Jewish influence there, but it was also an area where the influence of Hellenism was more overt. Others favor Alexandria, the center of Jewish Hellenism, noting similarities between the merger of Greek philosophy and Old Testament religion found in John and explicitly developed in the writings of Philo of Alexandria. If left to choose between the latter two proposals, most scholars would decide based on how they construe the relationship between John and the Synoptics. If the Gospel were composed in Syria, the community would probably have been aware of the traditions that inform the other Gospels, while Alexandria would provide a more out-of-the-way location where the Johannine church could conceivably have developed independently.

By the same token, a number of scholars return to the traditional location of Ephesus and indicate that it meets all of the criteria adequately. The picture of Ephesus provided in Acts 18 and 19 is of a pagan Greek city (19:23-

41) where varieties of Christianity were proclaimed (18:24-26). The stories there attempt to illustrate specifically the superiority of Christian ministry over that practiced by Jews (19:11-16). They even describe the incorporation of former disciples of John the Baptist into the Christian fold (19:1-7) in a manner analogous to John 1:35-36. In light of such correspondences, many are content to let the ancient tradition stand.[34]

## When?

The overall character of John's Gospel is reflective and retrospective. It does not so much report events as discuss their meaning, and it does so with depth and profundity that suggest reflection over a considerable period of time. In the early church John's Gospel was always thought to be the latest of the four, and most modern scholars concur. They believe that this Gospel evinces the most mature development of a number of theological themes and accordingly assign it a relatively late date. Other factors support this reasoning. The Gospel displays concern for Christians being systematically expelled from synagogues (9:22; 12:42; 16:2), an occurrence that historians believe was the result of a Jewish decision made around 85 c.e. Also, a late date helps to explain why John is quoted less by early Christian writers than the Synoptic Gospels.

A number of features, however, seem to indicate an early date, prior to 70 c.e. and before the writing of any of the other Gospels: references to Jesus as Rabbi (a term Christians soon dropped); allusions to the Temple complex as still standing (5:14); and material that appears to reflect competition between followers of Jesus and those of John the Baptist (1:20, 35-37; 3:22-23, 27-30; 10:41). Thus a minority of scholars have maintained that John's Gospel was actually the first of the four to be written and have assigned it a date fairly close to the life and ministry of Jesus.[35]

The puzzle is usually resolved by regarding the Gospel as a book that was written in stages. Some portions, such as those ascribed to the beloved disciple, may indeed come from an early time, but these were edited and more material was added as years passed. When was the process complete? Some scholars used to argue that John's Gospel did not reach its final form until well into the *second* century, possibly as late as 160–170 c.e. This now seems most unlikely. A tiny fragment of a papyrus manuscript (called p[52]) containing a few verses from John 18 has been dated to the beginning of the second century, suggesting that the Gospel was already being copied and circulated by that time. Thus John's Gospel is almost universally regarded today as a late first-century document, probably reaching its final form around 90–100 c.e.

# Why?

The purpose of John's Gospel is explicitly evangelistic. It records "signs" that are intended to bring its readers to believe "that Jesus is the Messiah, the Son of God," so that they "may have life in his name" (20:31). We should not think, however, that the work as a whole is directed toward unbelievers in the interests of converting them to the Christian religion. Much of the Gospel is clearly devoted to confirming the faith of those who already believe and to guiding them in understanding the implications of their faith.[36] The Gospel seeks to reveal "the truth" to people at various levels of apprehension, with the conviction that knowing this truth will have an immediate, qualitative effect on their lives (8:31-32).

More specific reasons for the Gospel's composition may be geared to the particular historical situation of the community that produced it. The Hellenistic environment demanded a work that would recast the Jewish story of Jesus in the language and style of the Greco-Roman world. The expulsion of Christians from synagogues also necessitated a telling of the story that explained how one confessed to be the *Jewish* Messiah had come to be known as Messiah to Christians instead. From a sociological perspective, first-century Christianity might be viewed as a sectarian movement that split off from Judaism and was rejected by the larger group. As a foundational document of that movement, John's Gospel attempts both to appropriate the traditions of Israel for the emerging sect and to reorient the movement away from the Hebraic world of its past toward the Hellenistic world that represents its future.

Clues to the specific concerns of the Johannine community may also be gathered from the letters of John. These letters reveal the community to be one that has suffered divisions over various doctrinal matters, divisions so grave that some members have left the church (1 John 2:19), and those who remain must be warned against "deceivers" who teach about Christ in ways that are not approved (2 John 7). Tension is high. In one letter, the elder tells the congregation not to show any hospitality to those whose teaching he does not approve (2 John 10-11); in another, he complains that his opponents are advocating a similar policy with regard to him and his friends (3 John 10). The material in the Gospel stressing the need for Jesus' followers to "love one another" is no doubt intended to address such problems of internal division.[37]

At the same time, the Gospel intends to define confessional boundaries for the community by interpreting the tradition in ways that will rule out ideas that some have taught. For instance, the author of 1 John insists that "every spirit that confesses that Jesus Christ has come in the flesh is from God" (4:2). Apparently, some teachers in the community had taught something to the contrary, perhaps that Christ was a heavenly being or an angel, but not a human being (see 2 John 7). We know that in the second century such teaching was characteristic of varieties of Christianity associated with Gnosticism.[38] Some gnostic Christians made a distinction between Jesus, who was a physical human being, and the Christ, who was the spiritual being that inhabited Jesus' body for a time. Although such ideas were ultimately rejected as heretical by the Christian church, they may have been present in embryonic form in the first-century Johannine community. Thus when John says his Gospel is written so that people may believe "Jesus is the Christ [Messiah]," this phrase, like so many others in his Gospel, may have multiple meanings. On the one hand, Jews and other non-Christians are encouraged to believe that Jesus is the Messiah of Israel. On the other, *Christians* are encouraged to believe that, contrary to what some teach, Jesus *is* the Christ and not just some disposable human form that the Christ used while on earth (see also 1 John 2:22). John's Gospel was written to reveal "the truth," but this truth must be presented in opposition to what is regarded as error and deception.

◆

# Major Themes

## Already and Not Yet

Salvation in John's Gospel has a decidedly present-tense orientation. Jesus does speak often about eternal life, but even then the concern is as much qualitative as quantitative. The point is not simply that Jesus offers people life that never ends, but that he offers them life that is worth living. The eternal or never-ending quality of this life is but one aspect of it: eternal life begins now and flows into the future. We see this clearly in a text such as 5:24, where Jesus says that anyone who believes God "has eternal life, and does not come under judgment, but has passed from death to life." For John, then, the passage from earthly existence to life eternal is not a future hope that believers await. It is a present reality, something that has already occurred. Theologians call this concept *realized eschatology*—that is, what is usually associated with the future or the end times is realized already in the lives of believers.[39]

To illustrate further, we may examine the way that the Johannine writings use the word *life*.[40] In the Synoptic Gospels, Jesus uses the word *life* to refer to life after death. For example, when Jesus says, "It is better for you

to enter life maimed than to . . . go to hell" (Mark 9:43), the phrase "to enter
life" refers to participation in the future kingdom of God, which will be
granted to some at the final judgment. But in John's Gospel the word *life* is
typically used to refer to the quality of one's existence here and now. Jesus
says he has come so that people "may have life, and have it abundantly"
(10:10). Indeed, the very reason for the book's existence is to report Jesus'
ministry in such a way that people may come to believe and "have life in his
name" (20:31). In this regard, a passage from one of the epistles is also revealing: "God gave us eternal life, and this life is in his Son. Whoever has
the Son has life; whoever does not have the Son of God does not have life"
(1 John 5:11-12). The negative, latter phrase does not refer literally to people
who have died but to people who, though physically alive, do not really
"have life." The Johannine perspective does hold that such people will eventually "perish" (John 3:16), that is, they will not live forever as will believers
(10:28). But John wants to maintain that there is a qualitative difference
even now between mere physical existence and eternal life, which for those
who "have the Son" is a current experience.

Realized eschatology is so prominent in John's Gospel that some scholars
have thought this evangelist denies or at least ignores traditional ideas concerning the future. The few scattered references to a future coming of Christ
can be interpreted existentially. For instance, Jesus says, "I will come again
and will take you to myself, so that where I am, there you may be also"
(John 14:3). Does this refer to the parousia, to the great event described in
the Synoptic Gospels in which Christ is expected to return to earth, coming
in clouds with great power and glory to enact the final judgment (Mark
13:26-27)? Some find the reference in John more intimate than cosmic and
take such verses as references, not to a parousia at the end of time, but to a
present experience through which Christ comes to believers today. If members of the Johannine community believe they are people who "have the
Son" (1 John 5:11-12), then they must believe that, in some sense, the Son
has already come to them.[41]

Other references, however, seem to point definitely to an event that
marks a boundary between present and future life. In chapter 21, the addendum to the Gospel, Jesus says of the beloved disciple, "If it is my will that
he remain *until I come,* what is that to you?" (John 21:23). Also, the epistles
speak of the present world as passing away (1 John 2:17) and look forward
to a time in the future when Christ will be revealed in a way that he is not
now (1 John 2:28; 3:2). Of course, the final chapter of the Gospel and the
epistles are ascribed to a late stage in the development of this community. A
common theory, therefore, is that the Johannine community focused almost
exclusively on present dimensions of Christian life until near the end of the
first century. Then, perhaps influenced by contact with other Christian

groups, some aspects of the traditional future expectations were incorporated into their theology as well.

In any case, the Gospel as we now have it presents dual concepts of key themes in the Christian faith. Jesus will come again in the future (21:21-23), but he also comes now to those who love and obey him (14:23). There will be a resurrection "on the last day" (6:39, 40, 44, 54), but those who believe in Jesus have experienced resurrection already so that, in some sense, they "never die" (11:26). Similarly, there will be a judgment on that last day (12:48), but judgment also occurs in the present so that those who believe "are not condemned; but those who do not believe are condemned already" (John 3:18). Such dual imagery is similar to the present and future dimensions that we observed in chapter 2 for the phrase "kingdom of God" in Mark's Gospel.

John's Gospel, however, clearly wants to stimulate interest in the present aspects of salvation. We see this in the story of the raising of Lazarus, which employs the characteristic motif of misunderstanding. Four days after Lazarus has died, Jesus tells the man's sister, Martha, "Your brother will rise again." She responds, "I know that he will rise again in the resurrection on the last day" (John 11:23-24). Martha misunderstands Jesus' prediction of an immediate resuscitation as a reference to the distant future. The dramatic subsequent event, in which Lazarus walks out of his tomb, demonstrates that the future is now. The Gospel of John preserves some dichotomy between what is "already" and what is "not yet," but encourages its readers to learn, as Martha does, that much of what is usually associated with the future is currently available.

## Knowing the Truth

People who "have life" may also be described in John's Gospel as persons who are being "born anew" or "born from above" (3:3), or as persons who are "made free" (8:32). The latter phrase recalls the Gospel of Luke, which also emphasizes the present-tense dimension of salvation and describes this as "release to the captives" (Luke 4:18). As in Luke, then, salvation in John can mean liberation, and this may have social or political implications in addition to spiritual ones.[42] The full context of the Johannine phrase, however, brings out a distinctive element less evident in Luke's writings. What Jesus says in John is, "If you continue in my word, you are truly my disciples; and you will know the truth, and the truth will make you free" (John 8:31-32). For John salvation is the result of an ongoing process of enlightenment. As people come to know the truth, they experience the qualitative difference in life that marks those who believe.

Modern theologians may observe that John discerns the human predicament differently than other biblical writers. Frequently, the New Testament presents salvation in terms of forgiveness of sins. The problem for humanity is that people have transgressed God's laws and are destined to suffer the present and future consequences of their transgressions. Jesus saves people by making atonement for their sins or by overcoming the power of evil that determines their fate. John does know and accept this tradition. Jesus is "the Lamb of God who takes away the sin of the world" (1:29), and evil has no power over him (14:30-31). But John also envisions humanity as enslaved by ignorance and deception. People do not experience the abundant, meaningful life that God intends because they do not know the truth.

"What is truth?" Pilate asks in John's Gospel (18:38), and the book's readers are no doubt expected to do the same.[43] It is not just any truth that is of interest here; it is ultimate truth, which for John means truth about God. Perhaps the most important thing Jesus does in this Gospel is to reveal God. The last verse of the Gospel's prologue makes this point succinctly: the basic problem is that "no one has ever seen God"; the solution to this problem is that, now, Jesus has made God known (1:18). Just how does Jesus make God known? As in the other Gospels, he teaches people about God, revealing through his words and deeds that God loves the world (3:16), that God is true (3:33), that God is spirit (4:24), that God is active (5:17), that God gives the Holy Spirit (14:16), that God answers prayer (16:23), and so on. But there is more to his revelation of God than this.

Many scholars note that John's Gospel presents Jesus as a messenger from God.[44] Time and again, the book speaks of God *sending* Jesus into the world with language that duplicates what was used in ancient messenger proceedings. Sent by God (7:28-29), Jesus is to deliver the message entrusted to him (3:34; 17:8) and then return to the one who sent him (7:33-34; 13:1, 3-4). Jesus refers to God regularly—a total of twenty-three times—as "the one [or the Father] who sent me." This imagery is confused, however, in that sometimes Jesus appears to be not only the messenger but the message itself. When the prologue identifies Jesus as "the Word [of God] made flesh" (1:14), it indicates that he himself is a physical representation of what God has to say. He is the self-revelation of God, and in him the truth about God is made real in a way that people can see, hear, and touch (1 John 1:1). Thus, when one of Jesus' disciples (Philip) says to him, "Lord, show us the Father, and we will be satisfied," Jesus responds, "Have I been with you all this time, Philip, and you still do not know me? Whoever has seen me has seen the Father" (John 14:8-9).

In John, then, not only does Jesus tell what God is like and show what God is like, but in a fundamental sense, Jesus *is* what God is like. He not only reveals the truth; he *is* the truth (14:6). Or, to put it differently, Jesus not only teaches people *about God* in John's Gospel, he also addresses people *as God,* that is, as the Word of God made flesh (1:14). Often, what Jesus says about himself in this book applies less to his own historical person than to the transcendent divine reality for whom he speaks. This is probably the case with the seven metaphorical "I am" sayings (see figure 25). Whatever the metaphors mean, they reveal not only who Jesus is but apply also to God for whom Jesus speaks. When the Word of God (Jesus) says, "I am the bread of life" (John 6:35, 51), we are expected to conclude that "God is the bread of life." To do otherwise, to apply the metaphors narrowly to the historical figure of Jesus, leads to misunderstanding (John 6:51-52).

Jesus also *acts* as the Word of God made flesh throughout the narrative of John's Gospel. His miracles may be called "signs" because they reveal what God is like. This explains why, as we noted above, the working of signs can be embraced in John's Gospel even though it is repudiated in the Synoptics. What is rejected in the other Gospels is the idea that miracles may serve as proofs to authenticate one's ministry (see Mark 8:11-12). In John's Gospel, the miracles are not called signs because of what they prove but because of what they reveal. The healing of the blind man, for instance, does not convince unbelievers that Jesus is God's agent (9:24-29), but for those who do believe Jesus is God's agent this miracle may reveal God's works (9:3). In a symbolic sense, removal of blindness may signify how Jesus enables people to see what they could not see otherwise (9:38-41), just as changing water into wine may symbolize the qualitative transformation that Jesus can effect in people's lives (2:1-11).

Even without unraveling the meaning of Jesus' symbolic actions and metaphorical speech, something basic about God is revealed through Jesus' ministry in John's Gospel. His words and deeds are consistently intended to benefit his audience. He does not, for instance, curse his enemies or work "punishment miracles" that bring affliction upon others. Accounts of such activity by divine agents were common in the ancient world and even turn up occasionally in the Bible (2 Kgs. 2:23-25; Acts 13:8-12). But if John presents Jesus as the one who has come to reveal what God is like, then the first thing that Jesus reveals is that God loves the world and desires to bless and to save rather than to punish or condemn (John 3:16-17). The metaphors and the miracles all point to this, summoning positive images of light and life, seeing and healing. God is not here likened to a raging fire that threatens to destroy the undeserving (Deut. 4:24). All the images chosen are inviting: running water (4:10-15), an open door (10:9), bread (6:32-35) and wine (2:1-11), birth (3:3-5) and resurrection (11:23-25). In fact, the Johannine writings present God as one who is not to be feared (compare Matt. 10:28), as one whose "perfect love casts out fear" (1 John 4:18).

The very coming of Jesus into this world is viewed as a demonstration of God's love (1 John 4:9), but nowhere is God's love more clearly revealed for John than in Jesus' death on the cross. "No one has greater love than this," Jesus says, "to lay down one's life for one's friends" (John 15:13). Thus the death of Jesus works for salvation in a different way than that found in the other Gospels. By presenting Jesus as the "Lamb of God" (1:29), John pays homage to the traditional notion that the death of Jesus may be likened to a sacrifice that atones for sins. But on another level, his voluntary death demonstrates in an ultimate way the greatness of God's love, and thus reveals the true nature of God.[45] People who come to know this truth are set free; people who believe what Jesus reveals about the love of God have life that does not perish, life that is abundant and eternal.

## Community of Love

The Johannine community is often described as a *sect,* that is, as a group that would have identified itself as distinct from other religious associations, including other varieties of Christianity.[46] This perspective is based in part on the distinctive character of the Gospel, but it also derives from discernible tensions that appear to be addressed implicitly there and explicitly in the epistles. As this community struggles for self-identification, it appears to be marking boundaries on at least three levels, with regard to the world, the Jews, and other Christians.[47]

*(a) The world.* John's Gospel begins with an allusion to the creation story in Genesis ("In the beginning . . ."), which presents the world as God's creation and therefore as intrinsically good (Gen. 1:31). Indeed John now says that "all things came into being" through the Word, which was to become flesh in the person of Jesus Christ (1:3, 14). If God (and God's Son) are responsible for the world's very existence, then it is no surprise to learn that God loves the world and does not wish to condemn it. God sent the Son into the world "that the world might be saved through him" (John 3:16-17). At the same time, the Johannine community has come to view the world as a pagan, hostile environment. It is a realm ruled by the devil (12:31; 14:30; 16:11), unable to receive the Spirit of truth (14:17). Jesus' kingdom is "not from this world" (18:36), and neither Jesus nor his followers "belong to the world" (17:16). The world either does not know Jesus (1:10) or else it hates him and his followers (7:7; 15:18-19; 16:20; 17:14).

The ambiguity with which the world is viewed in these writings suggests disparity between the community's expectations and experience. Its affirmation of the world as the work of God's creation and object of Christ's redemption (1:29) implies commitment to the world at least as a mission field for evangelism. As Jesus was sent by God into the world, so now he sends his disciples into the world (17:18; 20:21). Still, the epistles suggest that the community eventually adopted a largely defensive posture. There, believers are warned, "Do not love the world or the things in the world" (1 John 2:15). At this stage of its development at least, the community seems to have less interest in converting the world than in overcoming its dangers and influences (1 John 5:3-4; John 16:33). There is no talk here of transforming the world, of being "salt of the earth" (Matt. 5:13) or of turning "the world upside down" (Acts 17:6). Still, the Johannine community has not abandoned its mission. Ironically, it believes its mission to the outside world is fulfilled precisely through attention to internal concerns. Johannine Christians are to remain *in the world but not of it* (17:15-16). By living as a nonworldly community, embodying the ethic of mutual love and oneness, they believe they will become a living testimony. Through those who do not belong to the world, the world may come to know and believe the truth about Jesus and God's love (17:20-23).[48]

John's attitude toward the world is often compared with that of second-century Christian Gnosticism. The Gnostics viewed the world as evil, rejected the God of the Old Testament, and ascribed the very act of creation to demonic forces. Christ, they said, came as a spiritual being to free human spirits from the evil world of matter and flesh. The Johannine writings contain both ideas that appear to be compatible with this gnostic perspective and statements that utterly reject it. Some scholars have suggested that the negative attitude toward the world in this Gospel represents a step toward Gnosticism; others see the Gospel as struggling with some of the same problems that led to the gnostic rejection of the world, while denouncing that option as a viable conclusion. In any case, we know that John's Gospel was the most popular of the four among the Gnostics and that early church leaders such as Irenaeus and Origen had to argue against gnostic interpretations of this book when putting forward their own views concerning it.[49]

*(b) The Jews.* If the Johannine community regarded the pagan world of the Roman Empire as its enemy, then we might imagine that it would have found greater commonality with the Jews. To an outsider, at least, Johannine Christians and Jews would appear to have much in common: they share the same Scriptures and, by and large, agree on definitions of morality and ethical behavior.[50] Yet we have noted that John's Gospel presents Jews as the implacable opponents of Jesus and his followers.

In this Gospel, Jews are not worse than others in the world; they are simply no different—and *that* is significant! They have lost their privileged position of being God's chosen people. Jesus came to them as one coming to "his own," but their rejection of him caused them to become numbered among those who did not know him (1:10-11). Thus, whatever can be said of "the world" in general can now be said of "the Jews" in particular. The devil is the ruler of this world (12:31; 14:30) and the father of the Jews (8:44).

At the same time, John's Gospel appears to be friendly to some Semitic groups. First, John the Baptist leads a group of people who have experienced light and truth similar to that brought by Jesus (5:33-35). Recognizing this, the Gospel goes on to present John as one who testifies to Jesus, sometimes in such a way that his own followers become the latter's disciples (1:24-37). Second, a number of scholars have noted similarities between Johannine theology and Samaritan religion, particularly regarding the latter's concept of Moses as one who ascended to heaven, saw God, and returned to reveal God to humanity.[51] The language that this Gospel uses at certain points (3:13, 31; 5:20; 6:46; 7:16) is very close to that used in Samaritan writings, except that now the claim is that Jesus (not Moses) is the revealer from heaven. John's Gospel attempts to correct Samaritan thinking in other respects too (4:20-22), while nevertheless insisting that Jesus' teaching is close enough to that of Samaritan religion that he was actually called a Samaritan himself (8:48). Notably, in this Gospel, Samaritans respond favorably to Jesus and come to believe in him (4:39-42).

Thus, the hostility toward "the Jews" in John's Gospel is not directed at an ethnic group but at the religion associated with first-century Jewish synagogues. As we have indicated, references throughout the Gospel to synagogue expulsion (9:22; 12:42; 16:2) no doubt allude to crises in this community's history that have fueled this antipathy.[52] The boundary marking must also be understood in light of the great diversity of first-century Judaism, something that can be obscured by John's generic phrase "the Jews."[53] Comparisons are often noted between the Johannine community and the Jewish monastic community at Qumran which kept the library of documents now known as the Dead Sea Scrolls. These writings exhibit the same dualistic thinking as John's Gospel, describing community members as belonging to the light and to the truth and castigating those of the world as children of darkness and falsehood. The Qumran community also rejected the Jewish religion as it was represented in the synagogues (and in the Jerusalem Temple), while viewing themselves as true heirs of the faith.[54]

*(c) Other Christians.* Some scholars believe the Johannine community was seeking to define itself not only vis-à-vis other Semitic groups but also with reference to other Christians. Several of the passages dealing with the beloved disciple present that person so that he appears to be superior to the other disciples, particularly Peter (see figure 24). Closer to Jesus than Peter (13:23-25), he is also quicker, not only in getting to the tomb on Easter morning (20:4), but also in coming to faith (20:8) and recognizing the risen Lord when he appears (21:7). In the first century, Peter was widely regarded

as a pillar of the church (Gal. 2:9), if not as *the* rock on which the church was built (Matt. 16:18). Perhaps, then, the Johannine community treasured stories that presented Peter as secondary to the beloved disciple because they believed the version of the faith that he represented was inferior to that based on the latter's testimony—the faith articulated in this Gospel.[55]

Another story in John's Gospel can be read with similar effect. As Jesus hangs on the cross, he sees his mother and the beloved disciple. He says to his mother, "Woman, here is your son," and to the disciple, "Here is your mother." From that hour, John notes, the beloved disciple took Jesus' mother into his own home (19:26-27). On one level, this story simply indicates Jesus' concern in his hour of death to be sure his mother would be provided for after he was gone. Historically, however, such an action would have been unnecessary since Jesus had brothers who could have cared for her. Indeed the eldest of his brothers, James, became the leader of the church in Jerusalem (see Acts 15:13-21) and is mentioned alongside Peter and John the son of Zebedee as a pillar of the church (Gal. 2:9). In effect, then, this story presents Jesus as saying, "I regard the beloved disciple (not James) as my true brother!" The implication may be, once again, that the community founded on this beloved disciple's testimony is superior to that led by James.

Divisions between the Johannine community and other Christian groups are explicitly addressed in the epistles. The tenor there is much stronger, for some who claim to be followers of Jesus are identified as "deceivers" or even "antichrists" (1 John 2:18; 2 John 7). These persons, however, do not appear to be followers of Peter or James, but rather proponents of ideas that would have been rejected by all major leaders of the church known to us in the New Testament. Specifically, the group that the Johannine community regarded as heretical consisted of persons who considered themselves to be followers of Christ but who espoused what is known as *docetism,* the doctrine that Jesus was divine but not human.[56] The second-century Gnostics were but one group to espouse a docetic Christology.

We have observed that the Johannine writings emphasize love for one another as the most important of all commandments, the one which is definitive of the community (John 13:35). At the same time, the inward orientation of this community is evident in the absence of any explicit teaching regarding love for others: enemies, neighbors, or humanity in general. Today, the directive to "love one another" can be interpreted broadly, as calling upon all people to love each other. But in its original context, the command was addressed to disciples of Jesus who, accordingly, were to love other disciples of Jesus.

Apparently, the Johannine community did not feel obligated to love the world (1 John 2:15) or the Jews. Heretics, too, have gone out into the world and so are probably no longer to be considered among the "one another"

Johannine Christians are directed to love (1 John 4:5-7). Peter and the other disciples of Jesus, however, certainly *are* among this group. Even if these writings reflect competition and tension between the Johannine community and the varieties of faith found elsewhere in the New Testament, they do not employ the same sort of "us and them" vocabulary with reference to Jesus' disciples as that used with regard to the world, the Jews, or the heretics. Indeed, the Gospel contains Jesus' prayer that all of his disciples and those who believe in him through their word "may all be one" (John 17:20-21).[57]

To label the Johannine community a sect, then, may be too simplistic. The group is a marginal, distinctive Christian community that is seeking to define itself with relation to other religious movements. Apparently it has determined that its differences with synagogal Judaism on the one hand, and docetic (Gnostic?) Christianity on the other, are too great for there to be any rapprochement. Its differences with other Christian groups, however, are not so great. The community can seek unity with such groups even while maintaining that its understanding of the faith is superior. Such matters as the Johannine community's belief in the preexistence of Christ and its preference for realized eschatology could have been topics for early ecumenical dialogue.

In any case, Johannine Christianity can only be regarded as sectarian from a historical perspective. The eventual acceptance of the Gospel into the Christian canon is evidence that, even if this community was somewhat unique in the first century, its testimony to the faith came to be accepted by a wider audience. What was marginal became mainstream, and the controversial theological understandings that developed within this "sectarian" group ultimately came to be definitive of orthodoxy.[58]

---

◆

---

## The Gospel of John As Literature: Sample Studies

*Anatomy of the Fourth Gospel: A Study in Literary Design*
By R. Alan Culpepper, FF (Philadelphia: Fortress Press, 1983)
A comprehensive overview of how John may be read like a modern novel, with sections on plot, characterization, point of view, narrative time, the role of the narrator, and the implied reader.

*John As Storyteller*
By Mark W. G. Stibbe (Cambridge: Cambridge University Press, 1992)
Applies a narrative-historical criticism to John 18–19, analyzing the account of Jesus' passion in terms of its formal literary characteristics, genre, and social function.

*Rhetoric and Reference in the Fourth Gospel*
By Margaret Davies, JSNTSS 69 (Sheffield: Sheffield Academic Press, 1992)
Draws upon structuralism and reader-response criticism to elucidate key concepts and metaphors in John and then relates these to the Gospel's theological and anthropological perceptions.

*The Print's First Kiss: A Rhetorical Investigation of the Implied Reader in the Fourth Gospel*
By Jeffrey Lloyd Staley; SBLDS 82 (Atlanta: Scholars Press)
Considers the impact made on readers by a text intended for oral delivery and examines passages in John where readers are invited to embrace tensions between conscious contradictions.

◆

## Feminist Readings of John: Sample Studies

"John" in *The Women's Bible Commentary,* pp. 293–304
By Gail R. O'Day; ed. C. Newsome and S. Ringe (Louisville: Westminster/John Knox, 1992)
A brief survey of key texts in John that portray women, with an emphasis on establishing that these stories are especially important theologically to the Gospel's understanding of Jesus and of the nature of faithful discipleship.

"Men do not have a monopoly on witness and discipleship in John; rather, the Gospel of John narrates a faith world that would not exist without women's participation in it" (p. 294).

"The Gospel of John" in *Searching the Scriptures,* Vol. II, pp. 561–634
By Adela Reinhartz; ed. E. S. Fiorenza (New York: Crossroad, 1994)
Evaluates John from the perspective of a Jewish feminist reader, applauding the Gospel's attitude toward women while deploring its attitude toward Jews. Its portrayals of women characters, emphasis on love, and absence of gender as an explicit category are all positive features, but ultimately the liberation this Gospel offers is limited and conditional.

"The feminist reading of scripture . . . seeks to expose the question of liberation not only from the perspective of women qua women but from the point of view of the marginalized, whether defined in terms of gender, race, sexual orientation, physical capability, or in any other way" (p. 595).

# The Other Gospels

Matthew, Mark, Luke, and John were not the only Gospels written. Numerous other books that report sayings of Jesus and events of his life were produced by Christians in the first few centuries following his death.[1] These works are sometimes called the *apocryphal* Gospels to distinguish them from the four *canonical* works that came to be regarded as Scripture.[2]

Most of these books claim to be written by one of Jesus' disciples or close friends, but in no case is this claim taken seriously by historical scholars. Although they are difficult to date, most of the books were probably written later than the four canonical Gospels. All of them are short, and some have been preserved only in fragmentary form. Many of them reflect ideas associated with the religious movement called Gnosticism and, so, may owe their origin to a desire for gnostic Christians to have Gospels expressive of their particular interests.[3] In other words, with very few exceptions (mainly, the *Gospel of Thomas*), these books do not contribute anything to our understanding of the life and work of Jesus. Still, they are significant for historians because of what they reveal about the theology, piety, and politics of the early church.[4]

The nature and style of these writings vary greatly. Some, such as the *Gospel of the Egyptians* and the *Gospel of Truth,* are simply religious treatises that do not even purport to present the words or deeds of Jesus. Apparently the titles of such writings used the word *gospel* in a general sense to mean "religious truth" rather than to designate a particular genre of literature. Apocryphal writings that do claim to transmit information about Jesus fall into two broad categories: "Narrative Gospels" and "Sayings Gospels."

The Narrative Gospels were most similar to the four New Testament books, insofar as they told stories about Jesus. The ones that we still possess, however, usually focus on either the beginning of Jesus' life (*Infancy Gospel of Thomas* and *Protoevangelium of James*) or on his death and resurrection (*Gospel of Peter*) rather than on his life or ministry itself. We know, however, that other narrative Gospels existed, even though we no longer possess copies of them. Of special interest are the three "Jewish-Christian Gospels" from which early Christian writers sometimes quote: the *Gospel of the Nazareans*, the *Gospel of the Hebrews*, and the *Gospel of the Ebionites*. These works were apparently written and treasured by Christians who remained deeply rooted in Judaism.

Sayings Gospels reported teachings or words of Jesus with little interest in relating these to the events of his life. The most significant of these is the *Gospel of Thomas*, a collection of sayings similar in form to what scholars suppose for the Q document. Other works did not present individual sayings of Jesus so much as extended discourses on selected topics. These are stylistically reminiscent of Jesus' discourses in the Gospel of John, but in the apocryphal Gospels they are typically presented as postresurrection speeches. Usually, Jesus is described as appearing after Easter to one of his followers, and the ensuing dialogue becomes a pretext for the development of dogmatic ideas beyond what is found in the four New Testament Gospels. For example, in the *Gospel of Bartholomew*, Jesus describes his descent into Hades and the Annunciation to Mary; in the *Gospel of Philip*, he offers instruction on the sacraments.

# Narrative Gospels

### THE PROTOEVANGELIUM OF JAMES

This second-century work claims to be written by James, the "stepbrother" of Jesus, who is here described not as a child of Joseph and Mary, but of Joseph by a previous marriage. It is primarily concerned with Mary, the mother of Jesus, beginning with an account of how she was miraculously born to a pious couple (Joachim and Anna) and then sent to the temple where she was fed by the hand of an angel. Eventually, the narrative catches up with the stories in Matthew and Luke, on which it is clearly dependent. Still, these are embellished. We have now an account of how Herod tries to kill not only Jesus but also John the Baptist, whose father suffers martyrdom rather than reveal his whereabouts. Another such embellishment is the following story of Joseph and Mary being tested when the latter's pregnancy was discovered (on the "drink test," compare Num. 5:11-31):

> The high priest said, "I am going to give you the Lord's drink test, and it will disclose your sin clearly to both of you." And the high priest took the water and made Joseph drink it and sent him into the wilderness, but he returned unharmed. And he made the girl drink it, too, and sent her into the wilderness. She also came back unharmed. And everybody was surprised because their sin had not been revealed. And the high priest said, "If the Lord God has not exposed your sin, then neither do I condemn you."(16:3-7)

### THE INFANCY GOSPEL OF THOMAS

This highly fanciful work, probably from the latter half of the second century, claims to be authored by one of Jesus' twelve disciples. It provides a collection of miracle stories from "the lost years" of Jesus' life (ages five to twelve). Soundly condemned whenever it is mentioned by church leaders, the book does not appear to support any developed doctrinal aberrance, Gnostic or otherwise. Rather, it offers us a view of "how Jesus was regarded in the unsophisticated religious imaginations of ordinary early Christians, rather than in the more abstract theological affirmations of Christian intellectuals."[5] As a little boy, Jesus makes clay pigeons come to life, raises playmates from the dead, and stretches a board that his father Joseph accidentally cut too short. More disturbing is the story that follows:

> [Jesus] was going through a village when a boy ran by and bumped him on the shoulder. Jesus got angry and said to him, "You won't continue your journey." And all of a sudden he fell down and died. (4:1)

## THE GOSPEL OF PETER

An account of Jesus' death and resurrection attributed to Jesus' premier disciple, this work has been the subject of controversy since its discovery in 1886. Only fragments remain, but these provide an account of Jesus' passion and resurrection different from those found in the New Testament Gospels. Most scholars have understood the work to be a second-century document dependent upon the Gospels, partly because it seems to have a less historical and more overtly theological inclination. But this view has been sharply contested recently.[6] The work may have developed in stages, and if so, it could contain some material as early as what is found in the canonical Gospels. One theory even regards it as a witness to an early "Passion-Resurrection" source that provided the common origin for the four canonical accounts. The assumption, then, is that these events were first the subject of imaginative theological speculation and only later grounded in history.[7] The *Gospel of Peter*'s most famous passage is the intriguing tale of the walking-talking cross:

> They see three men leaving the tomb [two angels plus Jesus], two supporting the third, and a cross was following them. The heads of the two reached up to the sky, while the head of the third, whom they led by the hand, reached beyond the skies. And they heard a voice from the skies that said, "Have you preached to those who sleep?" And an answer was heard from the cross, "Yes!" (10:2-4)

## THE GOSPEL OF THE HEBREWS

The most widely quoted of the three Jewish-Christian Gospels, the text of this work is still impossible to establish. No copies remain, and the early Christians who cited this or the two similar works (*Gospel of the Ebionites* and *Gospel of the Nazareans*) did not always specify their source, so that we cannot always be certain which of the three books is being used. Nevertheless, a total of nine passages ranging from one to seven lines in length have been identified as likely to derive from this work. It appears to have been written sometime in the early second century, and the brief snippets we have reveal some distinctive ideas. The mother of Jesus is identified as the archangel Michael, who took on the form of Mary:

When Christ wanted to come to earth, the Good Father summoned a mighty power in the heavens who was called Michael, and entrusted Christ to his care. The power came down into the world and it was called Mary, and Christ was in her womb for seven months. (1:1-2; paraphrased by Cyril of Jerusalem, fourth century)

On the other hand, the "holy spirit" is also identified as Jesus' mother in another verse, probably from the story of his temptation: "(Jesus said), 'Just now my mother, the holy spirit, took me by one of my hairs and brought me to Tabor, the great mountain'" (4a; quoted by Origen; third century).

# Sayings Gospels

### THE GOSPEL OF THOMAS

Generally considered to be the most significant of the apocryphal works, this collection of Jesus' sayings may contain some material as old as anything in the New Testament Gospels. Indeed, the historians who make up the Jesus Seminar regard it as more reliable historically than the canonical Gospel of John. Scholars had known of its existence for some time, since it is referred to by certain early church leaders, but no copy was thought to have survived. Then, in 1945, a complete manuscript was unearthed in the Egyptian city of Nag Hammadi. The text was written in Coptic, and was recognized to be a translation of a Greek document, some fragments of which had been found previously.

The *Gospel of Thomas* was probably written in Edessa in Syria, but its date is a subject of great controversy. Some scholars place it firmly in the first century, around the same time as the four canonical writings.[8] Others argue adamantly that it belongs to the second century.[9] This debate sometimes influences decisions made by historical scholars attempting to write modern biographies of Jesus. In any case, the book claims to be written by Didymus Judas Thomas, a twin brother of Jesus. Often regarded as harboring a gnostic orientation, it emphasizes wisdom motifs and the possibility of experiencing paradise here and now. The latter concept is tied to a radical asceticism which, for instance, demands total sexual abstinence on the part of Jesus' followers. The latter may be reflected in the following quote:

Jesus said to [his disciples], "When you make the two into one, and when you make the inner like the outer, and the upper like the lower, and when you make male and female into a single one, so that the male will not be male nor the female be female . . . then you will enter the Father's domain." (22:4-7)

### THE GOSPEL OF MARY

Attributed to Jesus' friend Mary Magdalene, this gnostic-tinged work is probably from the second century, though estimates vary as to whether to place it early or late in that period. The book is of interest primarily because it reflects the power struggles over efforts to restrict roles of women within the early church. Unfortunately, about half of the pages are missing from our manuscripts. What we still possess opens with a scene of Jesus teaching his disciples. Then he departs and conversation between the disciples continues, revealing that only Mary and Levi have understood the Master's words. Mary then recounts a vision she had and the private explanation of it that the Lord provided her. The others are offended by this:

> Peter said, "Has the Savior spoken secretly to a woman and not openly so that we would all hear? Surely he did not wish to indicate that she is more worthy than we are?" Then Mary wept and said to Peter, "Peter, my brother, what are you imagining about this? Do you think that I've made all this up secretly by myself or that I am telling lies about the Savior?" Levi said to Peter, "If the Savior considered her to be worthy, who are you to disregard her? For he knew her completely and loved her devotedly. . . . We should announce the good news as the Savior ordered and not be laying down rules or making laws. (10:3-13)

### THE APOCRYPHON OF JAMES

As with the Gospel of Thomas, the only complete manuscript of this work is a Coptic translation of what was supposedly an original Greek document. It, too, was discovered at Nag Hammadi in 1945. The original may have been produced as early as the first half of the second century. The book describes a discourse given to James and Peter by Jesus just before his ascension. The discourse itself is similar in form to an epistle, but it contains parables, prophecies, and wisdom sayings. A principal theme is martyrdom, which seems to be encouraged:

> [Jesus said], "Become seekers of death, therefore, like the dead who are seeking life, for what they seek is manifest to them. So what can be of concern to them? When you inquire into the subject of death, it will teach you about election. I swear to you, none will be saved who are afraid of death; for [God's] domain belongs to those who are dead." (5:3-5)

### DIALOGUE OF THE SAVIOR

This treatise may have been compiled as early as the beginning of the second century, but our only copy is an incomplete fourth-century Coptic translation, once again discovered among the Nag Hammadi documents in 1945. It presents a putative conversation between Jesus and three of his followers: Matthew, Judas, and Mary. It appears to incorporate material from at least four different sources and organize material in a way that is loosely related to baptism. Gnostic concern for the life of the human soul is evident, as is reflection on the present and future possibilities for salvation.

> Matthew said, "Lord, I wish to see that place of life . . . where there is no wickedness, but only pure light." The Lord said, "Brother Matthew, you will not be able to see it as long as you bear flesh." Matthew said, "Lord, even if I will not be able to see it, let me know it." The Lord said, "Those who have known themselves have seen it in everything that is given for them to do for themselves, and they have come to be it in their goodness."(14:1-4)

# ABBREVIATIONS

| | |
|---|---|
| AB | Anchor Bible |
| AnBib | Analecta biblica |
| *ANQ* | *Andover Newton Quarterly* |
| BbB | Bonner biblische Beiträge |
| BI | Biblical Institute |
| BIS | Biblical Interpretation Series |
| BU | Biblische Untersuchungen |
| BWANT | Beiträge zur Wissenschaft vom Alten und Neuen Testament |
| *CBQ* | *Catholic Biblical Quarterly* |
| CBQMS | Catholic Biblical Quarterly—Monograph Series |
| CC | Continental Commentaries |
| EH | Euoropäische Hochschulschriften |
| FB | Forschung zur Bibel |
| FF | Foundations and Facets |
| GBS | Guides to Biblical Scholarship |
| GNS | Good News Studies |
| HTS | Harvard Theological Studies |
| *Int* | *Interpretation* |
| IRT | Issues in Religion and Theology |
| *JBL* | *Journal of Biblical Literature* |
| JSNTSS | Journal for the Study of the New Testament—Supplement Series |
| CBI | Literary Currents in Biblical Interpretation |
| LTPM | Louvain Theological and Pastoral Monographs |
| LTT | Library of Theological Translations |
| NA | Neutestamentliche Abhandlungen |
| NovTSup | Novum Testamentum, Supplements |
| NTL | New Testament Library |
| *NTS* | *New Testament Studies* |
| NTT | New Testament Theology |
| OBO | Orbis biblicus et orientalis |
| OBS | Oxford Bible Series |
| OBT | Overtures to Biblical Theology |
| PC | Proclamation Commentaries |
| SANT | Studien zum Alten und Neuen Testament |
| SB | Stuttgarter Bibelstudien |
| SBEC | Studies in Bible and Early Christianity |
| SBLDS | Society of Biblical Literature Dissertation Series |
| SBM | Stuttgarter biblische Monographien |
| SemS | Semeia Studies |

| SNT | Studien zum Neuen Testament |
| SNTSDS | Society for New Testament Studies Dissertation Series |
| SNTSMS | Society for New Testament Studies Monograph Series |
| SNTSU | Studien zum Neuen Testament und seiner Umwelt |
| SNTW | Studies of the New Testament and Its World |
| SS | Symposium Series |
| StNeo | Studia neotestamentica |
| TI | Theological Inquiries |
| TST | Toronto Studies in Theology |
| WUNT | Wissenschaftliche Untersuchungen zum Neuen Testament |
| *WW* | *Word and World* |
| *ZNW* | *Zeitschrift für die neutestamentliche Wissenschaft* |
| ZS | Zacchaeus Studies |

# NOTES

### INTRODUCTION: FOUR STORIES OF JESUS

1. See *The Works of Josephus,* trans. W. Whiston (Peabody, Mass.: Hendrickson, 1987).

2. See, for example, Paul J. Achtemeier, ed., *Harper-Collins Bible Dictionary,* rev. ed. (San Francisco: HarperSanFrancisco, 1996), and David Noel Freedman, *Anchor Bible Dictionary,* 6 vols. (New York: Doubleday, 1992). The latter work is actually more like an encyclopedia than a dictionary.

3. John J. Rousseau and Rami Arav, *Jesus and His World* (Minneapolis: Fortress Press, 1995).

4. Theodore H. Gaster, *The Dead Sea Scriptures in English Translation,* 3d ed. (New York: Doubleday, 1976).

5. James M. Robinson, ed., *The Nag Hammadi Library in English,* rev. ed. (San Francisco: HarperSanFrancisco, 1990).

6. John H. Elliott, *What is Social-Scientific Criticism?* GBS (Minneapolis: Fortress Press, 1993).

7. David Rhoads, "Social Criticism: Crossing Boundaries," in *Mark and Method: New Approaches in Biblical Studies,* ed. J. C. Anderson and S. M. Moore (Minneapolis: Fortress Press, 1992), pp. 135–61, esp. pp. 137–38.

8. Howard Clark Kee, *Knowing the Truth: A Sociological Approach to New Testament Interpretation* (Minneapolis: Fortress Press, 1989).

9. Bruce J. Malina, *The New Testament World: Insights from Cultural Anthropology,* rev. ed. (Louisville: Westminster/John Knox Press, 1993).

10. E. P. Sanders, *Judaism: Practice and Belief 63* B.C.E.–*66* C.E. (London: SCM Press, 1992).

11. Bo Reicke, *The New Testament Era: The World of the Bible from 500* B.C. *to* A.D. *100,* trans. D. Green (Philadelphia: Fortress Press, 1964).

12. Christians have traditionally designated dates before the birth of Jesus as B.C. (Before Christ) and dates after that time as A.D. (*Anno Domini,* Latin for "the year of our Lord"). In academic circles, however, dates are usually designated as B.C.E. (Before the Common Era) or C.E. (Common Era).

13. See Ellis Rivkin, *What Crucified Jesus? The Political Execution of a Charismatic* (Nashville: Abingdon Press, 1984); and Gerard S. Sloyan, *The Crucifixion of Jesus: History, Myth, Faith* (Minneapolis: Fortress Press, 1995).

14. Eduard Lohse, *The New Testament Environment*, trans. J. Steely (Nashville: Abingdon Press, 1976); and Calvin J. Roetzel, *The World That Shaped the New Testament* (Atlanta: John Knox Press, 1985).

15. D. S. Russell, *Divine Disclosure: An Introduction to Jewish Apocalyptic* (Minneapolis: Fortress Press, 1992).

16. Pheme Perkins, *Gnosticism and the New Testament* (Minneapolis: Fortress Press, 1993).

17. Charles Talbert, *What Is a Gospel? The Genre of the Canonical Gospels* (Philadelphia: Fortress Press, 1977).

18. Jack Kingsbury calls them "kerygmatic stories" in *Jesus Christ in Matthew, Mark, and Luke*, PC (Philadelphia: Fortress Press, 1981), p. 96.

CHAPTER I. FROM JESUS TO US

1. The classic work on the first quest is Albert Schweitzer, *The Quest of the Historical Jesus*, trans. W. Montgomery (New York: Macmillan, 1966; German original, 1906); a good sample of the second is Günther Bornkamm, *Jesus of Nazareth*, trans. I. and F. McLuskey (New York: Harper & Row, 1960); surveys of the recent quest (so far) include Ben Witherington III, *The Jesus Quest: The Third Search for the Jew of Nazareth* (Downer's Grove, Ill.: InterVarsity Press, 1995); and (forthcoming) Mark Allan Powell, *Jesus as a Figure in History* (Louisville: Westminster/John Knox Press).

2. Results of the Jesus Seminar's sessions are published in *The Five Gospels: The Search for the Authentic Words of Jesus* (New York: Macmillan, 1993); and (forthcoming) *The Acts of Jesus* (New York: Macmillan).

3. Stephen L. Harris lists eight criteria proposed by Norman L. Perrin for determining which sayings are most likely authentic: (1) orality (strikingly memorable, to be retained in an oral culture); (2) form (aphorisms and parables, not long discourses); (3) distinctiveness (peculiar or outrageous quality); (4) dissimilarity (with regard to both Judaism and the early Christian church); (5) multiple attestation (from different sources); (6) coherence (consistent with what is established by above criteria); (7) awkwardness (potentially embarrassing to the church); and (8) linguistic and environmental evidence (free of anachronism). See *The New Testament: A Student's Introduction*, 2d ed. (Mountain View, Calif.: Mayfield Publishing Co., 1995).

4. The terminology derives from the seminal work of B. H. Streeter, *The Four Gospels: A Study of Christian Origins* (New York: Macmillan, 1926). Although Streeter's view that M and L were actual documents has not fared well, his book is otherwise regarded as the classic statement of this position.

5. See Richard Edwards, *A Theology of Q: Eschatology, Prophecy, and Wisdom* (Philadelphia: Fortress Press, 1976); and Christopher M. Tuckett, *Q and the History of Earliest Christianity: Studies on Q* (Edinburgh: T. & T. Clark, 1996).

6. The classic statement of this position is contained in William R. Farmer, *The Synoptic Problem: A Form-Critical Analysis* (New York: Macmillan, 1964).

7. Griesbach was also the person who coined the term *Synoptics* to refer to these Gospels. His work is summarized in Werner Georg Kümmel, *The New Testament: The History of the Investigation of Its Problems,* trans. S. M. Gilmour and H. C. Kee (Nashville: Abingdon Press, 1972).

8. Here, three fundamental works form the basis for everything that has come after: Rudolf Bultmann, *The History of the Synoptic Tradition,* trans. J. Marsh (New York: Harper & Row, 1963; German original, 1921); Martin Dibelius, *From Tradition to Gospel,* trans. B. Woolf (New York: Charles Scribner's Sons, 1934; German original, 1919); and Vincent Taylor, *The Formation of the Gospel Tradition,* 2d ed. (London: Macmillan, 1935).

9. A useful guide to typical forms in the Gospels and other New Testament literature is James L. Bailey and Lyle D. Vander Broek, *Literary Forms in the New Testament: A Handbook* (Louisville: Westminster/John Knox Press, 1992).

10. The distinction between emendation analysis and composition analysis seems to have been drawn first by Ernst Haenchen, *Der Weg Jesus* (Berlin: Töppelmann, 1966).

11. On the making of ancient books, see Bruce M. Metzger, *The Text of the New Testament: Its Transmission, Corruption, and Restoration,* 3d ed. (New York: Oxford University Press, 1992), pp. 3–35.

12. Ibid., pp. 6, 247.

13. Metzger (*Text,* pp. 186–206) classifies errors as unintentional or intentional changes. The former category includes errors arising from faulty eyesight, hearing, memory, or judgment. The latter includes changes involving spelling and grammar; harmonistic corruption; addition of natural complements or adjuncts; clearing up of historical or geographical difficulties; and addition of miscellaneous details.

14. The essential volumes for this discipline are Metzger, *Text,* and Kurt Aland and Barbara Aland, *The Text of the New Testament,* rev. ed. (Grand Rapids: Eerdmans, 1989).

15. This phenomenon of similar endings occurs often enough to have been accorded its own technical term, the rather scary word *homoioteleuton.* An apparent bane of copyists, it was a frequent cause of error.

16. This maxim was first stated by Johann Albrecht Bengel (1687–1752), whom the Alands say "is due the laurel of the eighteenth century" (*Text,* p. 11).

17. This principle was first formulated by J. J. Griesbach (1745–1812), whom we have met previously (see above, n. 7). Numerous exceptions to the rule are noted, in cases where omissions are explicable.

18. The Greek text most widely used today is published in two editions: *The Greek New Testament,* 4th ed. (Stuttgart: United Bible Societies, 1993); and *Novum Testamentum Graece,* 27th ed. (Stuttgart: Deutsche Bibelgesellschaft, 1993). For convenience, these are respectively referred to as the UBS and Nestle-Aland editions, after their publisher and editors.

19. For a review of most versions up to 1982, see Sakae Kubo and Walter F. Specht, *So Many Versions?* rev. ed. (Grand Rapids: Zondervan, 1983).

20. The name Vulgate is usually applied to what was actually a revision of older Latin translations undertaken by St. Jerome at the instigation of Pope Damascus around 382 C.E.

21. The most significant English translation prior to that of Tyndale was the translation of the entire Bible from the Vulgate produced by John Wycliffe in 1382. Wycliffe viewed the accessibility of Scriptures as instrumental to the task of reforming the church. Like Tyndale, he was condemned as a heretic.

22. In 1982, some publishers came out with editions of a Bible called the New King James Version. This version was essentially the same as the KJV, but with modern vocabulary substituted for archaic and obscure words. For example, "ye" was replaced with "you," "dost" with "did," and so on. Still, the NKJV is no more accurate than the old KJV, since the numerous text-critical errors in the latter were not corrected.

23. Capt. J. Roger's paraphrase of the 23rd Psalm and Clarence J. Jordan's version of 1 Corinthians are cited in Kubo and Specht, *So Many Versions?* (p. 21) and discussed in John Beekman and John Callow, *Translating the Word of God* (Grand Rapids: Zondervan, 1974). Jordan's piece was published in Clarence Jordan, *The Cotton Patch Version of Paul's Epistles* (New York: Association Press, 1968).

24. See J. B. Phillips, *The New Testament in Modern English* (New York: Macmillan, 1958; rev. ed., 1973); and Ken Taylor, *The Living Bible, Paraphrased* (Wheaton, Ill.: Tyndale House, 1971).

25. See Kubo and Specht, pp. 80–81, 242. Phillips produced his less-free second edition precisely because the work he had intended for devotional reading was being used in study groups. Similarly, the NLT was produced by a team of evangelical scholars to provide a work in the spirit of the Living Bible that would stick closer to the original sense.

26. This version is not a distinct translation, but a special emended edition of the NRSV. See *The New Testament and Psalms: An Inclusive Version* (New York: Oxford University Press, 1995).

27. Ulrich Luz, *Matthew 1–7: A Commentary,* CC (Minneapolis: Augsburg, 1989), pp. 95–99.

28. See Mark Allan Powell, *What Is Narrative Criticism?* GBS (Minneapolis: Fortress Press, 1990).

29. Graham N. Stanton, *The Gospels and Jesus,* OBS (Oxford: Oxford University Press, 1989), p. 41.

30. See Robert M. Fowler, *Let the Reader Understand: Reader-Response Criticism and the Gospel of Mark* (Minneapolis: Fortress Press, 1991).

31. An excellent survey is found in Janice Capel Anderson, "Feminist Criticism: The Dancing Daughter," in *Mark and Method,* ed. Janice Capel Anderson and Ste-

phen D. Moore (Minneapolis: Fortress Press, 1992), pp. 103–34. This volume also contains useful surveys and examples of narrative, reader-response, deconstructive, and social criticism. On feminist criticism, see further Elisabeth Schüssler Fiorenza, ed., *Searching the Scriptures*, 2 vols. (New York: Crossroad, 1993–94).

32. Many feminist scholars appeal to this concept as it is developed in a work by a nonbiblical scholar, Judith Fetterley, *The Resisting Reader: A Feminist Approach to American Fiction* (Bloomington: Indiana University Press, 1978).

33. This term was coined by Alice Walker in *In Search of Our Mother's Gardens* (New York: Harcourt Brace Jovanovich, 1974).

34. To cite only examples of studies on the Gospel of Mark, see Fernando Belo, *A Materialist Reading of the Gospel of Mark* (Maryknoll, N.Y.: Orbis Books, 1981); Diarmuid McGann, *The Journeying Self: The Gospel of Mark through a Jungian Perspective* (New York: Paulist Press, 1985); John P. Keenan, *The Gospel of Mark: A Mahāyāna Reading* (Maryknoll, N.Y.: Orbis Books, 1995); and José Cádenas Pallares, *A Poor Man Called Jesus: Reflections on the Gospel of Mark* (Maryknoll, N.Y.: Orbis Books, 1986).

35. See A. K. M. Adam, *What Is Postmodern Biblical Criticism?* GBS (Minneapolis: Fortress Press, 1995).

CHAPTER 2. THE GOSPEL OF MARK

1. Notably, Robert H. Gundry, *Mark: A Commentary on His Apology for the Cross* (Grand Rapids: Eerdmans, 1993), pp. 1012–21.

2. Powell, *What Is Narrative Criticism?* p. 43.

3. J. Lee Magness, *Sense and Absence: Structure and Suspension in the Ending of Mark's Gospel,* SemS (Atlanta: Scholars Press, 1986).

4. For a brief summary and a bibliography regarding these sources, see Frank J. Matera, *What Are They Saying about Mark?* (New York: Paulist Press, 1987), pp. 58–62.

5. Burton Mack argues that Mark exercised a considerable amount of creativity in the composition of his Gospel, with little concern for or reliance on historical sources. See *A Myth of Innocence: Mark and Christian Origins* (Philadelphia: Fortress Press, 1988).

6. One recent study on the "little apocalypse" chapter of Mark 13 holds that the concern is epistemological—Mark is more concerned with teaching his readers *how* to know than *what* to know. See Timothy J. Geddert, *Watchwords: Mark 13 in Markan Eschatology,* JSNTSS 26 (Sheffield: Sheffield Academic Press, 1989).

7. Perhaps the best volume on Jesus as a teacher/philosopher in Mark is Vernon K. Robbins, *Jesus the Teacher: A Socio-rhetorical Interpretation of Mark* (Philadelphia: Fortress Press, 1984).

8. For a recent study, see Edwin H. Broadhead, *Teaching with Authority: Miracles and Christology in the Gospel of Mark,* JSNTSS 74 (Sheffield: Sheffield Academic Press, 1992).

9. Studies on the Markan passion narrative include Edwin K. Broadhead, *Prophet, Son, Messiah: Narrative Form and Function in Mark 14–16,* JSNTSS 97 (Sheffield: Sheffield Academic Press, 1994); John R. Donahue, *Are You the Christ? The Trial Narrative in the Gospel of Mark,* SBLDS 10 (Missoula, Mont.: Society of Biblical Literature, 1973); Werner H. Kelber, *The Passion in Mark: Studies on Mark 14–16* (Philadelphia: Fortress Press, 1976); and Frank J. Matera, *The Kingship of Jesus: Composition and Theology in Mark 15,* SBLDS 66 (Chico, Calif.: Scholars Press, 1982).

10. Martin Kähler, *The So-Called Historical Jesus and the Historic Biblical Christ,* trans. Carl E. Braaten (Philadelphia: Fortress Press, 1964), p. 80. The German original was published in 1892.

11. John C. Meagher, *Clumsy Construction in Mark's Gospel: A Critique of Form and Redaktionsgeschichte,* TST 3 (New York: Mellen, 1979).

12. Other devices include the use of concentric or chiastic patterns. See Joanna Dewey, *Markan Public Debate: Literary Technique, Concentric Structure, and Theology in Mark 2:1 — 3:6* (Chico, Calif.: Scholars Press, 1980); and Benoit Standaert, *L'Évangile selon Marc: Composition et Genre Litteraire* (Paris: Les Editions du Cerf, 1983).

13. Keith F. Nickle, *The Synoptic Gospels: An Introduction* (Atlanta: John Knox Press, 1980), p. 60.

14. David Rhoads and Donald Michie, *Mark as Story* (Philadelphia: Fortress Press, 1982), pp. 47–49; and Frans Neirynck, *Duality in Mark: Contributions to the Study of the Markan Redaction* (Louvain: Leuven University Press, 1972).

15. William Telford, *The Barren Temple and the Withered Tree,* JSNTSS 1 (Sheffield: Sheffield Academic Press, 1980).

16. See the recent study on the parables of Mark 4 by Joel Marcus, *The Mystery of the Kingdom of God,* SBLDS 90 (Atlanta: Scholars Press, 1986).

17. An exhaustive study of the traditions connected to Markan authorship is found in C. Clifton Black, *Mark: Images of an Apostolic Interpreter* (Columbia: University of South Carolina Press, 1994).

18. Eusebius, *The History of the Church from Christ to Constantine,* trans. G. A. Williamson (New York: Penguin Books, 1965), p. 152 (bk. 3, par. 39). For a list of other patristic evidence that associates this Gospel with Peter, see Vincent Taylor, *The Gospel according to Mark: The Greek Text with Introduction, Notes, and Indexes,* 2d ed. (New York: St. Martin's Press, 1966), pp. 1–8.

19. Kurt Niederwimmer, "Johannes Markus und die Frage nach dem Verfasser des zweiten Evangeliums," ZNW 58 (1967): 172–88. For a contrary argument, see Martin Hengel, *Studies in the Gospel of Mark* (Philadelphia: Fortress Press, 1985).

20. A prominent defender of this position is Hengel, *Studies in Mark.*

21. Willi Marxsen, *Mark the Evangelist: Studies on the Redaction History of the Gospel* (Nashville: Abingdon Press, 1969). Howard Clark Kee argues for Syria (north of Galilee) in *Community of the New Age: Studies in Mark's Gospel* (Philadelphia: Westminster Press, 1977).

22. On this point, for instance, Hengel (*Studies in Mark*) and Marxsen (*Mark the Evangelist*) agree.

23. S. G. F. Brandon, *Jesus and the Zealots: A Study of the Political Factor in Primitive Christianity* (Manchester: Manchester University Press, 1967); Werner Kelber, *The Kingdom in Mark: A New Place and a New Time* (Philadelphia: Fortress Press, 1974). Brandon favors Roman origin, and Kelber, Galilean.

24. Roger P. Booth, *Jesus and the Laws of Purity: Tradition History and Legal History in Mark 7,* JSNTSS 13 (Sheffield: JSOT Press, 1986).

25. Mary Ann Tolbert identifies the parable of the sower as "a plot synopsis" of the whole Gospel, with the four soils corresponding to four types of characters portrayed elsewhere in Mark's story. See *Sowing the Gospel: Mark's World in Literary-Historical Perspective* (Minneapolis: Fortress Press, 1989), pp. 127–75.

26. Benoit Standaert, *L'Évangile selon Marc.*

27. Justin Martyr, *1 Apology* 67.3.

28. For a sample of the vast literature on this topic see Bruce Chilton, ed., *The Kingdom of God in the Teaching of Jesus,* IRT 5 (Philadelphia: Fortress Press, 1984). On Markan references, see Aloysius M. Ambrozic, *The Hidden Kingdom: A Redaction-Critical Study of the References to the Kingdom of God in Mark's Gospel,* CBQMS 2 (Washington: Catholic Biblical Association of America, 1972).

29. Now available in English as *The Messianic Secret,* trans. J. C. Grieg, LTT (London: James Clarke, 1971).

30. James L. Blevins, *The Messianic Secret in Markan Research, 1901–1976* (Washington: University Press of America, 1981); and Christopher Tuckett, ed., *The Messianic Secret,* IRT 1 (Philadelphia: Fortress Press, 1983). For a more recent approach, see Heikki Räisänen, *The "Messianic Secret" in Mark's Gospel,* rev. ed., trans. C. Tuckett, SNTW (Edinburgh: T. & T. Clark, 1990).

31. Paul J. Achtemeier, "Gospel Miracle Tradition and the Divine Man," *Int* 26 (1972): 174–97. For a critique of this approach, see Otto Betz, "The Concept of the So-Called 'Divine Man' in Mark's Christology," in *Studies in New Testament and Early Christian Literature: Essays in Honor of Allen Wikgren,* ed. D. E. Aune (Leiden: Brill, 1972), pp. 229–40.

32. Theodore J. Weeden, *Mark: Traditions in Conflict* (Philadelphia: Fortress Press, 1971); Norman Perrin, *A Modern Pilgrimage in New Testament Christology* (Philadelphia: Fortress Press, 1974); and Paul J. Achtemeier, *Mark,* 2d ed., PC (Philadelphia: Fortress Press, 1986).

33. Morna D. Hooker, *The Son of Man in Mark* (Montreal: McGill University Press, 1967); and Barnabas Lindars, *Jesus Son of Man: A Fresh Examination of the Son of Man Sayings in the Gospels* (Grand Rapids: Eerdmans, 1983).

34. Four works are particularly important: Donald Juel, *Messiah and Temple: The Trial of Jesus in the Gospel of Mark,* SBLDS 31 (Missoula, Mont.: Scholars Press, 1977); Carl R. Kazmierski, *Jesus, the Son of God: A Study of the Markan Tradition and Its*

*Redaction by the Evangelist,* FB 33 (Würzburg: Echter Verlag, 1979); Jack Dean Kingsbury, *The Christology of Mark's Gospel* (Philadelphia: Fortress Press, 1983); and Hans-Jörg Steichele, *Der leidende Sohn Gottes: Eine Untersuchung einiger alttestamentlicher Motive in der Christologie des Markusevangeliums,* BU 14 (Regensburg: Friedrich Pustet, 1980).

35. Kingsbury, *Christology.*

36. Weeden, *Mark: Traditions in Conflict.*

37. Kelber, *Kingdom in Mark.*

38. Etienne Trocmé thinks the basic critique is ecclesiological: leadership in the community should not be limited to the original followers of Jesus. See *The Formation of the Gospel according to Mark* (Philadelphia: Westminster Press, 1975; French original, 1963).

39. Ernest Best, *Following Jesus: Discipleship in the Gospel of Mark,* JSNTSS 4 (Sheffield: University of Sheffield, 1981); C. Clifton Black, *The Disciples according to Mark: Markan Redaction in Current Debate,* JSNTSS 27 (Sheffield: Sheffield Academic Press, 1989); John R. Donahue, *The Theology and Setting of Discipleship in the Gospel of Mark* (Milwaukee: Marquette University, 1983); and Karl-Georg Reploh, *Markus-Lehrer der Gemeinde: Eine redaktionsgeschichtliche Studie zu den Jungerperikopen des Markus-Evangeliums,* SBM 9 (Stuttgart: Katholisches Bibelwerk, 1969).

40. The tension between Mark's apparent insistence on faith and tolerance of disbelief is evident in the comparison of two works: Christopher D. Marshall, *Faith as a Theme in Mark's Narrative* (Cambridge: Cambridge University Press, 1989); and Mary R. Thompson, *The Role of Disbelief in Mark: A New Approach to the Second Gospel* (New York: Paulist Press, 1989).

41. This is the view of Best, *Following Jesus.*

42. Robert C. Tannehill, "The Disciples in Mark: The Function of a Narrative Role," in *The Interpretation of Mark,* ed. William Telford (Philadelphia: Fortress Press, 1985), pp. 134–57.

CHAPTER 3. THE GOSPEL OF MATTHEW

1. See, for example, Stephenson H. Brooks, *Matthew's Community: The Evidence of His Special Sayings Source,* JSNTSS 16 (Sheffield: Sheffield Academic Press, 1987).

2. The Sermon on the Mount has become the subject of many books and commentaries in its own right. For a survey, see Warren Carter, *What Are They Saying about Matthew's Sermon on the Mount?* (New York: Paulist Press, 1994).

3. Dorothy Jean Weaver, *Matthew's Missionary Discourse: A Literary-Critical Analysis,* JSNTSS 38 (Sheffield: Sheffield Academic Press, 1990).

4. Jack Dean Kingsbury, *The Parables of Jesus in Matthew 13: A Study in Redaction Criticism* (Richmond: John Knox Press, 1969).

5. Wilhelm Pesch, *Matthäus der Seelsorger: Das neue Verständnis der Evangelien dargestellet am Beispiel von Matthäus 18,* SB 2 (Stuttgart: Katholisches Bibelwerk, 1966);

and William G. Thompson, *Matthew's Advice to a Divided Community: Mt. 17,22—18,35,* AnBib 44 (Rome: Biblical Institute, 1970).

6. Fred W. Burnett, *The Testament of Jesus-Sophia: A Redaction-Critical Study of the Eschatological Discourse in Matthew* (Washington: University Press of America, 1981).

7. Though nominally an Anglican, Jefferson actually espoused Deism, distinguishing between Jesus himself and "the charlatanism and superstition" that marked the religion erected in his name. He was especially hard on the apostle Paul (whom Jefferson called "the first great corrupter"), and on belief in sacraments, miracles, or anything else that smacked of the supernatural. See Edwin S. Gaustad, *Sworn on the Altar of God: A Religious Biography of Thomas Jefferson* (Grand Rapids: Eerdmans, 1996).

8. Benjamin W. Bacon, *Studies in Matthew* (London: Constable, 1930).

9. The idea is developed further theologically by Dale C. Allison, Jr., in *The New Moses: A Matthean Typology* (Minneapolis: Fortress Press, 1993).

10. Jack Dean Kingsbury, *Matthew: Structure, Christology, Kingdom* (Philadelphia: Fortress Press, 1975); and idem, *Matthew as Story,* 2d ed. (Philadelphia: Fortress Press, 1988).

11. Other structural outlines for Matthew have also been proposed. For a summary, see David R. Bauer, *The Structure of Matthew's Gospel: A Study in Literary Design,* JSNTSS 31 (Sheffield: Almond Press, 1989).

12. Bauer (*Structure*) offers a list of fifteen patterns not discussed here. Chiastic arrangements have held special interest for many scholars. See Peter F. Ellis, *Matthew: His Mind and His Message* (Collegeville, Minn.: Liturgical Press, 1974); and John P. Heil, *The Death and Resurrection of Jesus: A Narrative-Critical Reading of Matthew 26–28* (Minneapolis: Fortress Press, 1991).

13. See also Janice Capel Anderson, *Matthew's Narrative Web: Over and Over and Over Again,* JSNTSS 91 (Sheffield: Sheffield Academic Press, 1994).

14. For this reason, perhaps, studies on Peter have tended to be polemical or apologetic. A helpful ecumenical study is found in R. Brown, K. Donfried, and J. Reumann, eds., *Peter in the New Testament: A Collaborative Assessment by Protestant and Roman Catholic Scholars* (Minneapolis: Augsburg; New York: Paulist, 1973).

15. Two studies of Matthew's ecclesiology are Hubert Frankemölle's *Jahwebund und Kirche Christi,* NA 10 (Münster: Aschendorff, 1974); and Michael H. Crosby, *House of Disciples: Church, Economics, and Justice in Matthew* (Maryknoll, N.Y.: Orbis Books, 1988). The former grounds the concept in Old Testament covenant theology, while the latter focuses on the impact of Greco-Roman household communities.

16. At least one influential study holds that the Jewish opponents of Jesus in Matthew serve primarily as foils for addressing problems in leadership in the Christian church. See David E. Garland, *The Intention of Matthew 23,* NovTSup 52 (Leiden: Brill, 1979).

17. On this hotly debated topic, see Robert Banks, *Jesus and the Law in Synoptic Tradition,* SNTSMS 28 (Cambridge: Cambridge University Press, 1975); Gerhard

Barth, "Matthew's Understanding of the Law," in *Tradition and Interpretation in Matthew,* ed. G. Bornkamm, G. Barth, and H. J. Held, trans. P. Scott, NTL (Philadelphia: Westminster Press, 1963), pp. 58–164; John P. Meier, *Law and History in Matthew: A Redactional Study of Mt. 5:17-48,* AnBib 71 (Rome: Biblical Institute, 1976); and Alexander Sand, *Das Gesetz und die Propheten: Untersuchungen zur Theologie des Evangeliums nach Matthäus,* BU 11 (Regensburg: Friedrich Pustet, 1974). For a summary, see Donald Senior, *What Are They Saying about Matthew?* rev. ed. (New York: Paulist Press, 1996), pp. 62–73.

18. Matthew's use of the Old Testament and his understanding of what constitutes fulfillment have generated almost as much controversy as the question of his attitude toward the law. See Robert H. Gundry, *The Use of the Old Testament in St. Matthew's Gospel with Special Reference to the Messianic Hope,* NovTSup 18 (Leiden: Brill, 1967); G. D. Kilpatrick, *The Origins of the Gospel according to St. Matthew* (Oxford: Clarendon, 1946); Wilhelm Rothfuchs, *Die Erfüllungszitate des Matthäus-Evangeliums: Eine biblisch-theologische Untersuchung,* BWANT 8 (Stuttgart: W. Kohlhammer, 1969); and Krister Stendahl, *The School of St. Matthew and Its Use of the Old Testament* (Philadelphia: Fortress Press, 1968). For a summary, see Senior, *What Are They Saying about Matthew?* pp. 51–61.

19. The apocalyptic flavor of Matthew is just beginning to receive new appreciation in recent dissertations, not yet published, by Jeffrey Gibbs and Kathleen Weber. See also David E. Orton, *The Understanding Scribe: Matthew and the Apocalyptic Ideal,* JSNTSS 25 (Sheffield: Sheffield Academic Press, 1989); and David C. Sim, *Apocalyptic Eschatology in the Gospel of Matthew,* SNTSMS 88 (Cambridge: Cambridge University Press, 1996).

20. The theme is key to Frankemölle's *Jahwebund,* and is foundational to Mark Allan Powell, *God with Us: A Pastoral Theology of Matthew's Gospel* (Minneapolis: Fortress Press, 1995).

21. Eusebius, *History,* p. 152 (bk. 3, par. 39).

22. This is essentially the view of Robert H. Gundry, which informs his *Matthew: A Commentary on His Handbook for a Mixed Church Under Persecution,* 2d ed. (Grand Rapids: Eerdmans, 1994).

23. Notable exceptions include John Meier, *The Vision of Matthew: Christ, Church, and Morality in the First Gospel,* TI (New York: Paulist Press, 1979); Poul Nepper-Christensen, *Das Matthäusevangelium: Ein judenchristliches Evangelium?* (Århus: Universitetsforlaget, 1958); and Sjef Van Tilborg, *The Jewish Leaders in Matthew* (Leiden: Brill, 1972).

24. M. D. Goulder places Matthew in a rabbinic tradition similar to that of Hillel and Shammai. O. Lamar Cope avoids the historical identification but sees Matthew and his community as advocating a theological approach similar to that of rabbinic scribes. David E. Orton prefers the model of "apocalyptic scribes" such as those responsible for Daniel and certain Qumran writings. See Goulder, *Midrash and Lection in Matthew* (London: SPCK, 1974); Cope, *Matthew: A Scribe Trained for the Kingdom*

*of Heaven,* CBQMS 5 (Washington: Catholic Biblical Association of America, 1976); and Orton.

25. Reinhart Hummel, *Die Auseinandersetzung zwischen Kirche und Judentum im Matthäusevangelium* (Munich: Kaiser Verlag, 1963); J. Andrew Overman, *Matthew's Gospel and Formative Judaism: The Social World of the Matthean Community* (Minneapolis: Fortress Press, 1990); and Anthony J. Saldarini, *Matthew's Christian-Jewish Community* (Chicago: University of Chicago Press, 1994). This is also the general inclination of essays collected in David Balch, ed., *Social History of the Matthean Community: Cross-Disciplinary Approaches* (Minneapolis: Fortress Press, 1991).

26. Saldarini, *Matthew's Christian-Jewish Community.*

27. W. D. Davies, *The Setting of the Sermon on the Mount* (Cambridge: Cambridge University Press, 1966); Douglas Hare, *The Theme of Jewish Persecution of Christians in the Gospel According to St. Matthew,* SNTSMS 6 (Cambridge: Cambridge University Press, 1967); and Georg Strecker, *Der Weg der Gerechtigkeit: Untersuchung zur Theologie des Matthäus,* 2d ed. (Göttingen: Vandenhoeck & Ruprecht, 1966).

28. Davies (*Setting*) sees the immediate occasion for the Gospel as the addition of a famous eighteenth benediction to the liturgical prayers said in Jewish synagogues, condemning Christians as heretics.

29. Graham N. Stanton, *A Gospel for a New People: Studies in Matthew* (Edinburgh: T. & T. Clark, 1992).

30. Amy-Jill Levine, *The Social and Ethnic Dimensions of Matthean Social History,* SBEC 14 (Lewiston, N.Y.: Mellen Press, 1988).

31. Saldarini, *Matthew's Christian-Jewish Community.*

32. Jack Dean Kingsbury, *Matthew,* 2d ed., PC (Philadelphia: Fortress Press, 1981), pp. 99–100.

33. John P. Meier, "Antioch," in *Antioch and Rome: New Testament Cradles of Catholic Christianity,* by R. Brown and J. Meier (New York: Paulist Press, 1983), pp. 11–86.

34. Gundry (*Matthew*) accepts Matthean use of Mark but still dates the Gospel prior to 70 C.E.

35. See Kingsbury, *Matthew,* PC, pp. 93–107.

36. Davies, *Setting.*

37. Powell, *God with Us,* pp. 28–61.

38. One theory that has been advanced is that the Matthean divinization of Jesus is modeled after the personification of wisdom in the Old Testament. See M. Jack Suggs, *Wisdom, Christology, and Law in Matthew's Gospel* (Cambridge: Harvard University Press, 1970); Burnett, *Testament of Jesus-Sophia;* and Celia Deutsch, *Hidden Wisdom and the Easy Yoke: Wisdom, Torah, and Disciples in Matthew 11:25, 30,* JSNTSS 18 (Sheffield: Sheffield Academic Press, 1987).

39. On this interpretation, see Stanton, *Gospel for a New People,* pp. 207–31. For a contrary view, see Ulrich Luz, "The Final Judgment (Matt 25:31-46): An Exercise in

'History of Influence' Exegesis," in *Treasures New and Old: Contributions to Matthean Studies*, ed. David R. Bauer and Mark Allan Powell, SS (Atlanta: Scholars Press, 1996), pp. 271–310.

40. Meier, *Vision of Matthew*. See also Rolf Walker, *Die Heilsgeschichte im ersten Evangelium* (Göttingen: Vandenhoeck & Ruprecht, 1967).

41. Kingsbury, *Matthew: Structure, Christology, Kingdom*, pp. 25–39.

42. Frankemölle (*Jahwebund*) believes Matthew understands the relationship between the church and its risen Lord as analogous to that between Israel and Yahweh in Old Testament theology, articulated by the Deuteronomist and the Chronicler.

43. Powell, *God with Us*, p. 21 n. 36. A more detailed study, *Binding and Loosing*, is forthcoming.

44. See Klyne Snodgrass, "Matthew and the Law," in Bauer and Powell, *Treasures New and Old*, pp. 99–127.

45. Studies on Matthew's concept of discipleship include Michael J. Wilkins, *The Concept of Disciple in Matthew's Gospel as Reflected in the Use of the Term "Mathētēs,"* NovTSup 59 (Leiden: Brill, 1988); and Jean Zumstein, *La Condition du Croyant dans L'Évangile selon Matthieu*, OBO 16 (Göttingen: Vandenhoeck & Ruprecht, 1977).

CHAPTER 4. THE GOSPEL OF LUKE

1. Geoffrey F. Nuttall, *The Moment of Recognition: Luke as Story-Teller* (London: The University of London Athlone, 1978). John Drury likens Luke's style to midrash in *Tradition and Design in Luke's Gospel. A Study in Early Christian Historiography* (London: Darton, Longman, and Todd, 1976).

2. Michael D. Goulder, who does not accept the Q hypothesis, has suggested a completely different scheme wherein Luke uses Mark and Matthew to compose a Gospel structured for calendrical lectionary reading. See *Luke: A New Paradigm*, 2 vols., JSNTSS 20 (Sheffield: Sheffield Academic Press, 1989).

3. On this section, see Helmuth L. Egelkraut, *Jesus' Mission to Jerusalem: A Redaction-Critical Study of the Travel Narrative in the Gospel of Luke, Luke 9:51—19:48*, EH (Frankfurt: Peter Lang, 1976); and David P. Moessner, *Lord of the Banquet: The Literary and Theological Significance of the Lukan Travel Narrative* (Minneapolis: Fortress Press, 1989).

4. On these two chapters, see especially Raymond E. Brown, *The Birth of the Messiah: A Commentary on the Infancy Narratives in Matthew and Luke* (Garden City, N.Y.: Doubleday, 1979).

5. On these, see Stephen Farris, *The Hymns of Luke's Infancy Narratives: Their Origin, Meaning, and Significance*, JSNTSS 9 (Sheffield: JSOT Press, 1985).

6. So Hans Conzelmann, *The Theology of St. Luke*, 2d ed., trans. G. Buswell (Philadelphia: Fortress Press, 1982; German original, 1957).

7. So Robert H. Tannehill, *The Gospel according to Luke*, vol. 1 of *The Narrative Unity of Luke-Acts: A Literary Interpretation*, FF (Philadelphia: Fortress Press, 1986).

8. The scholar most responsible for discerning these parallels is Charles H. Talbert. See his *Literary Patterns, Theological Themes, and the Genre of Luke-Acts* (Missoula, Mont.: Scholars Press, 1974).

9. The nature of the unity between the two works is questioned in Mikeal C. Parsons and Richard I. Pervo, *Rethinking the Unity of Luke and Acts* (Minneapolis: Fortress Press, 1993). The argument is reviewed in Mark Allan Powell, *What Are They Saying about Acts?* (New York: Paulist Press, 1991).

10. Robert J. Karris, *Luke, Artist and Theologian: Luke's Passion Account as Literature*, TI (New York: Paulist Press, 1985), pp. 47–78.

11. The attitude toward rich and poor in this Gospel has been investigated from numerous perspectives with varying results. See Hans Degenhardt, *Lukas, Evangelist der Armen. Besitz und Besitzverzicht in den lukanischen Schriften* (Stuttgart: Katholisches Bibelwerk, 1965); Luke T. Johnson, *The Literary Function of Possessions in Luke-Acts*, SBLDS 39 (Missoula, Mont.: Scholars Press, 1977); Halvor Moxnes, *The Economy of the Kingdom: Social Conflict and Economic Relations in Luke's Gospel*, OBT (Philadelphia: Fortress Press, 1988); Walter Pilgrim, *Good News to the Poor: Wealth and Poverty in Luke-Acts* (Minneapolis: Augsburg, 1981); and David Seccombe, *Possessions and the Poor in Luke-Acts*, SNTSU (Linz: A. Fuchs, 1982).

12. A recent study on one aspect of "the excluded" theme is David A. Neale's *None but the Sinners: Religious Categories in Luke*, JSNTSS 58 (Sheffield: Sheffield Academic Press, 1991).

13. Jane Schaberg, for instance, calls Luke "an extremely dangerous text, perhaps the most dangerous in the Bible." See "Luke," in *The Women's Bible Commentary*, ed. Carol A. Newsom and Sharon H. Ringe (Louisville: Westminster/John Knox Press, 1992), pp. 275–92. Barbara Reid finds liberating potential in Luke's stories of women, though she recognizes it is sometimes necessary to "unravel patriarchal underpinnings of the text" or read "against Luke's intent" to do this. See *Choosing the Better Part? Women in the Gospel of Luke* (Collegeville, Minn.: Liturgical Press, 1996). For a sample of other views (some more positive), see Mark Allan Powell, *What Are They Saying about Luke?* (New York: Paulist Press, 1989), pp. 93–97.

14. William H. Shepherd, Jr., *The Narrative Function of the Holy Spirit as a Character in Luke-Acts*, SBLDS 147 (Atlanta: Scholars Press, 1994); and Roger Stronstad, *The Charismatic Theology of St. Luke* (Peabody, Mass.: Hendrickson, 1984).

15. Darrell Bock, *Proclamation from Prophecy and Pattern: Lucan Old Testament Christology*, JSNTSS 12 (Sheffield: Sheffield Academic Press, 1987); Craig A. Evans and James A. Sanders, *Luke and Scripture: The Function of Sacred Tradition in Luke-Acts* (Minneapolis: Fortress Press, 1993); Martin Rese, *Alttestamentliche Motive in der Christologie des Lukas*, SNT 1 (Gütersloh: Gütersloher Verlagshaus Gerd Mohn, 1969); and John T. Squires, *The Plan of God in Luke-Acts*, SNTSMS 76 (Cambridge: Cambridge University Press, 1993).

16.  Robert J. Karris, "Missionary Communities: A New Paradigm for the Study of Luke-Acts," *CBQ* 41 (1979): 80–97.

17.  Karris, *Luke, Artist and Theologian;* and Jerome Neyrey, *The Passion according to Luke: A Redaction Study of Luke's Soteriology,* TI (New York: Paulist Press, 1985). Two classic studies that try to find a midpoint between substitutionary and exemplary understandings of atonement in Luke are Gerhard Voss, *Die Christologie der Lukanischen Schriften in Grundzügen,* StNeo 2 (Brügge: Desclée de Brouwer, 1965); Gerhard Schneider, *Verleugnung, Verspottung, und Verhör Jesu Nach Lukas 22, 54-71,* SANT 22 (Munich: Kösel, 1969).

18.  For a brief summary and bibliography on this part of the argument, see Powell, *What Are They Saying about Acts?* pp. 32–37.

19.  The classic statement of this view is Philipp Vielhauer, "On the 'Paulinism' of Acts," trans. W. C. Robinson and V. P. Furnish, now found in L. Keck and J. Martyn, eds. *Studies in Luke-Acts* (Philadelphia: Fortress Press, 1980), pp. 33–50 (German original, 1950).

20.  Joseph A. Fitzmyer, "The Authorship of Luke-Acts Reconsidered," in *Luke the Theologian: Aspects of His Teaching* (New York: Paulist Press, 1989), pp. 1–26.

21.  One strong supporter of Jewish authorship for Luke-Acts is Jakob Jervell, *Luke and the People of God* (Minneapolis: Augsburg, 1972).

22.  Henry J. Cadbury, *Style and Literary Method of Luke,* HTS 6 (Cambridge: Cambridge University Press, 1920), pp. 39–72. Cadbury's most influential work was *The Making of Luke-Acts* (London: SPCK, 1958).

23.  I. Howard Marshall, *Luke: Historian and Theologian* (Grand Rapids: Zondervan, 1970).

24.  This motive provides the premise for Conzelmann's impressive synthesis (*Theology of St. Luke*). It is challenged by John T. Carroll, *Response to the End of History: Eschatology and Situation in Luke-Acts,* SBLDS 92 (Atlanta: Scholars Press, 1988); and A. J. Mattill, *Luke and the Last Things: A Perspective for the Understanding of Lukan Thought* (Dillsboro, N.C.: Western North Carolina Press, 1979).

25.  Views on this topic vary broadly. See Robert L. Brawley, *Luke-Acts and the Jews: Conflict, Apology, and Conciliation,* SBLMS 33 (Atlanta: Scholars Press, 1987); Robert L. Maddox, *The Purpose of Luke-Acts,* SNTW (Edinburgh: T. & T. Clark, 1985); David Ravens, *Luke and the Restoration of Israel,* JSNTSS 119 (Sheffield: Sheffield Academic Press, 1995); Jack Sanders, *The Jews in Luke-Acts* (Philadelphia: Fortress Press, 1987); Joseph Tyson, ed., *Luke-Acts and the Jewish People: Eight Critical Perspectives* (Minneapolis: Augsburg, 1988); Stephen G. Wilson, *The Gentiles and the Gentile Mission,* SNTSMS 23 (Cambridge: Cambridge University Press, 1973); and idem, *Luke and the Law,* SNTSMS 50 (Cambridge: Cambridge University Press, 1983).

26.  Charles H. Talbert, *Luke and the Gnostics: An Examination of the Lucan Purpose* (Nashville: Abingdon Press, 1966).

27.  So, Cadbury, *Making of Luke-Acts,* pp. 299–316; and Conzelmann (*Theology of St. Luke*). This thesis is opposed rather vigorously by Richard J. Cassidy in *Jesus,*

*Politics, and Society: A Study of Luke's Gospel* (Maryknoll, N.Y.: Orbis Books, 1978). On related political issues in Luke, see Powell, *What Are They Saying about Luke?* pp. 82–102.

28.  Philip Esler and David Tiede develop different models according to which they believe Luke addressed identity crises brought on by the social upheavals of his day. See Esler, *Community and Gospel in Luke-Acts* (Cambridge: Cambridge University Press, 1987); and Tiede, *Prophecy and History in Luke-Acts* (Philadelphia: Fortress Press, 1980).

29.  A recent study attempts to find coherence in Luke's portrait of Jesus as the Lord who humbles himself to serve, in a way analogous to that presented in the hymn in Philippians 2:5-11. See H. Douglas Buckwalter, *The Character and Purpose of Luke's Christology,* SNTSMS 89 (Cambridge: Cambridge University Press, 1996).

30.  Mark L. Strauss, *The Davidic Messiah in Luke-Acts: The Promise and Its Fulfillment in Lukan Christology,* JSNTSS 110 (Sheffield: Sheffield Academic Press, 1995).

31.  Lindars, *Jesus Son of Man,* pp. 132–44.

32.  Paul S. Minear, *To Heal and to Reveal: The Prophetic Vocation according to Luke* (New York: Seabury Press, 1976), pp. 102–21.

33.  Frederick W. Danker, *Luke,* 2d ed., PC (Philadelphia: Fortress Press, 1987), pp. 67–71.

34.  Talbert, *Literary Patterns,* pp. 125–41.

35.  Charles Talbert, "The Concept of Immortals in Mediterranean Antiquity," *JBL* 94 (1975): 419–36.

36.  Danker, *Luke,* pp. 28–46.

37.  See Anton Wessels, *Images of Jesus: How Jesus Is Perceived and Portrayed in Non-European Cultures* (Grand Rapids: Eerdmans, 1986).

38.  Thus, scholars like Helmuth Flender and Eric Franklin regard the ascension rather than the parousia as the definitive eschatological event for Luke: salvation typically associated with the last days is available now. Hans Bartsch disagrees, arguing that Luke wants to arouse those who are content with this world to hope for the next. Flender, *St. Luke: Theologian of Redemptive History,* trans. R. and I. Fuller (Philadelphia: Fortress Press, 1967); Franklin, *Christ the Lord: A Study in the Purpose and Theology of Luke-Acts* (Philadelphia: Westminster Press, 1975); and Bartsch, *Wachet aber zu jeder Zeit! Entwurf einer Auslegung des Lukasevangeliums* (Hamburg-Bergstedt: Herbert Reich-Evangelischer Verlag, 1963).

39.  Mark Allan Powell, "Salvation in Luke-Acts," *WW* 12 (1992): 5–10.

40.  Conzelmann, *Theology of St. Luke.*

41.  Initially, it met with widespread acceptance, influencing such prominent scholars as Jacques Dupont, Ernst Haenchen, Günter Klein, Ernst Käsemann, and Gerhard Schneider. See Powell, *What Are They Saying about Luke?* pp. 76–78; and idem, *What Are They Saying about Acts?* pp. 58–74.

42. To cite but one recent example, J. Bradley Chance believes that Luke portrays Jesus as inaugurating the new age in its fullest eschatological sense, such that the "time of the church" is actually the messianic reign of Christ. See *Jerusalem, the Temple, and the New Age in Luke-Acts* (Macon, Ga.: Mercer University Press, 1988).

43. Gerhard Lohfink, *Die Himmelfahrt Jesu: Untersuchungen zu den Himmelfahrts und Erhöhungstexten bei Lukas* (Munich: Kösel, 1971). Compare Mikeal Parsons, *The Departure of Jesus in Luke Acts,* JSNTSS 21 (Sheffield: Sheffield Academic Press, 1987).

44. Flender, *St. Luke;* Franklin, *Christ the Lord.*

45. Gerhard Krodel, *Acts,* PC (Philadelphia: Fortress Press, 1981), pp. 4–5.

46. Tannehill, *Gospel according to Luke,* pp. 201–4.

47. Schuyler Brown, *Apostasy and Perseverance in the Theology of Luke,* AnBib 36 (Rome: Biblical Institute, 1969); and Richard J. Dillon, *From Eye-Witnesses to Ministers of the Word: Tradition and Composition in Luke 24,* AnBib 82 (Rome: Biblical Institute, 1978).

48. The term "early catholicism" was applied to Luke by Ernst Käsemann, who meant it pejoratively. See, for example, *Jesus Means Freedom* (Philadelphia: Fortress Press, 1970), pp. 116–29. For rebuttal, see Werner Georg Kümmel, "Current Accusations against Luke," *ANQ* 16 (1975): 131–45.

49. See Susan R. Garrett, *The Demise of the Devil: Magic and the Demonic in Luke's Writings* (Minneapolis: Fortress Press, 1989).

50. Again, the foremost accuser is Ernst Käsemann. See, for instance, "Ministry and Community in the New Testament," in *Essays on New Testament Themes* (Philadelphia: Fortress Press, 1982), pp. 63–94 (German original, 1949).

51. The success of the mission to Israel in Luke-Acts is a debated matter: Does Luke represent the gentile mission as replacing a failed mission to Israel, supplementing a continuing mission to Israel, or growing out of a successful mission to Israel? For discussion, see Powell, *What Are They Saying about Acts?* pp. 67–72.

### CHAPTER 5. THE GOSPEL OF JOHN

1. Robert Gordon Maccini, *Her Testimony is True: Women as Witnesses according to John,* JSNTSS 125 (Sheffield: Sheffield Academic Press, 1996).

2. See James D. G. Dunn's well-titled article, "Let John Be John," in *The Gospel and the Gospels,* ed. Peter Stuhlmacher (Grand Rapids: Eerdmans, 1990), pp. 293–322.

3. The title of a book by Robert Kysar offers an apt description—*John, The Maverick Gospel,* rev. ed. (Louisville: Westminster/John Knox Press, 1993).

4. D. Moody Smith, *John among the Gospels: The Relationship in Twentieth-Century Research* (Minneapolis: Fortress Press, 1992).

5. See Thomas L. Brodie, *The Quest for the Origin of John's Gospel: A Source-Oriented Approach* (Oxford: Oxford University Press, 1993).

6. Rudolf Bultmann, *The Gospel of John* (Philadelphia: Westminster Press, 1971; German original, 1941).

7. Robert T. Fortna, *The Gospel of Signs: A Reconstruction of the Narrative Source Underlying the Fourth Gospel* (New York: Cambridge University Press, 1970); idem, *The Fourth Gospel and Its Predecessor: From Narrative Source to Present Gospel* (Philadelphia: Fortress Press, 1988); and Urban C. Von Wahlde, *The Earliest Version of John's Gospel: Recovering the Gospel of Signs* (Wilmington, Del.: Michael Glazier, 1989).

8. The stages in figure 22 are based on a popular proposal in Raymond E. Brown, *The Gospel according to John,* 2 vols., AB 29, 29A (Garden City, N.Y.: Doubleday, 1966–70). For other proposals, including those of such significant scholars as C. K. Barrett, Marie-Emile Boismard, Rudolf Bultmann, Oscar Cullmann, Wolfgang Langbrandtner, Barnabas Lindars, J. Louis Martyn, Georg Richter, John A. T. Robinson, and D. Moody Smith, see Gerard S. Sloyan, *What Are They Saying about John?* (New York: Paulist Press, 1991), pp. 3–49; and Raymond E. Brown, *The Community of the Beloved Disciple* (New York: Paulist Press, 1979), pp. 171–82.

9. See Craig A. Evans, *Word and Glory: On the Exegetical and Theological Background of John's Prologue,* JSNTSS 89 (Sheffield: Sheffield Academic Press, 1993); and Elizabeth Harris, *Prologue and Gospel: The Theology of the Fourth Evangelist,* JSNTSS 107 (Sheffield: Sheffield Academic Press, 1994).

10. On the Hellenistic background (especially Philo), see Harris, *Prologue and Gospel,* pp. 196–201; on the Jewish background, see Evans, *Word and Glory.*

11. Some recent studies have likened John's presentation of Jesus as the incarnate Word of God to the Old Testament personification of wisdom, which is also said to have been present with God at creation (Prov. 8:22–31; John 1:1–3) and to be the source of life (Prov. 8:35; 1 John 5:12). See D. Moody Smith, *The Theology of the Gospel of John,* NTT (Cambridge: Cambridge University Press, 1995), pp. 17–18. See also Martin Scott, *Sophia and the Johannine Jesus,* JSNTSS 71 (Sheffield: Sheffield Academic Press, 1992).

12. See Marianne Meye Thompson, *The Humanity of Jesus in the Fourth Gospel* (Philadelphia: Fortress Press, 1988). She argues that the Gospel of John assumes the humanity of Jesus without seeking to prove it.

13. One example of how the two natures get played off against each other in Johannine studies is in discussions of the term "Son of (the) Man." Compare Francis Moloney, *The Johannine Son of Man,* 2d ed. (Rome: Ateneo Salesiano, 1979); and Delbert Burkett, *The Son of the Man in the Gospel of John,* JSNTSS 56 (Sheffield: Sheffield Academic Press, 1991). For Moloney, the title emphasizes the humanity of Jesus; for Burkett it is an enigmatic synonym for "Son of God" ("the Man" referring to God, not humanity).

14. Bultmann (*John*) saw the beloved disciple as an ideal figure. R. Alan Culpepper thinks he was a historical figure, but in John's narrative is identified with the "implied author" of the Gospel so as to become a literary representation of the dominant point of view. See *Anatomy of the Fourth Gospel: A Study in Literary Design,* FF (Philadelphia: Fortress Press, 1983).

15. Floyd V. Filson, "Who Was the Beloved Disciple?" *JBL* 68 (1949): 83–88; and Joseph N. Sanders, "Those Whom Jesus Loved," *NTS* 1 (1954): 29–41.

16. The latter is the preference of James H. Charlesworth in the most exhaustive study of this topic to date, *The Beloved Disciple: Whose Witness Validates the Gospel of John?* (Valley Forge, Pa.: Trinity Press International, 1995).

17. See David Mark Ball, *"I Am" in John's Gospel: Literary Function, Background, and Theological Implications,* JSNTSS 124 (Sheffield: Sheffield Academic Press, 1996); and Phillip B. Harner, *The I-Am of the Fourth Gospel: A Study in Johannine Usage and Thought* (Philadelphia: Fortress Press, 1971).

18. On the function of such language, see the interdisciplinary study by Norman R. Petersen, *The Gospel of John and the Sociology of Light* (Valley Forge, Pa.: Trinity Press International, 1993).

19. Paul Diel and Jeannine Solotareff, *Symbolism in the Gospel of John,* trans. N. Marans (San Francisco: Harper & Row, 1988); Craig R. Koester, *Symbolism in the Fourth Gospel: Meaning, Mystery, and Community* (Minneapolis: Fortress Press, 1995); and Dorothy A. Lee, *The Symbolic Narratives of the Fourth Gospel: The Interplay of Form and Meaning,* JSNTSS 95 (Sheffield: Sheffield Academic Press, 1994).

20. Bultmann (*John*) viewed the Johannine community as essentially nonsacramental, while Oscar Cullmann held John was profoundly interested in the sacraments. See Cullmann, *Early Christian Worship,* trans. A. S. Todd and J. B. Torrance (London: SCM, 1953). For an example of a mediating view, see G. R. Beasley-Murray, *Gospel of Life: Theology in the Fourth Gospel* (Peabody, Mass.: Hendrickson, 1991), pp. 85–101.

21. Culpepper, *Anatomy,* pp. 152–65; and Herbert Leroy, *Rätsel und Missverständnis: Ein Beitrag zur Formgeschichte des Johannesevangeliums,* BhB 30 (Bonn: Peter Hanstein, 1968).

22. The phenomenon of irony is much more complex than this single example suggests. For a basic introduction see Culpepper, *Anatomy,* pp. 165–80; and Paul D. Duke, *Irony in the Fourth Gospel* (Atlanta: John Knox Press, 1985). On the hermeneutical implications of Johannine irony, see Gail R. O'Day, *Revelation in the Fourth Gospel: Narrative Mode and Theological Claim* (Philadelphia: Fortress Press, 1986).

23. William S. Kurz, *The Farewell Addresses in the New Testament,* ZS (Collegeville, Minn.: Liturgical Press, 1990), pp. 71–120; Fernando F. Segovia, *The Farewell of the Word: The Johannine Call to Abide* (Minneapolis: Fortress Press, 1991); and Bruce Woll, *Johannine Christianity in Conflict: Authority, Rank, and Succession in the First Farewell Discourse* (Chico, Calif.: Scholars Press, 1981).

24. Studies on the Spirit in John include Gary M. Burge, *The Anointed Community: The Holy Spirit in the Johannine Tradition* (Grand Rapids: Eerdmans, 1987); George Johnston, *The Spirit Paraclete in the Gospel of John,* SNTSMS 12 (Cambridge: Cambridge University Press, 1970); Felix Porsch, *Pneuma und Wort: Ein exegetische Beitrag zur Pneumatologie des Johannesevangeliums* (Frankfurt: Josef Knecht, 1974); Hans Windisch, *The Spirit-Paraclete in the Fourth Gospel* (Philadelphia: Fortress Press,

1968); and John Wijngaards, *The Spirit in John,* ZS (Wilmington, Del.: Michael Glazier, 1988).

25.  See further, Wolfgang J. Bittner, *Jesu Zeichen in Johannesevangelium* (Tübingen: Mohr, 1987); Raymond F. Collins, *These Things Have Been Written: Studies on the Fourth Gospel,* LTPM 2 (Grand Rapids: Eerdmans, 1990), pp. 158–97; Daniel J. Harrington, *John's Thought and Theology: An Introduction,* GNS (Wilmington, Del.: Michael Glazier, 1990); and W. Nicol, *The Sēmeia in the Fourth Gospel: Tradition and Redaction* (Leiden: Brill, 1972).

26.  On the Johannine passion see Godfrey Nicholson, *Death as Departure: The Johannine Descent-Ascent Schema,* SBLDS 63 (Chico, Calif.: Scholars Press, 1983); I. de la Potterie, *The Hour of Jesus: The Passion and Resurrection of Jesus according to John* (New York: Alba House, 1989); and Beasley-Murray, *Gospel of Life,* pp. 34–58.

27.  For discussion and debate, see C. K. Barrett, *The Gospel of John and Judaism* (Philadelphia: Westminster Press, 1975); and John Bowman, *The Fourth Gospel and the Jews* (Pittsburgh: Pickwick Press, 1975).

28.  Bruce E. Schein defends the translation "Judeans" in *Following the Way: The Setting of John's Gospel* (Minneapolis: Augsburg, 1980). The NRSV (Inclusive Version) often uses "religious authorities."

29.  On the Johannine love command, see further Raymond E. Brown, *The Community of the Beloved Disciple* (New York: Paulist Press, 1979); Victor Paul Furnish, *The Love Command in the New Testament* (Nashville: Abingdon Press, 1972), pp. 132–58; Fernando F. Segovia, *Love Relationships in the Fourth Gospel* (Atlanta: John Knox Press, 1982); and Sjef Van Tilborg, *Imaginative Love in John,* BIS 2 (Leiden: Brill, 1993).

30.  For an exhaustive study of traditions concerning this person, see R. Alan Culpepper, *John the Son of Zebedee: The Life of a Legend* (Columbia: University of South Carolina Press, 1994).

31.  This is the view of Martin Hengel, *The Johannine Question,* trans. J. Bowden (Philadelphia: Trinity Press International, 1989).

32.  Oscar Cullmann, *The Johannine Circle,* trans. J. Bowden (Philadelphia: Westminster Press, 1976); Alan R. Culpepper, *The Johannine School,* SBLDS 26 (Missoula, Mont.: Scholars Press, 1975).

33.  The Jesus Seminar, for instance, does not find a single verse in the entire Gospel of John that it is willing to print in red type, indicating that Jesus actually said the words. One verse, John 4:44, is printed in pink type, indicating that Jesus might have said the words. See Funk, *Five Gospels.* On the historicity of John, see also the classic study by C. H. Dodd, *Historical Tradition in the Fourth Gospel* (Cambridge: Cambridge University Press, 1963).

34.  Sjef Van Tilborg, *Reading John in Ephesus,* NovTSup 83 (Leiden: Brill, 1996).

35.  John A. T. Robinson, *The Priority of John,* ed. J. F. Coakley (London: SCM, 1985). But even Robinson grants that the Gospel may have been edited to achieve its final form at a later date.

36. A text-critical problem at John 20:31 prevents us from knowing with certainty whether the evangelist originally wrote "come to believe" (as the NRSV indicates) or "continue to believe."

37. Urban von Wahlde, *The Johannine Commandments: 1 John and the Struggle for the Johannine Tradition* (New York: Paulist Press, 1990).

38. See Pheme Perkins, *Gnosticism and the New Testament* (Minneapolis: Fortress Press, 1993).

39. The concept was developed by C. H. Dodd in his work on parables, though he was also a Johannine scholar. See *The Parables of the Kingdom*, rev. ed. (New York: Charles Scribner's Sons, 1961; original, 1935).

40. Beasley-Murray, *Gospel of Life*, pp. 1–14.

41. Robin Scroggs, *Christology in John and Paul*, PC (Philadelphia: Fortress Press, 1988), pp. 96–99.

42. Frederick Herzog, *Liberation Theology: Liberation in the Light of the Fourth Gospel* (New York: Seabury Press, 1977); Robert Karris, *Jesus and the Marginalized in John's Gospel*, ZS (Collegeville, Minn.: Liturgical Press, 1990); David Rensberger, *Johannine Faith and Liberating Community* (Philadelphia: Westminster Press, 1988).

43. On the Johannine concept of truth, see I. de la Potterie, *La Vérité dans S. Jean*, 2 vols. (Rome: Pontifical Biblical Institute, 1977).

44. Beasley-Murray, *Gospel of Life*, pp. 15–33; J. A. Bühner, *Der Gesandte und sein Weg im 4. Evangelium*, WUNT (Tübingen: Mohr, 1977); Marinus de Jonge, *Jesus, Stranger from Heaven and Son of God* (Missoula, Mont.: Scholars Press, 1977); and J. P. Miranda, *Die Sendung Jesu im vierten Evangelium: Religions- und theologiegeschichtliche Untersuchungen zu den Sendungsformeln* (Stuttgart: Katholisches Bibelwerk, 1977).

45. J. Terence Forestell, *The Word of the Cross: Salvation as Revelation in the Fourth Gospel* (Rome: Pontifical Biblical Institute, 1974).

46. Jerome H. Neyrey uses sociological models to analyze the developing theology of the Johannine community as expressive of its experience of alienation and estrangement, but he sees the ultimate mood as "more one of revolt against discredited systems than sectarian defense" (p. 205). See *An Ideology of Revolt: John's Christology in Social-Science Perspective* (Philadelphia: Fortress Press, 1988).

47. Brown, *Community of the Beloved Disciple*, pp. 59–91.

48. See Teresa Okure, *The Johannine Approach to Mission: A Contextual Study of John 4:1-42*, WUNT 31 (Tübingen: Mohr, 1988).

49. Elaine Pagels, *The Johannine Gospel in Gnostic Exegesis: Heraclon's Commentary on John* (Missoula, Mont.: Scholars Press, 1973).

50. Most discussions of the law in John concur that this Gospel intends to present Jesus as one who was faithful to Torah. See A. E. Harvey, *Jesus on Trial: A Study in the Fourth Gospel* (Atlanta: John Knox Press, 1977); and Severino Pancaro, *The Law*

*in the Fourth Gospel: The Torah and the Gospel, Moses and Jesus, Judaism and Christianity according to John* (Leiden: Brill, 1975).

51. See Marie-Emile Boismard, *Moses or Jesus: An Essay in Johannine Christology,* trans. B. T. Viviano (Minneapolis: Fortress Press, 1992); Thomas F. Glasson, *Moses in the Fourth Gospel* (Naperville, Ill.: A. R. Allenson, 1963); and Wayne A. Meeks, *The Prophet-King: Moses Traditions and the Johannine Christology* (Leiden: Brill, 1967).

52. J. Louis Martyn links the consolidation of the Johannine community to the introduction into synagogue liturgies of an "Eighteenth Benediction" condemning Christians as heretics, but just when and where this benediction was actually used is disputed. See *History and Theology in the Fourth Gospel,* 2d ed. (Nashville: Abingdon Press, 1979).

53. Some scholars, for instance, note that John distinguishes between "the Jews" (whom he regards unfavorably) and "Israel" (whom he regards favorably). Brown (*John,* p. lxxi) regards "the Jews" as "almost a technical term for the religious authorities, particularly those in Jerusalem who are hostile to Jesus."

54. James H. Charlesworth, ed., *John and the Dead Sea Scrolls,* 2d ed. (New York: Crossroad, 1990).

55. C. K. Barrett argued that Peter and the beloved disciple had equal but distinct roles for the community, the former viewed as the head of its evangelistic and pastoral work, the latter as the guarantor of its tradition (*The Gospel according to St. John,* 2d ed. [Philadelphia: Westminster Press, 1978]).

56. Udo Schelle, *Antidocetic Christology in the Gospel of John,* trans. L. Maloney (Minneapolis: Fortress Press, 1992). Thompson (*Humanity of Jesus*) believes the Gospel is more concerned with affirming paradox than combating docetism.

57. Brown (*Community of the Beloved Disciple,* pp. 71–91) distinguishes three groups of those whom John would regard as "other Christians" with varying degrees of tolerance: Christian-Jews within the synagogues, Jewish Christians of inadequate faith (represented by James), and Christians of apostolic churches (represented by Peter).

58. T. E. Pollard, *Johannine Christology and the Early Church,* SNTSMS 13 (Cambridge: Cambridge University Press, 1993); and F.-M. Braun, *Jean le Théologien et son évangile dans l'église ancienne,* 2 vols. (Paris: J. Gabalda, 1959–64).

### Appendix Notes

1. For the texts of several significant works, see Robert J. Miller, ed., *The Complete Gospels,* rev. ed. (San Francisco: HarperSanFrancisco, 1992); Robinson, *Nag Hammadi Library;* and Wilhelm Schneelmelcher, ed., *Gospels and Related Writings,* vol. 1 of *New Testament Apocrypha,* rev. ed., trans. R. McL. Wilson (Louisville: Westminster/John Knox Press, 1990). Quotations of documents in this chapter are from Miller.

2. The process through which writings came to be regarded as canonical was complex and, at times, remains unclear. It involved the eventual coherence of both accep-

tance at a "grassroots level" (which books got used the most) and sanction by official authorities. See H. Von Campenhausen, *The Formation of the Christian Bible* (Philadelphia: Fortress Press, 1972). Other Gospels were used, especially in the Eastern church, but by the beginning of the third century, collections of Matthew, Mark, Luke, and John were being widely circulated and appear to have achieved definitive scriptural standing as a group.

3. See especially, Elaine Pagels, *The Gnostic Gospels* (New York: Random House, 1979).

4. For one assessment of these works and their significance, see Helmut Koester, *Ancient Christian Gospels: Their History and Development* (Philadelphia: Trinity Press International, 1990).

5. Miller, *Complete Gospels*, p. 370.

6. Notable scholars who have argued that the Gospel of Peter is independent of the four New Testament Gospels include Helmut Koester and John Dominic Crossan. See Koester, *Ancient Christian Gospels*, pp. 216–40; and Crossan, *The Cross That Spoke: The Origins of the Passion Narrative* (San Francisco: Harper & Row, 1988).

7. Crossan, *Cross That Spoke*. The argument is updated somewhat in his *Four Other Gospels: Shadows on the Contours of Canon* (Sonoma, Calif.: Polebridge Press, 1992), pp. 85–127.

8. Miller, *Complete Gospels*, pp. 302–3.

9. N. T. Wright, *The New Testament and the People of God* (Minneapolis: Fortress Press, 1992).

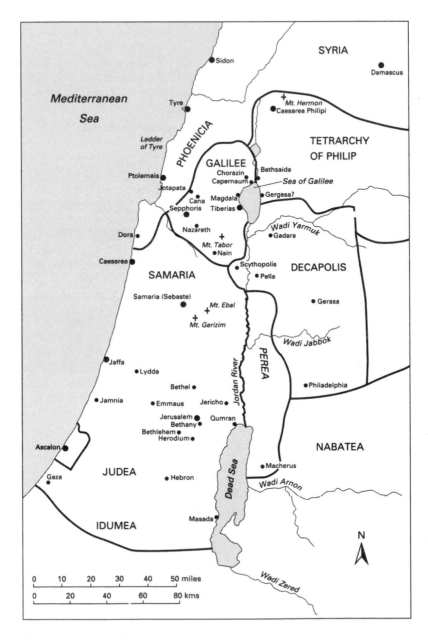

Palestine in the time of Jesus

# GLOSSARY

◆————————————————————◆

**Antitheses.** the six passages in Matthew 5:21-48 in which Jesus contrasts his teaching with that of others.

**apocalyptic.** a dualistic perspective that regards the present as an evil age soon to be ended by divine intervention.

**Apocrypha.** ancient writings that are similar to those found in the Bible but are not regarded as scripture.

**atonement.** the Christian belief that Jesus provided for the salvation of humans so that they may be spared divine or eternal punishment for their sins.

**baptism.** a ritual involving symbolic bathing that became the primary entrance rite of the Christian religion.

**Beatitudes.** announcements of blessing, such as those found in Matthew 5:3-12 and Luke 6:20-23.

**canonical.** ancient writings that are considered to be scripture, that is, regarded as authoritative within a particular religious system.

**chiasm.** a poetic arrangement of elements in an ABCB'A' pattern.

**Christology.** the study of various perspectives on the enduring significance of the person and work of Jesus.

**codex.** a manuscript that is written on bound pages (like a book) rather than on one sheet rolled up like a scroll.

**composition analysis.** the study of how the Gospel writers have ordered and arranged individual units into the work as a whole.

**corrective Christology.** the theory that explains the motif of the messianic secret in Mark's Gospel as an attempt to correct false understandings of messiahship.

**crucifixion.** a Roman form of execution that consisted of nailing or binding people to wood crosses and leaving them to die.

**cultural anthropology.** comparative study of phenomena that occur in diverse cultures.

**Dead Sea Scrolls.** a collection of Jewish writings from around the time of Jesus discovered at Qumran between 1947–1956.

**deconstruction.** a postmodern perspective that critiques all methods for interpreting the Gospels by challenging the possibility of determining "meaning" in any definitive sense.

**Didache.** a second-century Christian writing intended to serve as a manual for community life.

**docetism.** the belief, regarded as heretical by most Christians, that Jesus was not truly a human being.

**dualism.** the perspective that radically distinguishes between contrasting phenomena (good and evil, matter and spirit) with little allowance for overlap.

**dynamic equivalence.** an approach to translation that tries to produce a message that will have the same effect as the original rather than reproducing the message word-for-word.

**ecclesiology.** the study of different understandings of the church.

**emendation analysis.** the study of how the Gospel writers altered their source materials.

**eschatology.** the study of different perspectives concerning the future, especially the end of the world and life beyond death.

**Essenes.** a monastic Jewish subgroup active at the time of Jesus (but never mentioned in the New Testament) who preserved the library called the Dead Sea Scrolls.

**eucharist.** the ritual Christian meal involving bread and wine, instituted by Jesus the night before his death.

**evangelist.** a technical term for the author (or compiler) of any one of the four Gospels.

**exorcism.** a form of healing that involves the expulsion of an evil spirit.

**feminist criticism.** an approach to the Gospels that challenges patriarchal interpretations of texts or the patriarchal values conveyed by the texts themselves.

**form criticism.** the study of how Gospel traditions were shaped and transmitted orally before they were put into writing.

**framework.** in form criticism, the portion of a Gospel text that the author is believed to have had added to what was inherited from earlier sources.

**fulfillment citations.** a shorthand reference for the twelve passages in Matthew's Gospel that claim Old Testament prophecies were fulfilled by events in the life of Jesus.

**genre.** the classification of a document as to literary type.

**Gentile.** people who are not Jewish, also referred to as "the nations."

**Gnosticism.** a dualistic religious system which taught that people's spirits could be saved from the evil world of matter through the acquisition of secret knowledge.

**Golden Rule.** the words of general advice attributed to Jesus in Matthew 7:12 and Luke 6:31 ("Do to others as you have them do to you").

**gospel.** a word meaning "good news," used by Christians for the message of Jesus or for the story of his life, death, and resurrection.

**Great Commission.** a shorthand expression for Matthew 28:16-20, the passage in which Jesus tells his followers to "make disciples of all nations."

**Hellenism.** the influence of Greco-Roman culture on the rest of the world.

**historical present.** the use of a present-tense verb to describe an event in the past, usually taken as a sign of unrefined grammar.

**incarnation.** the Christian doctrine that God became a human being in the person of Jesus.

**intercalation.** the inserting of one story within another.

**irony.** a form of speech in which an author or character intends a different meaning than that which the words would usually convey.

**itinerant radicalism.** the lifestyle attributed to Jesus' disciples (especially in Q) according to which they renounce all worldly security and travel about as missionaries.

**Jamnia.** a city where councils were held toward the end of the first century to define the religion that would come to be known as Judaism.

**Jesus Seminar.** a group of scholars that have tried to determine which sayings and deeds attributed to Jesus can be regarded as historically authentic.

**justification.** the Christian doctrine concerning how sinful people are accepted by God and made right with God.

**Kingdom of God.** not necessarily a place, but a concept; the term may denote the phenomenon of God ruling in ways that are not limited by time or space.

**koinē.** the variety of Greek in which the New Testament was written, a variety more representative of the common people than of the educated class.

**L.** the label given to material that is unique to Luke's Gospel.

**law.** the commandments and moral codes of scripture that reveal God's intentions for how people are to live.

**lectionary.** a prescribed list of scripture passages to be read on certain days.

**M.** the label given to material that is unique to Matthew's Gospel.

**Messiah (or "Christ").** a descendant of King David whom some Jews believed would come to redeem the fortunes of Israel; identified with Jesus in the Gospels.

**messianic secret.** the puzzling motif in Mark's Gospel that portrays Jesus seeking to keep his identity a secret.

**minuscules.** late biblical manuscripts written in cursive with upper and lower case letters, a style developed in the ninth century.

**Nag Hammadi.** a village in Egypt where gnostic writings (including the Gospel of Thomas) were discovered in 1945.

**narrative criticism.** an approach to the Gospels that draws on modern literary theory to interpret them as coherent short stories.

**Palestine.** a general term for the geographical region that the Jewish people viewed as their homeland.

**papyrus.** a brittle writing material made from plant fibers that was used for the very earliest biblical manuscripts.

**parables.** short, memorable stories that usually function as extended figures of speech.

**Paraclete.** the term used for the Holy Spirit in the Gospel of John.

**paraphrase.** a non-literal approach to translation that attempts to render a similar message in a popular or understandable style.

*parousia.* the technical term for the Second Coming of Jesus anticipated by Christians.

**passion narrative.** the story of Jesus' suffering and death.

**Pentateuch.** the first five books of the Old Testament.

**Pharisees.** a Jewish subgroup at the time of Jesus whose religious practice was closely associated with the study of scripture in synagogues.

**prophecy.** in the Gospels, this term usually refers to an inspired saying thought to predict or foreshadow events that occur at a later time.

**polyvalence.** the concept that a text can convey multiple meanings.

**Q.** the label given to material that is found in both Matthew and Luke but not in Mark, thought by many to derive from an early, now lost, document.

**Qumran.** the area in which the Essenes are thought to have lived, where the Dead Sea Scrolls were found.

**rabbi.** a Jewish teacher.

**reader-response criticism.** an approach to the Gospels that tries to discover how a text is able to generate different effects and mean different things to people.

**redaction criticism.** the study of how the Gospel writers edited the traditions and source material that they inherited.

**realized eschatology.** the view that benefits usually associated with life after death are available here and now.

**reign of God.** an alternative translation of the biblical phrase, "Kingdom of God."

**resistant reading.** an approach to interpretation that self-consciously defies perspectives that may have informed the author's work.

**Sadducees.** a Jewish subgroup at the time of Jesus whose practice of religion was closely associated with the Temple sacrifices in Jerusalem.

**salvation history.** a theological concept of how God has related to humanity in different periods of time.

**Samaritans.** a group of Semitic people who claimed that they, not the Jews, were the true descendants of Abraham and Moses.

**sanctification.** the Christian doctrine concerning how sinful people may be transformed by God to live righteous lives.

**Sanhedrin.** a Jewish council headed by the high priest in Jerusalem that was granted authority in certain matters by the controlling Roman powers.

**scriptoriums.** schools where biblical manuscripts were mass produced.

**Septuagint.** the Greek translation of the Hebrew scriptures (called the Old Testament by Christians) that was in use at the time of Jesus.

**Sermon on the Mount.** the name given to the body of Jesus' teaching material found in Matthew 5–7.

**Signs Gospel.** an early account of Jesus' miracles (and possibly more) that some scholars believe was used as a source for the Gospel of John.

*Sitz im Leben.* German for "setting in life"; the function that a particular unit of tradition was expected to serve in the early church.

social history. the science of determining the social effects of historical transitions on people.

sociology of knowledge. the study of how different societies define knowledge and its acquisition.

synagogue. Jewish houses of worship where sacrifices were not performed but the scriptures were interpreted at regular sabbath services.

synoptic problem. the puzzle of trying to explain similarities between the first three Gospels, usually by reference to common sources they may have used.

Synoptics. the first three Gospels (Matthew, Mark, and Luke), so-named because much of their material is similar or parallel.

Talmud. an authoritative body of Jewish tradition from before and after the time of Jesus, offering interpretations of scripture for contemporary life.

Temple. the principal site for sacrificial worship among the Jewish people; located in Jerusalem, the Temple was destroyed in 70 C.E.

text criticism. the study of manuscripts that underlie modern editions of the Bible.

text types. families into which most ancient manuscripts of the Bible can be classified.

Torah. the law of God, as revealed in the Jewish scriptures.

tradition. in form criticism, the portion of a Gospel text that the author is believed to have inherited from an earlier source.

transfiguration. the event recorded in the Synoptic Gospels in which Jesus' physical appearance is temporarily changed (Mark 9:2-8).

Travel Narrative. the section of Luke's Gospel (9:51—19:44) that places numerous stories within the framework of Jesus' journey to Jerusalem.

uncials. the earliest biblical manuscripts, printed in all capital letters.

variants. readings in ancient biblical manuscripts that differ from what the original text is believed to have said.

vellum. a type of leather on which some biblical manuscripts were copied.

*Wirkungsgeschichte.* German for "history of influence"; the study of different ways in which biblical texts have been understood under diverse circumstances.

womanist. an African-American feminist approach to reading or to scholarship.

# SCRIPTURE INDEX

OTHER NEW TESTAMENT WRITINGS

# INDEX OF NAMES